D1453276

ART
AGAINST
IDEOLOGY

by Ernst Fischer

Translated by Anna Bostock

Allen Lane The Penguin Press · London 1969

CONTENTS

Chapter 1

ENDGAME AND IVAN DENISOVICH

Hamm, whose name hints vaguely at myth, literature and cheap histrionics, is rotting alive in his refuge. The world from which he came is dead. After an unspeakable catastrophe, all that remains are *objects*, only the inorganic, nothing that grows or breathes. 'End, it is the end, it's coming to the end, perhaps it's coming to an end.' There is no world left, no future, only the hiding-place in the middle of nothing.

MASTER AND SERVANT

Hamm, a wreck of a man, sits crippled and blind in his chair. The fact that he can still keep alive in his bunker, motionless, helpless, a lump of flesh with vague recollections and desires, he owes to Clov, his servant and general factotum. This Clov, a dismal clown, loathes his master more profoundly, more desperately than his tougher ancestors hated their healthier masters: more than Grazioso hated Hidalgo, more than Hanswurst hated the Prince or Doctor Faustus, whose service he entered later.

The game they are both playing is a double one. They are playing at the end of the world – the master not without pathos: 'Can
there be misery – (*he yawns*) – loftier than mine?' Clov plays with
a laugh of surprise and disgust at whatever still exists, that brief
laugh when he looks out of the window, attends to the rubbish bins,
contemplates the swollen Hamm. But also they are playing the
end-game in the struggle between master and servant: who is going
to checkmate whom? Or will it be just stalemate or a draw? Hamm
cannot live without Clov. Can Clov live without Hamm?

> HAMM: Get me ready. (*Clov does not move.*) Go and get the sheet.
> (*Clov does not move.*) Clov!
> CLOV: Yes.
> HAMM: I'll give you nothing more to eat.
> CLOV: Then we'll die.
> HAMM: I'll give you just enough to keep you from dying. You'll be
> hungry all the time.
> CLOV: Then we shan't die. . . .
> HAMM: . . . Why do you stay with me?
> CLOV: Why do you keep me?
> HAMM: There's no one else.
> CLOV: There's nowhere else.

The master–servant relationship, too, is touched with decay. In
Waiting for Godot there was a transposition of roles between Pozzo
and Lucky, the revolution that alters none of the essential nature of
power. In *Endgame* Clov stays with Hamm, not only because he is
paralyzed by habit and inaction, but also because he dreads going
out into a world which may no longer be there, away from his
master's dwindling provisions, into the unknown, into the wreckage
of the great disaster.

THE WORLD OF HAVING

It is the fashion in both West and East to classify Samuel Beckett's
great plays under the heading of 'Theatre of the Absurd'. In it,
they say, the riddle of human existence is revealed or suggested
outside and beyond all social implications, by images with a multitude of possible meanings. Great imaginative writing always takes
the form of images, and these always have many meanings; but
neither Hamm nor Clov is a creature from outer space: they come
from a society of haves and have-nots, masters and servants, a

world of having; they are not merely allegorical characters, they also wear disintegrating social masks. It is foolish to trace works of the imagination back to social realities alone, to regard them purely as a 'reflection' of social conditions: but equally it is dogmatic to interpret them solely as the result of an autonomous imaginative process, an internal spectacle independent of the social world.

Hamm has lived a life of prosperity and greed. He tries to hold on to what he once was, now reduced to memories – the land he owned, the grain he stored, the beggar to whom he offered philosophy instead of bread. With the attitude of a writer working on a story he seeks to justify his senseless existence, his still-being-there. He tells the story not without complacency.

The man came crawling towards me, on his belly. . . . It was an extraordinarily bitter day, I remember, zero, by the thermometer. But considering it was Christmas Eve there was nothing . . . extraordinary about that. . . . (*Pause.*) Well, what ill wind blows you my way? He raised his face to me, black with mingled dirt and tears. . . . Come on, man, speak up, what is it you want from me, I have to put up my holly. (*Pause.*) Well to make it short it finally transpired that what he wanted from me was . . . bread for his brat. Bread? But I have no bread, it does not agree with me. Good. Then perhaps a little corn? (*Pause. Normal tone.*) That should do it. (*Narrative tone.*) Corn, yes, I have corn, it's true, in my granaries. But use your head. I give you some corn, a pound, a pound and a half, you bring it back to your child and you make him – if he's still alive – a nice pot of porridge. . . . Use your head, can't you, use your head, you're on earth, there's no cure for that! . . . But what in God's name do you imagine? That the earth will awake in spring? That the rivers and seas will run with fish again? That there's manna in heaven for imbeciles like you? . . . In the end he asked me would I consent to take in the child as well – if he were still alive. . . .(*Pause. Normal tone.*) I'll soon have finished with that story . . .

Clov asks how the story goes on. Isn't it also *his* story that the master is telling? A story for Hamm; the truth for him? Hamm thinks he can remember offering the beggar a job as a gardener. Clov bursts out laughing:'A job as a gardener!'

HAMM: What is there so funny about that?
CLOV: A job as a gardener!
HAMM: Is that what tickles you?
CLOV: It must be that.
HAMM: It wouldn't be the bread?

CLOV: Or the brat.
    Pause.
HAMM: The whole thing is comical, I grant you that. What about
having a good guffaw the two of us together?
CLOV (*after reflection*): I couldn't guffaw again today.

Was not Clov the child whom the rich man took into his house?
And would he not – his hatred asks him – have climbed the trees?
Hamm replies coldly: 'All the little odd jobs.' Trees don't grow
for the beggar's child. But he – how was it with him?

CLOV: And then he would have grown up.
HAMM: Very likely.
    Pause.
CLOV: Keep going, can't you, keep going!
HAMM: That's all. I stopped there.
    Pause.
CLOV: Do you see how it goes on?
HAMM: More or less.
CLOV: Will it soon be the end?
HAMM: I'm afraid it will.

The world of having is sketched as economically as that. Beckett presumes our knowledge of it. It is present in each concentrated detail.
It is introduced into the play only to the extent that it carries the
action forward. For inside the simulated standstill there in movement, development. We have learnt to recognize as great a dynamism in the atom as in the universe. Something is going on. Hamm
wants Clov to tell him that it is an evening like any other. But
Clov refuses to reassure him. Hamm is afraid: 'What's wrong?'
And Clov: 'Something is taking its course.'

SOMETHING IS TAKING ITS COURSE

What is 'taking its course' is not only time, whose stealthy silence
becomes audible, dripping with fear, ticking away into nothingness;
not only the irresistible process of decay, but Clov's stuggle to
liberate himself, to get free from the master to whom he is bound
by habit, the power of the father-image, hatred and the larder,
the accumulated stores. This is taking its course. It begins with
the master's certainty that Clov cannot go free: 'Very well, then
go!', and Clov does not move, and Hamm in his chair sits up again,
still representing power, although he is blind and crippled: 'I

thought I'd told you to go?' and Clov says: 'I'm trying' – and goes to the cupboard and stops: 'Ever since I was born.' This cat-and-mouse game then leads to the sly question to Clov: 'Do you remember when you came here?' and Clov, exasperated by the frozen situation, replying: 'You've asked me these questions millions of times'; then the master's patriarchal hypocrisy: 'It was I was a father to you. . . . My house a home for you. . . . But for me, no father. But for Hamm, no home.' It begins with this dictum of all rulers, that without them there is no world-father, no home for the little ones, never mind if the home is a bunker and the world a hell. It ends with the discovery that the provisions have been used up. It begins with the question: 'And where were *you*?' It ends with the undisguised insolence of one who always served as a servant, never as a son.

HAMM: I was never there.

CLOV: Lucky for you.

HAMM: Absent, always. It all happened without me. I don't know what's happened . . .

CLOV: When? Where?

HAMM (*violently*): When! What's happened! Use your head, can't you! What has happened?

CLOV: What for Christ's sake does it matter?
    He looks out of window.

HAMM: I don't know.
    Pause. CLOV *turns towards* HAMM.

CLOV (*harshly*): When old Mother Pegg asked you for oil for her lamp and you told her to get out to hell, you knew what was happening then, no? (*Pause.*) You know what she died of, Mother Pegg? Of darkness.

HAMM (*feebly*): I hadn't any.

CLOV (*as before*): Yes, you had.

Something is taking its course. Hamm reviews his past, toned down by consideration for his own feelings, for the crippled self is hyper-sensitive. If life has been a dream, he need not be held responsible for it. 'What dreams! . . . Those woods!' The fact that he is losing his hair, his teeth, his earthly possessions, he shares with Clov; but the thing that raises him above Clov, so he boasts, are the lost *ideals* which he tries to smuggle fraudulently into his past. Clov has nothing to lose.

HAMM: Have you not had enough?

CLOV: Yes! (*Pause.*) Of what?

HAMM: Of this ... this ... thing.
CLOV: I always had. (*Pause.*) Not you?

Hamm is a gentleman with an ideology, with a false and falsifying consciousness. Clov does not fool himself. For Hamm, cosmic suffering is a way of ennobling his own shoddiness; Clov suffers without self-deception. The words, the symbols at Hamm's command are not without grandeur; in the master's mouth they represent the power of subjugating the servant inwardly as well as outwardly.

CLOV: There's one thing I'll never understand. . . . Why I always obey you. Can you explain that to me?
HAMM: No. . . . Perhaps it's compassion. (*Pause.*) A kind of great compassion. (*Pause.*) Oh you won't find it easy, you won't find it easy.

The master proves to be a master of psychology. You have to play on the servant's feelings, celebrate his obedience as a kind of great compassion, as Christianity, as humanity, and at the same time appeal to his uncertainties: poor fellow, you won't find it easy without me! How do you expect to manage in the world without my experience, my intellect, my store of material and spiritual wealth?

IF WE MEAN SOMETHING

And so, in order to set himself free, Clov must see through the master's false consciousness. He must prevent Hamm from escaping into the ptahos of established ideas and force him to acknowledge his part in what he has done, in what he has known he has done. Hamm, on the other hand, in order to excuse his existence, his doing and not-doing and the fact that Mother Pegg died of darkness because of him, must postulate total meaninglessness, the world as Nothing in which we mean nothing. Otherwise they come out of the darkness, encircling him: 'All those I might have saved. (*Pause.*) Helped! (*Pause.*) Saved. (*Pause.*) Saved! (*Pause.*) The place was crawling with them! (*Pause. Violently.*) Use your head, can't you, use your head, you're on earth, there's no cure for that! (*Pause.*) Get out of here and love one another! Lick your neighbour as yourself!'

CLOV: Something is taking its course.
> *Pause.*

HAMM: Clov!

CLOV (*impatiently*): What is it?

HAMM: We're not beginning to . . . to . . . mean something?

CLOV: Mean something! You and I, mean something! (*Brief laugh.*) Ah that's a good one!

HAMM: I wonder. (*Pause.*) Imagine if a rational being came back to earth, wouldn't he be liable to get ideas into his head if he observed us long enough. . . . And without going so far as that, we ourselves . . . (*with emotion*) . . . we ourselves . . . at certain moments. . . .(*Vehemently.*) To think perhaps it won't all have been for nothing!

If we mean something, if perhaps it won't all have been for nothing, Hamm has lost the end-game. He is then to be *judged*. How can he bear it if it all means something, if the worldlessness of his refuge is only illusory? Was the catastrophe inevitable? Was the cripple always crippled, the blind man always blind? Could he not have done something instead of never being there, when it was a matter of saving or helping? What he *possessed* was there; but he as an 'I', a self, beneath all those *things* and beneath the conventions and institutions relating to them, was never there: so he was without responsibility.

It is the same order, the same powerful domination of *things*, that has also robbed Clov of the capacity to realize his 'I', his self, that is to say to *be there*, to decide in relative freedom.

Beyond the refuge, which is suggestive of Max Weber's 'casing of enslavement', beyond the old wall, a world is – perhaps – being created in which it is possible to *be there* as a human being; possible for Clov, not for Hamm. Hamm lays his hand on the wall: 'Old wall! (*Pause.*) Beyond is the . . . other hell.'

THE PRISONERS

According to his dossier, Ivan Denisovich Shukhov had been sentenced for high treason. He had testified to it himself. Yes, he'd surrendered to the Germans with the intention of betraying his country and he'd returned from captivity to carry out a mission for German intelligence . . .

Shukhov reckoned simply. If he didn't sign he'd be shot. If he signed he'd still get a chance to live. So he signed.

But what really happened was this. In February 1942 their whole army was surrounded on the north-west front. No food was parachuted to them. . . . They'd no ammunition left. So the Germans rounded them up in the forest, a few at a time. Shukhov was in one of those groups, and remained in German captivity for a day or two. Then five of them managed to escape. They stole through the forest and marshes again and, by a miracle, reached their own lines. A tommy-gunner shot two of them on the spot, a third died of wounds, but two got through. Had they been wiser they'd have said they'd been wandering about the forest, and then nothing would have happened. But they told the truth: they said they were escaped P.O.W.s. P.O.W.s, you fuckers!

And so they passed from German into Soviet captivity – because the 'positive hero' Stalin insisted on was supposed to die rather than be taken prisoner.

ONE DAY IN THE LIFE OF IVAN DENISOVICH

One Day in the Life of Ivan Denisovich, by Alexander Solzhenitsyn. 'So it's a day like any other day!' Hamm says again and again in *Endgame*, because he fears and senses that something is taking its course, that an end is coming on this day of all days. The day Solzhenitsyn describes is really a day like any other. It is one of the 3,653 days of Ivan Denisovich Shukhov's sentence. 'The three extra days were for leap years.' It had been a good day, not one of the bad ones; they hadn't put Shukhov in the cells, they hadn't sent him to the 'Socialist Way of Life' settlement, that dreaded bare field covered with snowdrifts where prisoners, before beginning the actual work, had to dig holes, put on posts and stretch barbed wire across in order to cut off their own escape from this hell; he'd pinched a bowl of kasha at dinner; he'd built a wall and enjoyed doing it; he'd smuggled that bit of hacksaw-blade through the guard post; he'd earned something from Tsezar; he'd bought some tobacco. And there is something else which is not mentioned, yet which is the unspoken *leitmotiv* of the whole novel: he had *preserved his dignity as a human being* and would defend it with all his strength, even if the worst happened. I am reluctant to use grand words like 'human dignity' at a time when all such words – freedom, justice, humanity – have been so tarnished, so discredited and debased that they can barely escape the suspicion of being empty phrases. Yet we must be permitted to use them. For it is the formation of man, the negation of his dignity and the dignity itself which are the subject-matter of Beckett's play and Solzhenitsyn's novel. The two works invite comparison because the problems they deal with are the same.

What distinguishes the one from the other is obvious. It has nothing to do with the view generally held in the East that Beckett is a 'decadent anti-realist', nor with the one prevalent in the West that Solzhenitsyn is a respectable, though not outstanding, representative of Socialist Realism. Beckett is a great artist in complete control of his means of expression. Solzhenitsyn is a writer of considerable stature in search of new means of expression commensurate with the almost inexpressible things he has to say. The one is able to assume that his readers are familiar with the outside world from which the characters in his play have come; the other is compelled to reproduce the world of the labour camps not by symbolic imagery but with naturalistic precision. The one inherits all the modern experiments of artistic concentration; the other has to overcome a literary legacy of 'epic' diffuseness where nothing may be left unsaid.

THE SUN IN THE BARBED WIRE

The extent to which Solzhenitsyn succeeds in finding a style of his own in his first work is remarkable. It is a hard, economic, telling style without the least over-emphasis, a style tending towards Anglo-Saxon understatement. Solzhenitsyn tries to describe details in such a way that they grow larger than themselves, suggesting something universal in the narrow world of the camp. 'The lock-up was the only brick building in the camp.' A sentence such as this, the permanent prison in the midst of temporary replaceable huts, enters our memory and stays there. Or this: 'The cold made Shukhov gasp. Two powerful searchlights swept the camp from the farthest watch-towers. The border-lights, as well as those inside the camp, were on. There were so many of them that they outshone the stars.' Or, like the collapsed lighthouse in *Endgame* whose foundations are now sinking into the sea, the sun over the camp: '. . . red and enormous, rising in haze, its beams cutting obliquely through the gates, the whole building-site and the fence'. Symbols of two worlds: the sunken lighthouse, the sun caught in the barbed wire.

Can this sun be trusted? Is it still part of autonomous nature or is it already ruled by a dictatorial bureaucracy?

Shukhov says it must be noon, because the sun has reached its peak.

'If it's reached its peak,' said the captain reflectively, 'it's one o'clock, not noon.'

'What do you mean?' Shukhov demanded. 'Every greybeard knows that the sun stands highest at dinner-time.'

'Greybeards, maybe,' snapped the captain. 'But since their day a new decree has been passed, and now the sun stands highest at one.'

'Who passed that decree?'

'Soviet power.'

If in the camp the natural order of things is so denied – the prisoners so powerless, the blind tyranny so absolute ('They'd given Kilgas twenty-five years. Earlier there'd been a spell when people were lucky: everyone to a man got ten years. But from '49 onwards the standard sentence was twenty-five, irrespective.'), why should it not be possible to control the sun, too?

THE REALISTIC RUBBISH BINS

Solzhenitsyn's book is full of such passages in shorthand, such signs which any Soviet reader can understand without further commentary. Beckett is able to go further in his use of signs. Nagg and Nell, Hamm's parents, have been crushed under the wheels of technical civilization – literally so, for they have lost their legs in a motor accident. Their son takes them reluctantly along into his refuge and houses them in rubbish bins. The sawdust on which they were at first put is later replaced by sand. And this sand is not changed again.

Advocates of a pedantic 'realism' may object that it is not usual – therefore not 'realistic' – to keep parents who have lost their usefulness in rubbish bins. Certainly it is not usual, it is against nature, against recognized reality. But is it usual to kill children in gas chambers, putting their shoes aside for a future 'winter rescue' campaign? Is it natural to 'liquidate' innocent people or to put hundreds of thousands of them behind barbed wire? And the subhuman *Realpolitik* of atomic warheads, the 'military metaphysic' as C. Wright Mills calls it, this permanent end-game in which dogmas, clichés, outdated half-truths are passed off as reality, in which thoughtfulness is viewed as naïvety and rationality as treason – is that realistic? Is the world we live in still capable of being represented by the old 'realistic' methods? We do not throw our human rubbish into bins – we consign it to old people's homes and other haunted institutions, we give it old-age pensions and so appease our conscience. We have added a Mother's Day and a Father's Day to the holiday calendar: commerce bids us give presents to our dear ones. Is not everything in order? No, it is not: and it is the writer's task to show that nothing is in order, that indifference and dehumanization have taken over in this iron age, that at the back of convention and hypocrisy there is a very different kind of reality crouching before a leap into nothingness. Often this task is better achieved by apparent exaggeration, by concentrated images and shock, than by traditional realism.

Nagg and Nell in their rubbish bins, interested in nothing now but their biscuit, their pap, the loss of their last tooth and the milling-over of imbecile memories: Hamm, the affectionate son who cannot restrain his hatred: and his father, cheated of his sugar-plum, who flings back at him: 'I hope the day will come when you'll really need to have me listen to you, and need to hear my voice, any voice. (*Pause.*) Yes, I hope I'll live till then, to hear you calling me like when you were a tiny boy, and were frightened, in the dark, and I was your only hope,' all this is extraordinarily compacted reality, forcing the spectator to make alarming connections and disclosing a dehumanized world behind the curtains of self-deceit.

A MAN IS MORE PRECIOUS THAN GOLD

The human beings in Hamm's bunker, like the convicts behind their barbed wire, are in an exceptional situation which is a recognizable consequence of the regular, established one. In the former case, the world of having is rotting away because it is already dead: in the latter, the world of power – whose mechanism manipulates man as a mere quantum, a *quantité négligeable* – is becoming petrified. When the convicts leave the camp to go to work, they are carefully counted. 'A man is more precious than gold. If there was one head short when they got past the wire you had to replace it with your own.' Stalin used to speak of Russia's population as 'the gold fund', the most precious capital of socialism. But at the

B

same time man was degraded to an abstract work unit. Once when a man was run over by a tram in Moscow, I heard a bus conductress say: 'There goes another pair of hands – a pity.' The horrifying phrase was spoken in a voice that was neither heartless nor cold: it was the voice of recognized necessity, the heroism – which had become the norm – of too-rapid industrialization, the sacrifice of the present for the sake of the future. The nature of work as a process in which man makes and forms himself implies a future. Even reduced to specialized labour in the service of commodity production, it still retains something of this anticipation. But in the work of convicts the sense of a future is completely extinguished. Its essence is total dehumanization. The worker, or 'pair of hands', is not even taken to the labour market: he has lost even his character as a commodity: and the fact that he is considered more precious than gold, the dead substance that serves as a measure of value, is a hollow mockery.

The convicts were not thrown back into a state of barbarism but were condemned to something incomparably worse – to an *unnatural condition* maintained by the achievements of technical civilization: barbed wire, watch-towers, searchlights, automatic pistols and statistical accuracy. To reduce everything to quantity, to what is measurable, countable, exchangeable, is the tendency of technical civilization. Man, however, is the quintessence of the qualitative, the unaccountable, the immeasurable potential. Thus the dehumanized existence of the camps appears as a primitive model of technical civilization which turns man into an object among objects, a means of its means, a tool of its purpose – just as existence in Hamm's bunker, where technology after its self-destruction has shrivelled to a telescope and two rubbish bins, a handful of dadaist ready-mades, can serve as a model of the perfect parasitic consumer society after the catastrophe it has brought upon itself.

NO MORE FUTURE

In both cases, the future – the dimension which determines man – has been abolished. Hamm, Nagg, and Nell are present only as shadows in the mirror of the past; they are no more than fragments of memory. It is the same with Ivan Denisovich's companions: 'The days rolled by in the camp – they were over before you could say "knife". But the years, they never rolled by; they never moved by a second.' There is only the trickling away of the present and there is memory in which man finds himself once more in his incredible identity. The present is composed of a multitude of small, sharp-edged interlocking fragments, with human beings caught in the mesh. They too are fragments of themselves, component parts of an anti-human mechanism, trying in the stories they tell to recreate as historical beings the whole men they once were.

'. . . AND NO NATURE'

Dehumanization in the novel corresponds to denaturalization in the play. Not only the future has been abolished. The windows of the huts have become opaque with hoar-frost. Outside there is only cold – twenty-seven degrees below zero – biting fog, pinching frost, sharp, vicious wind. The convicts pray for a snowstorm, although its advantages are small. 'The prisoners sat locked in; the coal was delivered late and all the warmth was blown out of the hut. Flour didn't reach the camp, so there was no bread. . . . All the same, the prisoners loved snowstorms and prayed for them.' Nature is their enemy, and the unnaturalness of the camp is almost felt as natural, as a kind of security and protection. For, outside,

the steppe was barren and windswept, with a dry wind in summer and a freezing one in winter. Nothing could ever grow in that steppe, less than nothing behind four barriers of barbed wire. Bread comes only from the bread-cutter, oats are threshed only in the store-house. And however much blood you sweat at work, however much you grovel on your belly, you'll force no food out of that earth; you'll get no more than the damned authorities give you. And you don't even get that – because of the cook and the 'help' and all the other trusties in cushy jobs. They fleece you here, they fleece you in camp, they fleece you even earlier – in the stores. And those who do the fleecing don't swing picks. But you – you swing a pick and take what they give you. And get away from the serving-hatch!

Nature is dead, the steppe yields nothing, you live off the skilly arbitrarily doled out to you for the sake of that same skilly. 'All that matters is that the skilly's good today.' When the convict is back from the cold, the forced labour, the degradation, when he starts spooning up the watery food from the tin bowl, nothing can worry him any more. Although the food is thinner in the evening than in the morning – 'if they're to work, prisoners must be fed in the morning; in the evening they'll go to sleep anyway' – the returning columns race wildly towards it. Ivan Denisovich begins to eat. 'First he only drank the liquid, drank and drank. As it went down, filling his whole body with warmth, all his guts began to flutter inside him at their meeting with that skilly. Goo-ood! There it comes, that brief moment for which a zek lives.' The nature of man? His denaturalization as a man, his dehumanization.

NAGG (*appearing out of his bin*): Me pap!
HAMM: Accursed progenitor!
NAGG: Me pap!...
HAMM: Give him his pap.
CLOV: There's no more pap.

There's no more nature. No more corn grows. The stocks are dwindling. The fact that nature is dead justifies Hamm's dehumanization. Civilization has murdered nature and is now dying itself as a result of the same murder.

HAMM: Nature has forgotten us.
CLOV: There's no more nature.
HAMM: No more nature! You exaggerate.
CLOV: In the vicinity.

The windows in Ivan Denisovich's camp are opaque with hoarfrost. Clov needs a ladder to look out of the window, a telescope in order to view the outside world. He gets up on the ladder and looks through the telescope: Zero . . . (*he looks*) . . . zero . . . (*he looks*) . . . and zero.

HAMM: Nothing stirs. All is –
CLOV: Zer –
HAMM (*violently*): Wait till you're spoken to! (*Normal voice.*) All is . . . all is . . . all is what? (*Violently.*) All is what?
CLOV: What all is? In a word? Is that what you want to know? Just a moment. (*He turns the telescope on the without, looks, lowers the telescope, turns towards Hamm.*) Corpsed. (*Pause.*) Well? Content?
HAMM: No gulls?
CLOV (*looking*): Gulls!
HAMM: And the horizon? Nothing on the horizon?
CLOV (*lowering the telescope, turning towards Hamm, exasperated*): What in God's name could there be on the horizon?
Pause.

HAMM: The waves, how are the waves?
CLOV: The waves? (*He turns the telescope on the waves.*) Lead.
HAMM: And the sun?
CLOV (*looking*): Zero.
HAMM: Is it night already then?
CLOV (*looking*): No.
HAMM: Then what is it?
CLOV (*looking*): Grey. (*Lowering the telescope, turning towards Hamm, louder.*) Grey! (*Pause. Still louder.*) GREY!

It is the grey of smoke and ashes, the grey that rises like an exhalation of objects, drowning the bright colours, the lights, the promises of artificial paradises; the all-absorbing grey of indifference, of dehumanization, the indeterminate state of the no-longer or the not-yet, the condition of our world. The only living creature which unexpectedly appears in Hamm's bunker is a rat. Hamm: 'A rat? Are there still rats?' Horrified, he orders it to be killed, so that the vanished life may not return like this, like the restless, greedy, cruel rat-race of life. It must be over and done with, no return to a world which has become absurd, to a nature which is inaccessible, which 'has no notion of staying and has put its curse on standing still', to a civilization which devours man and feverishly produces disasters. The waves have turned to lead, the hearts to stone, the greyness which is neither day nor night has driven the sun from the sky, and Clov stares at the wall and says 'I see my light dying'.

LET US PRAY!

'What do you want outside?' Alyosha asks his companions in the camp. 'Why d'you want freedom? In freedom your last grain of faith will be choked with weeds. You should rejoice that you're in prison. Here you have time to think about your soul.' He invites them to pray. 'Of all earthly and mortal things our Lord commanded us to pray only for our daily bread.'

'Our ration, you mean?' asks Shukhov.

'Ivan Denisovich, you shouldn't pray to get parcels or for extra skilly, not for that. Things that man puts a high price on are vile in the eyes of our Lord. We must pray about things of the spirit . . .'

'Let us pray to God!' says Hamm after ordering Clov to exterminate the rat.

CLOV: Again!

NAGG: Me sugar-plum!

HAMM: God first! (*Pause.*) Are you right?

CLOV (*resigned*): Off we go.

HAMM (*to* NAGG): And you?

NAGG (*clasping his hands, closing his eyes, in a gabble*): Our Father which art –

HAMM: Silence! In silence! Where are your manners? (*Pause.*) Off we go. (*Attitudes of prayer. Silence. Abandoning his attitude, discouraged.*) Well?

CLOV (*abandoning his attitude*): What a hope! And you?

HAMM: Sweet damn all! (*To* NAGG.) And you?

NAGG: Wait! (*Pause.*) Nothing doing!

HAMM: The bastard! He doesn't exist!

CLOV: Not yet.

NAGG: Me sugar-plum!

HAMM: There are no more sugar-plums!

Alyosha: 'There you are, Ivan Denisovich, your soul is begging to pray. Why, then, don't you give it its freedom?'

Ivan Denisovich: 'Well, Alyosha . . . it's this way. Prayers are like those appeals of ours. Either they don't get through or they're returned with "rejected" scrawled across 'em.' Outside the staff-hut were four sealed boxes – they were cleared by a security officer once a month. Many were the appeals that were dropped into them. The writers waited, counting the weeks: there'll be a reply in two months, in one month. . . . But the reply doesn't come. Or if it does it's only 'rejected'.

'But, Ivan Denisovich, it's because you pray too rarely, and badly at that. Without really trying. That's why your prayers stay unanswered. One must never stop praying.'

But all communication has ceased. There is no more world. No nature. No God. 'Not yet!' says Clov. Astounding words, and easily missed in the no-more of this end-game. Clov has not lost any 'ideals' like Hamm, he thinks nothing of prayer and nothing of grand words, but it is he who says 'Not yet': God, man, the world. In the greyness, a future quivers.

WHY THE NEGATIVITY?

'What is the point of all this greyness, this harping on negatives?' The question is asked not only by generals whose job it is to train positive heroes filled with disciplined optimism. 'Was there nothing but forced labour, injustice and darkness even at the time of the "personality cult"? Let us speak of the victories, the upsurge of the people, of the glorious motherland, of shining examples, not of unedifying side-effects!' The people who condemn Solzhenitsyn as defeatist are often the same as those who condemn Beckett as decadent, although one might have expected them to take a kindlier view of an author who so mercilessly depicts the world of having in decay.

I do not believe that, in the dark times in which we live, literature must *only* be negative. But the affirmative, even when it is critical of the 'side-effects', is inevitably tainted with hypocrisy.

The sacrifices and achievements of the Soviet people have been enormous. Yet in order that the results should to some degree match the effort expended, it is necessary for the past *as a whole* to be recognized and admitted. Those who speak of the 'Russian miracle' and not of its cost are doing an ill service to the Soviet people. For the 'liquidation' of the old Bolsheviks, the terror of the police régime, the arbitrary arrests and deportations, the convict labour, endless days flying away over a waste of frozen time – these were not 'side-effects' but essential features of a system of rule which now has to be transformed into a socialist one. Calculating the relative percentages of 'good' and 'bad' in Stalin, trying to separate the personality cult from the power apparatus as though it were something accidental and superficial, can only hold back the development towards socialist democracy. Ivan Denisovich not only has a right to be heard: to hear him is the inescapable duty of all those who feel responsible for the future of socialism. The radiographer who takes the X-ray showing the fragments of shell in a human body, the surgeon who extracts them, are not 'poking about in old wounds' but saving a life. Every evil thing that has happened should be called by its name; and our consciousness of why it happened is the decisive prerequisite of a more humane, socialist future.

Likewise, there is more than just Hamm or Clov, Nell and Nagg, in the Western world – the world of having. The extreme situation and the extreme characters are, as it were, in an abyss covered over with the growth of years of habit. Conventional 'realism', 'objectively' apportioning light and shade, suggests an equilibrium which no longer exists. For the conventional 'realist' the time-bomb ticking away in the basement is just one more thing among a thousand others in the house, the ticking only a background noise – and anyone who insists on speaking only of the bomb, anyone for whom the ticking drowns every other sound, is accused of distorting reality. The bosses of our mass media, press, radio, film and television, succeed in their aim of taking our minds off disaster. Thus, the distraction they offer demands the antidote of maximum concentration on disaster. To provoke dreams of terror in the slumber of prosperity has become the moral duty of literature. The negative has, in our time, become so much part of everyday life that we are prepared not only to be reconciled to it but even to discover its 'good side'. We turn the dialectic of modern science and technology, which create progress and disaster simultaneously, into something banal and cosy. Yet this is not the only reason why the creative writer feels he must stress the negative side of life. The negative oppresses him on all sides, clearly definable, distinct: whereas the positive is indefinite, appearing only as an opposition. The negative, in its definiteness, is like a black angel of the annunciation, carrying in its folded wings the still unformed positive. This angel's horizon is the *other possibility*. It is this angel which allows us to apprehend the great 'perhaps'. It invites us to hope.

THE STRUGGLE TO REMAIN HUMAN

The struggle for existence, the law of the steppe, the right of the strongest is not all. The question still has to be answered: who will be the strongest? The wolf among wolves, the one who adapts unconditionally to a dehumanized world, the one who accepts his own humiliation – or the one who defends his human essence? At the very beginning of the novel Solzhenitsyn makes the team-leader Kuziomin, who in 1943 had already been a prisoner for twelve years, say to the newcomers: 'Here, lads, we live by the law of the *taiga*. But even here people manage to live. Do you know who are the ones the camps finish off? Those who lick other men's left-overs, those who set store by the doctors, and those who peach on their mates.'

On the face of it, the wolves have the better chance. No one can avoid partially adapting to the anti-human world around him; those who do not harden themselves, die. Man fights for existence in so far as he is an animal. His destiny as man is always to rise above his existence, his *being-here*, and to reach forward into *being-there*. Those who have turned into wolves, retaining their more-than-animal intelligence, will be the more successful ones. Yet those who survive the camp as human beings will – perhaps – be the stronger.

Man keeps his humanity alive in seemingly small ways. Shukhov noticed that his team-mate Tsezar was smoking, and smoking a cigarette, not a pipe. That meant he might be able to cadge a smoke. But he didn't ask straight away, he stood quite close up to Tsezar and, half turning, looked past him . . .

'. . . Fetuikov, that jackal, had come up closer too and now stood opposite Tsezar, watching his mouth with blazing eyes.'

Shukhov wanted the rest of that cigarette 'more than freedom itself'. 'But he would never lower himself like that Fetiukov, he would never look at a man's mouth.'

The apparently slight nuance, the fact that Shukhov will not look at the smoking man's mouth, is the defence of his identity, of that minimum which makes a human being a human being. Ivan Denisovich's self-discipline belies the fact that the convict lives only for the moment when he can be spooning up the food from his bowl.

THE ABSOLUTE 'NO'

Solzhenitsyn describes, without becoming didactic, a number of possible ways of resisting dehumanization. There is the old man who can never escape the camp, condemned to another ten years at the end of every ten.

He held himself straight – the other *zeks* sat all hunched up – and looked as if he'd put something extra on the bench to sit on. There was nothing left to crop on his head: his hair had dropped out long since – the result of high living, no doubt. His eyes didn't dart after everything going on in the mess-hall. He kept them fixed in an unseeing gaze at some spot over Shukhov's head. His worn wooden spoon dipped rhythmically into the thin skilly, but instead of lowering his head to the bowl like everybody else, he raised the spoon high to his lips. He'd lost all his teeth and chewed his bread with iron gums. All life had drained out of his face but it had been left, not sickly or feeble, but hard and dark like carved stone. And by his hands, big and cracked and blackened, you could see that he'd had little opportunity of doing cushy jobs. But he wasn't going to give in, oh no! *He* wasn't going to put his three hundred grammes on the dirty, bespattered table – he put it on a well-washed bit of rag.

The old man is self-discipline personified, a conservative self-discipline which draws its strength from form. He will never surrender, but neither will he ever return to the world of the living. In his dignity he resembles the house of stone among all the wooden huts. In order to withstand imprisonment, he has turned himself into a prison, a stony loneliness. His absolute 'no' has no future.

THE CARPETS

Hamm, walled up in his hiding-place, has less self-discipline, yet to the end he refuses to give up his right to metaphor-making, transformation, creative ecstasy. Between his wretched state and nothingness, he puts *the word*. He wants it to be beautiful, poetry in the midst of darkness. When all necessities are lacking, he produces the superfluous, thus affirming that, after all, he is a man.

A little poetry. (*Pause.*) You prayed – (*Pause. He corrects himself.*) You CRIED for night; it comes – (*Pause. He corrects himself.*) It FALLS: now cry in darkness. (*He repeats, chanting.*) You cried for night; it falls: now cry in darkness. (*Pause.*) Nicely put, that. (*Pause.*) And now? (*Pause.*) Moments for nothing, now as always, time was never and time is over, reckoning over and story ended.

Moments for more than nothing, which thus cancel out the negativity of the nothing which follows. In the pure uselessness of the word whose sound dies unheard, in this sadness and this beauty, Hamm transcends himself, his selfishness, his indifference, his dehumanized existence. The melodiousness of his farewell to the world is a message from a new, perhaps still possible one, protected by the night that falls; perhaps the day dawning.

The objection to this is that the aesthetic makes things too easy, that through art man can slip furtively into the realm of freedom instead of fighting steadfastly on in the realm of necessity. Hamm never gave the bicycle to Clov although Clov cried for it, Hamm refused the oil to Mother Pegg in the darkness – does a beautiful line of poetry acquit him? Is art the negation of negation? Is it not winged irresponsibility? Shukhov suspects this when his wife writes to him that only old men, women and children are now still working in the *kolkhoz*; the younger men have discovered a new, easier trade: that of art.

The new trade, his wife writes, is carpet-making.

Someone had brought stencils back from the war and from that time the thing became popular and the number of those carpet-painters grew and grew. They had no steady jobs, they didn't work anywhere, they helped the *kolkhoz* for a month or so, just at the hay-making or the harvesting, and for that the *kolkhoz* gave them a chit saying that so-and-so, a member of the *kolkhoz*, had been released to carry on his work and that the *kolkhoz* had no claim on him. And they travelled all over the country, they even flew in aeroplanes to save time, and they piled up roubles by the thousand and painted carpets all over the place. Fifty roubles a carpet made out of any old sheet you could spare – and it didn't seem to take them more than an hour to make a carpet of it . . .

There were three sorts of carpets, she wrote: the 'Troika', an officer of the hussars driving a beautiful troika; the 'Reindeer'; and a third with a Persian-style pattern. They had no other designs, but people all over the country were glad to get these and snatch them out of the painters' hands. Because a real carpet cost not fifty but thousands of roubles.

Shukhov did not much like the idea of the carpets. Behind this new but suspect activity he sensed the decline of the village, the disorganization of agriculture, the fruits of an administration alienated from reality, progressive demoralization. More telling than a hundred pages of long-winded reports, this small detail represents the whole situation in the last years of Stalin's rule – these cheap carpets painted from stencils covering up the greyness, a whole world of illusion, of *ersatz* gratification and unproductive propaganda. Yet the double aspect must not be overlooked: the men who paint carpets from these three stencils are escaping from an unprofitable form of production into a more profitable one, and the buyers long for something different, superfluous, non-utilitarian. '*Les choses superflues sont les choses les plus nécessaires.*' In this nostalgia for 'something higher', something not in the service of material consumption – even if it is an utterly fatuous stencil representing reindeer in a forest or a pretty troika being driven by a pretty hussar officer – we recognize the nature of man as a being who transcends himself. If human labour served only the production of useful objects and not man's intellectual, moral and aesthetic development and the cause of making a more beautiful, better and more human world, it would have no meaning.

PUTTING THINGS IN ORDER

In the disorder of the refuge, in the midst of that desolate mess, Clov suddenly begins to pick up the objects thrown down by Hamm.

HAMM: What are you doing?
CLOV: Putting things in order. (*He straightens up. Fervently.*) I'm going to clear everything away!
  He starts picking up again.
HAMM: Order!
CLOV (*straightening up*): I love order. It's my dream. A world where all would be silent and still and each thing in its last place, under the last dust.
  He starts picking up again.
HAMM (*exasperated*): What in God's name do you think you are doing?
CLOV (*straightening up*): I'm doing my best to create a little order.
HAMM: Drop it!

In this 'putting things in order' which Clov undertakes with sudden fervour there is an inherent inner contradiction. True, Clov dreams of a world where everything would be silent and still and each thing in its last place: he dreams of the harmonious perfection of an ultimate state: but precisely this dream of perfection drives him to constant activity, to the restlessness of putting things in order, to continual changing of the *status quo*. Even before the disorder which Hamm brought into the world, things were not in their last place, and Clov's dream that they should be so, his utopia of the finality of paradise, will not let him rest; anticipation of the future prevents him standing still, and may even persuade him to continue his putting-things-in-order outside the refuge. Once work has begun – work as the transformation of the outside world, founded on human planning and striving, work as the great putting-things-in-order – it cannot stop, for order achieved becomes at once a new disorder requiring another order, and so on *ad infinitum*. The master in his armchair may say 'Drop it!', but in the long run the servant cannot drop it, because it is his function to act, to clear everything away, to create order.

Shukhov's work team arrives at the building site.

At one place the panels of the prefabs lay under the snow; at another a start had been made on the brickwork, and abandoned when no higher than the foundations. Here lay a broken excavator lever, there a scoop, further on a pile of scrap-metal. A network of ditches and trenches criss-crossed the site with a pit or two here and there. The building of the automobile repair shop was ready for roofing. On a rise stood the power-station itself, built up to the second storey.

The power station left unfinished, abandoned in late autumn – what disorder, what confusion of planning and execution! Slave labour is unproductive, under the icy layer of discipline there is indifference, irresponsibility, blind self-interest.

Shukhov was seeing only his wall – from the junction where the blocks rose in steps, higher than the waist, to where it met Kilgas's. . . . At the spot he was working on, the wall had previously been laid by some mason who was either incompetent or had scamped the job. . . . There, he saw, was a cavity that couldn't be levelled up in one row. . . . And there the outer wall bellied a bit – it would take two rows to straighten that.

The wall on which Shukhov is working, the growing wall that soon reaches to his chest, what is it to him? Yet because in it the material fuses with his own energy, he begins to feel it as a continuation of himself, as a victory over the prevailing disorder. He begins the work under duress; he wants to complete it as his own, in hazardous freedom.

The rail clanged. The signal went dinning all over the site and reached the power-station. They'd been caught with some unused mortar. Eh, just when they'd got into the swing of it!

'Mortar! Mortar!' Tiurin shouted.

A new boxful had only just been mixed. They had to go on laying, there was no other way. If they left anything in the box, next morning they could throw the whole lot of it to hell – the mortar would have petrified, it wouldn't yield to a pickaxe.

But the team leader changes his mind.

'Eh,' Tiurin shouted 'Don't spare the shit. Carriers! Go and scrape the big box, and out with what's left into that hole there and scatter some snow on it to keep it hidden. . . .'

'Listen, lads,' Shukhov said, 'give your trowels to Gopchik. Mine's not on the list. There's no need to hand it in. I'll keep going.'

But if the team is not complete for counting, there will be trouble, and everyone is against Shukhov.

'To hell with the mortar,' says the team leader. 'Sling it over the wall.'

Shukhov replies: 'Don't wait, leader. Go ahead, you're needed there.' (Shukhov usually addressed Tiurin, more respectfully, as Andrei Prokofievich, but now, after working like that, he felt equal to the team leader. He didn't put it to himself, 'Look, I'm your equal', he just knew it.)

He is left alone with the deaf man.

Mortar. Block. Mortar. Block . . .

'Finish, curse you,' shouts Senka. 'Let's hop it.'

What Shukhov has done is to create order. Gripped by the very essence of labour, he becomes absorbed in it and so finds himself. The nature of work is deformed even in ordinary wage labour, degraded from a creative art to a mere earning process: in convict labour it undergoes total perversion. Yet by setting himself a task above and beyond the duress imposed upon him, Shukhov throws off the enforced nature of the work. Becoming personified in his work and anticipating the future, he gains permanence and continuity beyond the brief moment of his action and puts a little order into the world. Herbert Marcuse says that the nature of work is founded on 'there being an essential surplus of human existence over any possible situation of man himself or of the world: man's *being* is always more than his existence at any given moment . . .'[1]

Through such a 'surplus', which overcomes mere existence and strives towards possible *being*, Ivan Denisovich catches a glimpse of freedom. But will there be more than a glimpse of freedom? And where? For what?

FOR THE SAKE OF THE CAUSE

Many such Ivans, in face of the arbitrary power of the apparatus, have preserved human dignity under senseless coercion and pressure, and carried forward the cause of the Soviet Union. Gripped by this cause, hoping against hope, Mortar! Block! Mortar! Block!, disappointed again and again, Mortar! Block! Mortar! Block!, they will keep on building and believing. 'A year, there's nothing for it, we'll have to stick it out for another year in the old place.' These are the last words of a story by Solzhenitsyn called *For the Sake of the Cause*. In it he sums up what happened after Stalin's death and the return from the camps.

A technical college in a provincial town is temporarily housed in an inadequate building. The 'temporary' situation draws out indefinitely. At last the municipality assigns a plot of ground to the college. Two sets of foundations are laid, one for the school, one for a students' hostel. Three more years pass – until the students decide to build the school and the hostel themselves in their spare time. The students are transformed beyond recognition, filled with enthusiasm. 'Enthusiasm is probably a natural state of man, and, I suppose, the most beautiful one. Only the word has become . . . so humdrum, so shallow with us. We use it much too thoughtlessly,' says one of the teachers. Suddenly it's all over. A commission arrives, the powerful director Khabalygin, a comrade from the Ministry and two further comrades from a couple of committees for something-or-other. Ministry decision: a research institute to be housed in the new buildings.

The principal of the college appeals in vain to the secretary of the town Party Committee. An appeal to Knorozov, the instructor at the area committee, confirms the finality of the decision, 'for the sake of the cause', against the interest, the initiative, the enthusiasm of the students. 'Knorozov was proud of the fact that he never took back anything he had said. Like Stalin's word in Moscow in earlier days, so Knorozov's word in this area was never taken back and none of his decisions was ever altered. Stalin had been dead a long time, but Knorozov was still there.' This time it is Grachikov, the secretary of the town committee, who goes to plead with Knorozov.

The provincial Stalin's cold 'No!' exasperates Grachikov. 'Communism is built for human beings, not for stones!' he shouts as if possessed. 'It takes longer, it's more difficult. Even if we build everything in stone tomorow, we still won't have communism.'

The powerful director Khabalygin, who has pulled strings at the Ministry to get the decision he wants, becomes principal of the new research institute. Grachikov, 'not sufficiently mature to remain secretary of the town committee', becomes a labourer.

And the students?

'So we've got to start everything all over again,' thought the old principal of the college. 'We'll call the nine hundred together and tell them: we haven't got a building. It's got to be built. If we all help, it'll be built sooner.

'At first they'll grumble.

'Then they'll get swept into it, the way work always sweeps you in.

'They'll believe.

'And build.

'A year, there's nothing for it, we'll have to stick it for another year in the old place.'

And then?

The fact that the narrator does not ask the question but leaves the reader to ask and answer it, gives suggestive power to the story, although its literary quality is not as high as that of *Ivan Denisovich*. The style is undecided: the necessary reduction to the matter itself as a model of reality is successfully achieved, but the element of novelty, of something rising above literary realism, is still missing. It is no longer the old prose and yet not a new one; it lacks Joyce, Kafka, Faulkner with their means of expression still condemned as 'Western decadence'. But the subject is strong and clear, handled with courage and candour.

THE INVISIBLE REALITY

What matters is not the wall of the power station but the fact that, by means of it and with it, Shukhov is growing. Richness of life is not guaranteed by stone being added to stone with increasing speed and in increasing quantities – metals, plastics, motor cars, television sets, moon rockets, the accumulation of objects, goods and arms, useful and useless products: indeed, it is precisely in this world of objects that the living space of the human essence can shrink to a minimum, like the tiny space left for the man in the midst of his own furniture in Ionesco's one-act play. Surrounded by the glamour and swagger of a world of consumption, the artist's moral need is to reveal the inner nature of that world, its bleak emptiness, its invisible reality, Hamm's last retreat where there is no bicycle, no pap and no pain-killer, the wretchedness behind the prosperity, the negative. And likewise, behind the national song which proclaims '... For there is no other land on earth/Where man's heart can beat so freely', behind the gigantomania of the monuments and the power apparatus, lurks the 'other hell', the stone prison in the midst of wooden huts, the labour camp, the arrogance of officials, the dust on the red flags, the greyness of negativity. The worst thing is that one *becomes used to it*, becomes reconciled, adapts oneself, accepts the inhuman as normal. Ivan Denisovich, who has observed the old man's escape into his rigid 'no' and Alyosha's religious resignation, no longer knows at the end of the day – which, remember, has been a 'good day' – whether or not he should trust the glimpse of freedom he caught that evening.

Now he didn't know either whether he wanted freedom or not. At first he'd longed for it. Every night he'd counted the days of his stretch – how many had passed, how many were coming. And then he'd grown bored with counting. And then it became clear that men of his like wouldn't ever be allowed to return home, that they'd be exiled. And whether his life would be any better there than here – who could tell? Freedom meant one thing to him – home. But they wouldn't let him go home.

THE GREAT PERHAPS

Clov, too, does not know what he wants. To stay – what for? To go – where? How much future has to be mixed into the present to prevent it petrifying?

A gleam of hope. . . . Clov suddenly sees through the telescope something he has not seen before: in the midst of the disintegrating world, a child.

CLOV (*dismayed*): Looks like a small boy!
HAMM (*sarcastic*): A small . . . boy!
CLOV: I'll go and see. (*He gets down, drops the telescope, goes towards door, turns.*) I'll take the gaff.

For Hamm, this possible return of life, not merely of a rat you exterminate but of a human being, spells horror and damnation. His situation is still worse than that of Joseph K. in Kafka's *The Trial* when, just before his execution in the quarry, his glance falls on the top storey of a near-by house.

With a flicker as of a light going on, the casements of a window there suddenly flew open; a human figure, faint and insubstantial at that distance and that height, leaned abruptly far forward and stretched

C

both arms still farther. Who was it? A friend? A good man? Someone who sympathised? Someone who wanted to help? Was it one person only? Or were they all there? Was help at hand?

Hamm is denied this gleam of hope, the great perhaps. Joseph K. has become guilty only by not-doing; Hamm has refused Mother Pegg oil in the darkness. To justify his inhumanity man has to perish. But for Clov, the child may represent hope; what appears to be a part of the past may carry a vague hope of a future.

For Shukhov, too, the gate has opened. He will pick up the trowel and walk out, in order to *be there*, to help in the laborious putting-things-in-order.

CLOV: . . . That order! They said to me, Come now, you're not a brute beast, think upon these things and you'll see how all becomes clear. And simple! They said to me, What skilled attention they get, all these dying of their wounds.

HAMM: Enough!

CLOV: I say to myself – sometimes, Clov, you must learn to suffer better than that if you want them to weary of punishing you – one day. I say to myself – sometimes, Clov, you must be there better than that if you want them to let you go – one day.

It is true that he adds: 'But I feel too old, and too far, to form new habits.' And yet: 'I open the door of the cell and go. I am so bowed I only see my feet, if I open my eyes, and between my legs a little trail of black dust. I say to myself that the earth is extinguished, though I never saw it lit.'

Hamm is no more now than the past, a story he tells himself, filled with sound and fury, signifying nothing. But Clov, if he learns to be there better than that, that is to say if he learns how to be a human being, not a convict imprisoned by some outside power but holding judgement over his own self, if he learns how to be a human being, there is – perhaps – a future for him, a world more human, more reasonable than the old one, bursting into flower out of the black dust.

Clov and Ivan will meet – perhaps – somewhere along the way to this other world.

Note

1. Herbert Marcuse, *Kultur und Gesellschaft* (Frankfurt: Suhrkamp, 1965)

Chapter 2

COEXISTENCE AND IDEOLOGY

Perhaps the catastrophe can still be averted.

All those who resist the mechanism constitute this 'perhaps'. There is no fate. There are only alternatives.

In a letter written on 28 September 1945, Klaus Mann, Thomas Mann's lovable and unhappy son, wondered which way things would turn now that the war was over.

It depends on us: one has a choice at every turning point. We can opt for the right direction or the wrong one. . . . A sincere understanding between East and West is the *conditio sine qua non*; without it, nothing is possible. Every step that brings this understanding closer or con-solidates it is a step in the right direction. Every step that takes us further from this aim is a step towards the abyss.

The steps towards the abyss followed without delay – in the form of the cold war. George F. Kennan, one of the most intelligent American politicians, realized at the time and later wrote that the greatest obstacle to a reasonable policy was the fact that the West, and particularly America and Germany, have to a great extent decided upon the aim of the final annihilation of communism. . . . The question can be reduced to whether the world is seen from the viewpoint of an irreconcilable and deadly struggle between all those who call themselves communists and those who do not – a struggle which must inescapably, in the relatively near future, end with the total annihilation of one or both sides – or whether it is recognised that the socialist cause in the world can be furthered in more complex, more subtly graduated, less dramatic and less direct forms . . .[1]

The Twentieth Congress of the Communist Party of the Soviet Union in 1956 pronounced itself in favour of these 'more subtly graduated, less dramatic and less direct forms' and of competition between different social systems without recourse to arms. It is unfortunate that no greater personality was at hand to fill the world-historical role which Khrushchev assumed. Nevertheless he did have the courage to shake the Stalin myth, even though by Stalin's own methods. He spoke of a possibility of avoiding a third world war. He represented the will for coexistence. For this he deserves our thanks.

An old man, John XXIII, one of the most moving and admirable figures of the century, became the head of the Roman Catholic Church. What this dying man achieved within two years can no longer be undone by any conspiracy of the living.

In the United States, John F. Kennedy outlined the concept of a new policy against the military, a policy for peace and reason. The words of the American sociologist C. Wright Mills seemed to be coming true:

From the standpoint of mere survival, let alone progress toward a world of properly developing societies, there is now one and only one paramount goal and only one general means to it: coexistence.

The United States élite must give up the illusion that 'this bunch of Reds' will somehow go away, that their societies will collapse, or that there is any action short of mutual annihilation that the United States can take to make them collapse. They must recognize the world historical meaning of the Russian Revolution: that there now exists in the world an alternative way of industrialization . . .

We must demand that the coexistence of these two world-established models of industrialization be fully recognized and that the competition between them be conducted in economic and cultural and political ways, rather than by means of the idiot's race.

The military metaphysic must be abandoned.[2]

It seemed as though a new age had begun, as though the hopes of 1945 had returned to take on a new shape.

But the old age, which seemed on the way out, fought back. John Kennedy was assassinated. John XXIII died. Khrushchev proved unequal to his task.

THE WORKS OF MAN

'The works of man will lead to the death of man,' prophesied Leonardo.[3]

With increasing momentum, increasingly large masses of human beings, goods, arms, inventions and technical achievements are moving towards a future whose face is veiled and whose body is a chimera, a machine with an archangel's wings, a fantastically rapid alternation of ultra-light and deep, terrible night.

The more precisely computers calculate this future, the less we are capable of facing the incalculable. The more closely we predict what will happen in twenty years' time, the more unexpected are the events of today. We are lost in a perfectly constructed maze of facts, dates and information. Ariadne's thread has multiplied a hundred-fold; we do not know which one we should follow, and stumble from one dead-end into another. A plethora of means has devoured the end.

We are lagging behind ourselves. We are unable to catch up with what we have done. We overfeed the sky with the accomplishments of our technology whilst two thousand million people on earth are undernourished. What ought to serve us, dominates us. What frees us from effort, robs us of our freedom. What the mind devises, power abuses.

Sputniks, moon rockets, astronauts, encounters in space watched by millions on the television screen: what progress! Whose progress? Progress of man? Of reason? Of humanity? The 'soft' landing on the moon, what comfort when elsewhere things are so hard for us! Science tells us of all the things she has achieved to help the suffering and the living, and suddenly, beneath the healer's white coat, we glimpse the general's uniform.

Some have hoped that mankind, now that for the first time in world history it can destroy itself and commit collective suicide, is bound to become what it still is not – humanity; is bound to listen to the voice of reason, which power is still successfully trying to silence. Mankind must become reasonable, or it will cease to be.

QUESTIONS

Are power and reason compatible? Power and intellect? Power and freedom?

Can the development to full humanity be accomplished in our time without concentration of power?

Is it not precisely this concentration of power which paralyzes the development to full humanity?

Is it conceivable that a withdrawal into the small collective, into the creative community remote from the centres of power, can offer a hope of creating small islands of freedom even within the world of power?

Is it possible that, although the State does not wither away and a specialized bureaucracy continues to carry out the necessary work of administration, a parallel 'realm of freedom' can be created on the basis of the enormous productive forces and the increasing wealth of society?

Is it possible that a complete de-ideologization of power, the withdrawal from it of any messianic function and its limitation to merely administrative purposes, might stop power from being an obstacle to human development?

Are we right when we consider democracy in all areas of social existence to be the only panacea? Can it be that when the social mechanism is functioning almost automatically, democracy may begin to lose its significance?

Are humanism and the idea of the free personality outdated? Is our struggle a form of quixotism which blocks our view of other, completely different, possibilities and forms of humanity?

> *Against stupid giants*
> *mounted on the narrow back of tragic and valiant Rosinante*
> *Don Quixote canters into the unknown.*
> *When a heart is heavy with great longing,*
> *and on fire, no snow or wind can cool it;*
> *there is nothing you can do, my Quixote,*
> *but wage your struggle against windmills . . .*[4]

Yet the windmills are really monstrous, death-dealing machines:

Don Quixote sees it and Sancho Panza does not; Don Quixote is right, he is a tragi-comic figure like everyone who is right, and since the windmills have grown, becoming more terrible in their devouring passion than any dragon of ancient myth, Don Quixote has not remained alone. Millions have helped him to tame the monsters and to humanize the world.

Is his day over? May we in our highly industrialized societies still expect social, intellectual and moral renewal through revolutions on the old lines? Will the intellectuals, the technical intelligentsia and the highly skilled workers produce the core, the *avant-garde* of a new, bold yet thoughtful, revolutionary and democratic movement? Will such an *avant-garde* be capable of gaining the confidence, not only of progressive forces in the West, but also of the peoples of Asia, Africa and Latin America? Will it be possible in that way to preserve the world from the catastrophe which is bound to happen if 'the wretched of the earth' are not liberated through the solidarity of an international *class war* waged with new perspectives and by new methods, so that they may join with us in building a new humanity? Or will the last and bloodiest act of world revolution be a mankind-destroying *race war*, a last judgement after which no one shall rise from the dead?

In the most highly developed industrial society, the U.S.A., with its almost total integration of the workers into the ruling system, only Negroes, both black and white, the declassed and groups of young intellectuals remain outside. In these explosive social strata without any cohesion or common goal, Norman Mailer and others see the chance for the great revolt. 'If there are ten million Americans who are more or less psychopathic (and the figure is extremely modest), there are probably not more than one hundred thousand men and women who consciously see themselves as hipsters.'[5] These, however, are thought by Mailer to form the élite of a possible rebellion. The psychopath, he says, is the 'perverted and dangerous front-runner of a new kind of personality which could become the central expression of human nature before the twentieth century is over.'[6] If the Negro problem is not solved in the foreseeable future, 'Hip may erupt as a psychically armed rebellion' leading to 'a time of violence, new hysteria, confusion and rebellion' which will have incalculable consequences.

The same disillusionment with the working class and its historical function has led in Asia and Africa to the theory of an alliance of the national revolutionary intelligentsia and the undeveloped peasantry against all 'whites'. Frantz Fanon, in his manifesto *The Wretched of the Earth*, develops the thesis of the struggle of the disinherited and starving peasants against the '*colons*', the privileged town dwellers, among whom he includes not only employers, tradesmen and officials, but also workers. 'The starving peasant, outside the class system, is the first among the exploited to discover that only violence pays.'[7] Franz Marek, from whose book *Philosophie der Weltrevolution* I obtained this quotation, adds:

Fanon's final conclusions are incorrect, but the facts to which they relate are facts. New models of development towards socialism have come into being which go beyond the ideas of Marx and even Lenin, and which are also inadequately dealt with in the theoretical generalisations of the Chinese revolution . . .[8]

Will the new working class, will all those who represent reason in the highly developed industrial society and are prepared to assume responsibility in the future, recognize in time the magnitude of the decision confronting us?

Questions such as these demand to be asked if 'coexistence' is not to become part of the *danse macabre* of empty phrases – if it is to become something more than a threadbare agreement between the world powers not to drop bombs on one another while extending, somewhat modestly, their trade relations and 'cultural exchanges' (consisting of a few itinerant professors, artists and ballet companies).

THE UNDERDEVELOPED CONSCIOUSNESS

Until today, our consciousness has always been able, in the process of technical, economic and social development, to perceive the changed nature of the 'I', to translate the external into the internal and to establish a precarious equilibrium between man and the surrounding world. Every possibility realized has been surrounded not only by a multitude of rejected possibilities, but also by a vast number of newly created ones. It has not been a simple case of technology forging ahead and forcing society to follow in its wake; dreams have prophesied the achievements yet to come and thus have stimulated reason to devise means of forcing inert matter into the shape of an anticipated future. But while the imagination preceded the facts, it was the tendency of established social conditions, institutions and ideologies to linger behind the development of the productive forces – of which the imagination is one of the most powerful.

Hegel spoke of man's impulse

to assert himself in that which is presented to him in immediacy, in that which is at hand as an external something to himself, and by so doing at the same time once more to recognize himself therein. . . . And man does all this, in order that he may as a free agent divest the external world of its stubborn alienation from himself – and in order that he may enjoy in the configuration of objective fact an external reality simply of himself. . . . This human need runs through the most varied phenomena up to that particular form of self-reproduction in the external fact which is presented us in human art. And it is not merely in relation to external objects that man acts thus. He treats himself, that is, his natural form, in a similar manner: he will not permit it to remain as he finds it; he alters it deliberately.[9]

Marx disagreed with vulgar materialism as he did with Hegel's brilliantly one-sided views.

The materialistic doctrine concerning the changing of circumstances and education forgets that circumstances are changed by men and that the educator himself must be educated. . . . The coincidence of the changing of circumstances and of human activity or self-changing can only be comprehended and rationally understood as *revolutionary practice*.[10]

Today, however, we are confronted for the first time not only with the danger of total self-annihilation but also with the possibility of the *automation of man*, for our consciousness has not yet managed to cope with the new form of being. We need not fear that the human organism and intelligence are not malleable enough to adapt themselves to the new conditions; but we do have to worry about what Günther Anders calls 'the antiquatedness of man'. Perhaps it is only our humanist view of man that is antiquated, the dream of the *whole man* which European philosophy, the ancient world, Christianity, the Renaissance, utopian and scientific socialism have encouraged. Perhaps the model of the new man is already being made in American laboratories – a perfectly functioning being composed of carefully chosen genes, equipped with replaceable organs and always available spare parts, his stability not threatened by any emotion or sense of identity with himself, an automaton with a well-adjusted mechanism for the satisfaction of instincts, a biological shell into which the experience, the memory, the 'I' of other still living or already dead members of the species can be injected and withdrawn again when another kind of 'I' is required. But required by whom? By society, that is to say by those who govern society. For such a plan the only question asked is: what kind of man does society want? Never: what kind of a society does man need in order to attain humanity?

Man has become manipulable to the extreme. But who is to manipulate him in the future? The underdeveloped consciousness of rulers who use the means of an overdeveloped technology and who know the meaning of power and nothing else.

Or is it conceivable that man is crouching before a leap that will carry him far beyond himself? Biological mutations are generally regressive. But cannot the social mutation of our time be progressive?

Elias Canetti has spoken of the 'double aspect of things to come'. No one, he maintains, can escape from this double aspect of the future.

Everyone sees a dark figure and a bright one simultaneously, both approaching at startling speed. You may try to cover up one of them so as to see only the other, but both are inexorably there. . . . It is especially this double aspect of the future, actively desired and actively feared, that distinguishes the reality of our century from that of the last.[11]

Since this is so and since all these things-to-come are rushing towards us with gathering speed, can we afford to look only at our own group, our own party or system, for answers to questions which, if they are to be answered at all, must be answered *jointly*?

WHAT IS IDEOLOGY?

Since Napoleon spoke disparagingly of '*ideologues*', the concept of ideology has been defined and interpreted in a multitude of ways. The pejorative sense has predominated from the start: ideology as 'false consciousness' (Engels), as reality stood on its head (Marx). In his work *The German Ideology* Marx writes:

. . . in all ideology men and their circumstances appear upside down as in a *camera obscura*. . . . The phantoms formed in the human brain are also, necessarily, sublimates of their material life-process, which is empirically verifiable and bound to material premises. Morality, religion, metaphysics, all the rest of ideology and their corresponding forms of consciousness thus no longer retain the semblance of independence.[12]

The totality of the moral, religious, metaphysical, juridical and political ideas and prejudices of a society, the largely false consciousness that society has of itself, is seen as its 'ideology' or 'ideological superstructure'. The ideology of the ruling class at any given period is the dominant one at that time; the prevailing material relationships are *mystified*, that is to say the relationships 'which make the one class the ruling one, therefore the ideas of its dominance'.[13]

Such a definition of the concept of 'ideology' leads to considerable difficulties. First: is the ruling ideology a *unified* one, or, given the contradictions inevitable in any tradition of government, given the new social factors and the numerous compromises involved, is it a multi-layered, variegated ideology capable of different interpretations – but with a framework of common, irrefutable principles?

Further: are the ruled prepared under all circumstances to accept the ideology of their rulers? Or do certain *ideas of protest* arise (although these may in part be submerged within the ruling ideology), to become an anti-ideology? And does this anti-ideology mean that the class struggle (or the struggle between other social groupings) becomes also a struggle between ideologies? Marx and Engels occasionally used the concept of 'ideology' in this sense as well (Engels more frequently than Marx); generally, however, the pejorative interpretation predominates in their writings. Ideology is made distinct from cognition or science or the philosophy of practice.

Lastly, cannot false consciousness contain fragments of genuine understanding, cannot false morality include ethical postulates of general validity? Are not even 'the phantoms formed in the human brain' sublimates of reality? Is any ideology wholly 'false consciousness'? Every ideology must contain vague or confused reflections of reality, distorted insights and half-truths, or it is ineffective. With the development of a given society the ratio of the mixture changes. New reality triumphs over or at least modifies the consciousness which falsifies it. New insights and ideas then cause the outdated ideology's collapse or force it substantially to reconstruct itself.

The multitude of meanings which can inevitably be attached to the concept of 'ideology' has given rise to a variety of contradictory definitions. Leszek Kolakowski's definition seems to me excellent:

> We understand by ideology the sum of ideas which serves a social group (a class, but not exclusively) for the organization of the *values* which express the mystified consciousness of that group and its activity. . . . Ideology therefore is not 'pure' theory, and cannot be this, because knowledge of reality *per se* cannot impel anyone to action; ideology contains evaluative or descriptive judgements, which either are already the mystified expression of belief in certain values, or which subordinate their content to strengthening such belief and such values.[14]

Thus, in every ideology, it is not the amount of truth but the 'proof of strength' which is decisive, and if false consciousness proves more effective, then knowledge of the truth is subordinated to it, trimmed for its benefit, kept secret or discredited as 'hostile propaganda'. Historical development, then, is not merely a matter of ideological struggle reflecting the struggle between classes, nations or systems, but at the same time, although in a less spectacular fashion, the struggle of the *practice and recognition of truth* against the domination of ideology. Science, the arts, philosophic cognition are, it is true, capable of being influenced by ideology – generally to their detriment; but by their nature they are the revolt of reality against false consciousness.

CONFRONTATION OF IDEAS

New ideas opposing petrified ideologies cause unrest, stimulate opposition, eventually grip the masses and turn into actual power.

The concept of 'idea' is likewise difficult to define. A process of vulgarization has taken place between the time Plato first used it to designate the essential image behind the reproduced image, *that which is* behind *that which appears*, and our own time in which any useful suggestion is described as 'a good idea'. Yet what we call 'idea' is surrounded by a Platonic aura even today. 'Idea' is connected with intimation, thought, hypothesis, concept, theory, postulate, utopian anticipation. It is neither scientific knowledge nor exact thought, but a combination of reason and imagination, nature and vision, concept and appearance. It can be defined as *the notion seen*, as *thought borne on the wings of imagination*. Because it does not address itself to the intellect alone but to the whole human being, it has the power, in the form of an emotion, a desire or a demand – such as the demand for 'freedom', 'justice' or 'humanity' – to influence the masses. The 'idea of socialism' is a whole made up of such ideas, among which freedom, justice, humanity – the utopia of mankind and mankind as a utopia – are the determining ones.

In every ideology ideas are arrested so that they become *idées fixes*, immovable supports of a class, a system, a ruling group. What is lost is the movement of the idea, therefore its dialectic and therefore its reality. The idea is placed in a coffin of dogma. Ideologies are fortresses. Ideas operate in open territory, measure their forces in direct combat, test one another, learn through contradiction, come home enriched by experience; it may even happen that an idea, although challenging another, will recognize its own inadequacy and allow itself to be corrected by its opponent. This is a most alarming possibility for the commanders of ideological fortresses.

Such commanders have much in common with General Stumm von Bordwehr. In *The Man Without Qualities* Robert Musil relates how this general, appointed by the Ministry of War to keep an eye on the 'Parallel Action', begins to build up 'a catalogue of the ideas-in-chief' of the twentieth century. As a result, he discovers, groaning, that

you will notice . . . if you look at one of the idea-units in action at present, that it receives its supplies of fighting-troops and intellectual war-material, not only from its own bases, but also from those of its enemy. You will see that it is continually shifting positions and suddenly, without any cause, it turns its front and fights against its own lines of communication. And then again you will see that the ideas are ceaselessly going over to the enemy, and then back again, so that you will find them now in one, now in another line of battle. In short, one can't draw up a decent plan of communications or a line of demarcation or anything else, either, and the whole thing, if I may say so without offence, looks – not that I can really bring myself to believe it! – like what every commanding officer would call a hell of a mess.[15]

In a world of militarized ideologies, of ideological 'camps' and 'fronts', 'cultural fronts', etc., General Stumm von Bordwehr would do very well as Ideologist-in-Chief, warning against any free contest of ideas and predicting an ideological 'hell of a mess'. For nothing endangers the peace and security of an ideology so much as ideas, which have no respect for ideological walls.

THE 'BOURGEOIS' IDEOLOGY

For communist dogmatists there exists a bourgeois ideology under which anything undesirable at that moment, from existentialism to the theory of reality, from genetics to surrealism, and from nationalism to cosmopolitanism, can be subsumed. In bourgeois society there have in fact been (and still are) several more or less developed, mutually contradictory and hostile ideologies: humanism, puritanism, liberalism, nationalism, fascism and a number of other 'isms', all competing with one another but prepared to compromise. Even imperialism with its drive towards concentration and monopoly has failed to produce a monolithic ideology; racialism, voluntarism, pragmatism, irrationalism, scepticism and nihilism, which are described as the components of such an ideology, differ too widely from each other to produce an ideological coincidence of opposites. As a result of uneven social development, certain of these ideological compounds acquire primary importance in certain countries and situations, while others are relegated to the second rank as being less useful, or are rejected altogether. Thus, for example, the puritanical ideology of saving and of renouncing pleasure can, in a highly developed industrial society, become a sin against production, so that extravagance then becomes a virtue. The dominant ideology in imperialist Germany at the time of Hitler was substantially different from that in the no less imperialist United States at the time of Roosevelt, and the ideology now prevalent in England is not identical with that of Portugal.

'Bourgeois' or 'capitalist' ideology is imprecise, variegated, and flexible. Thus, for example, irrationalism has been (and, in part, still is) central to European and especially German ideology; at the same time, various forms of pragmatism, a down-to-earth 'rationalism' based on performance and success, are dominant in America. Irrationalism and pragmatism are not, of course, mutually exclusive; sometimes they combine together to form a curious blend. The dogmatists of rigid 'ideological fronts' should not forget that it was precisely at Stalin's time, when fundamental discoveries of modern science were being condemned as 'Western', that elements of irrationalism (in the form of voluntarism) and of pragmatism penetrated the communist ideology.

The view that scepticism, pessimism and nihilism are characteristic features of the bourgeois or capitalist ideology of today is based on a misconception. The rulers want confidence, optimism, affirmation; scepticism is often a protest against the prevalent ideology, a negative and by no means welcome result of it. It is true that shrewd 'ideologues' of power are able to enlist even scepticism in the service of the system, especially when new, revolutionary ideas become dangerously attractive. The sceptic and even the cynic are less of a threat to those in power than the man gripped by new revolutionary ideas. Scepticism can have a neutralizing effect. The apparent ideological weakness of the ruling group can often be its strength. The less an ideology insists on being recognized, the less resistance it provokes. Ideological 'agnosticism' and 'non-conformism' let in ideology through the back door of consciousness. In times of crisis, of course, there is plenty of ideological noise made: save freedom! honour the nation! the most sacred possessions of mankind, God and the Fatherland, etc., etc.

The *ideology of having*, adapted to the requirements of the rulers at any given time, is the only thing that has ideological substance in the world of having. For decades, this ideology of having has found its most effective support in anti-communism. The false consciousness which regards *having* as the essential guarantee of *freedom* draws from anti-communism arguments which play on both the intelligence and the emotions. The lack of freedom in the communist world, the contempt with which overbearing, arrogant communist officials speak of an 'abstract', 'petty-bourgeois' or 'anarchic' freedom in order to dismiss the people's desire for a very concrete kind of freedom indeed – for the right to decide freely between two alternatives – this makes it easier for the rulers of the capitalist world to claim that the largely illusory, manipulated freedom of private life, controlled by hidden persuaders, is the quintessence of freedom. In the ideology of having, the idea of freedom (even if much reduced in scope and scale) has become an effective force – and will remain so for as long as in the communist-ruled countries freedom is admitted only as the 'recognition of necessity' and as long as the area of free decision is not substantially enlarged. Even the appearance of freedom (especially if it reflects certain genuine liberties) is more attractive than the invitation to recognize dictatorship as freedom.

But the real ideological fuel, now as in the past, is *nationalism*. Today it forms part of all social systems, from the most backward to the most advanced. Through identification with the nation, the man not yet or no longer sure of his identity becomes capable of anything, any aggression directed inwards or outwards, murder and self-sacrifice, crime and heroism. Nationalism, whose home is Europe, has infected all the peoples of the world, producing in the oppressed a national hatred of the national arrogance of their rulers. Much as the nationalism of peoples fighting for national independence and equality differs from that of the 'master races' by its premises and motives, it nevertheless resembles it in its forms of expression and its tendency to elevate the nation's advantage to the status of a moral value of the highest order. Justified as the national struggle for liberation is, and unjustified as the oppression of foreign peoples in the name of civilization has been, we must recognize that the oppressed have learned from the oppressors not to shrink from anything in matters of national interest. Not only the nationalist training for cruelty is alarming, but also its epidemic spread. Nationalism, this fundamental substance of bourgeois ideology, has infected communists too.

CHRISTIANITY AND COMMUNISM

No less remarkable, but much more significant than the infection of a rigid ideology by the *evils* of the opposing ideology is the cooperation possible between the *good* elements of two contradictory ideologies.

Today the unified 'closed' ideologies which oppose communism are the great religions, and especially Roman Catholicism. For decades, emphasis was placed by both sides on the antagonistic and irreconcilable nature of these ideologies. Agreement on any point was thought to be impossible. Today, however, both sides have begun to think again. Although the profound conflict in fundamental ideas cannot be glossed over, it becomes clear that certain humanist values and aims are held in common.

The concept of 'ideological coexistence' is showing its weakness. It is not enough that Christianity and communism 'coexist'. What is at stake (let it be said to reassure the ideologues) is less than coexistence, or rather more: namely cooperation. In his declaration at Bergamo in March 1963, which has since become famous, Palmiro Togliatti spoke of the need for the Catholic Church and the communist party to work together, and rejected as 'naïve and erroneous' the view of the Enlightenment and of eighteenth-century materialism according to which increased education and social change automatically guaranteed the disappearance of religion. The roots of religion go deeper than that. The Christian and the marxist conception of man and society are based on common ethical values. A classless society

will, by freeing believers and unbelievers from the yoke of capitalism, give practical reality to moral values. The religious consciousness will not only be respected: it will be given real democratic scope for development, in which all historically positive values can find expression and make their contribution to the nation's progress.[16]

The great Council convoked by John XXIII, the course it took and the results it yielded, have brought us nearer to such cooperation. The common responsibility for the future of mankind is beginning to be visible beyond the separating ideologies.

The marxist Roger Garaudy quotes the words of the Catholic philosopher Teilhard de Chardin about the 'common front of all those who believe that the universe is still progressing and that we have been entrusted with the task of enabling it to progress'. Garaudy adds:

Hundreds of millions . . . find the meaning of their life and death – even, indeed, the meaning of the history of mankind – in religious faith. For hundreds of millions of men and women, communism gives a face to the world's hopes and a meaning to our history. It is therefore an irrefutable fact of our century that the future of mankind cannot be built in opposition to the believers, nor even without them; likewise, the future of man cannot be built in opposition to the communists, nor even without them.[17]

. . . It would be a historical tragedy and a tragic waste of time if the dialogue between Christians and marxists, their co-operation towards mutual enrichment, and their common effort to build the future home of mankind for the total man, were to remain poisoned or actually frustrated by the weight of the past.[18]

. . . The surest basis for the dialogue, the best guarantee of its sincerity is the deep certainty that, if every man thinks about the essentials of what he believes – the one of his faith in God, the other of his faith

D

in the mission of man – he will discover a common will to extend the creative energies of man to a maximum towards the realization of total man, and will become aware of the mutual enrichment derived from the dialogue, the co-operation and the competition between the promethean humanism of the marxists and the humanism of Christianity.[19]

As 'ideologies', communism and Christianity are indeed irreconcilable. The dogmas of, say, Roman Catholicism are as unacceptable to the marxist as the atheistic ideas of marxism are to the Catholic.

And yet: if I, by no means a religious man, had the power to 'abolish' religion, I would not do it, for countless millions of people would lose their last glimmer of hope, their last moral hold, their only defence against dehumanization. (Furthermore, it is an error of dictators, who despise mankind, to think that convictions can be 'abolished'.)

At the very moment when we step out from the fortresses of ideology into the open air, we discover ideas closely akin to one another, common values, the possibility and the necessity of co-operating and competing. It was all very well for the Young Hegelians to expect liberation to come from the triumph of atheism: our task today is to concentrate all our forces on the triumph of humanism, together with all others who are willing to join us.

MARXISM AND IDEOLOGY

Marxism is not an ideology: but the communist parties constructed an ideological system and named it 'Marxism–Leninism'.

Jean-Paul Sartre calls marxism 'the philosophy of our epoch', and we agree with him.

It will be a long time yet before marxism is exhausted; it is still quite young, almost a child; it has barely begun to develop. It remains, then, the philosophy of our epoch; it is not yet out of date, because the temporal circumstances which produced it are not yet out of date. Our whole thinking can grow only on this soil; thinking must stay within this framework, or be lost in a vacuum or become retrograde.[20]

The unique quality of this 'philosophy of practice' is its *combination of science and utopia*. Its aim is cognition, not for its own sake but in order to change the world of man and to arrive at a scientific interpretation of the social factors which condition its tendency towards socialism. Admittedly, false consciousness, too, can change the world. But marxism does not depend upon a test of strength but upon the truth, measurable against reality, of its scientific findings. In every science there are errors: to rectify them is the principle of science. If a science does not wish to do so, it must abdicate.

Marxism as a science aims at the *truth*, the closest approximation to the truth; therefore it is always prepared to criticize, correct, revise itself. Its goal – its utopia – is *the whole man*, man no longer alienated, his every capacity developed, creative man. It is with this utopia that marxism began. Exploring the laws of development of society, it has built a scientific foundation for this utopia. The progress from utopian to scientific socialism therefore does not mean the rejection but the synthesizing of the utopia. In scientific marxism as the 'philosophy of practice', the utopia is grasped, preserved and synthesized *as a realistic possibility*. The apparent contradiction in the statement that marxism is both science and utopia is resolved at the very moment that it is uttered. In this synthesis, scientific method makes no concession to the wish; yet a gleam of light from the future falls always on the analysis of the present, for any social analysis without anticipation of the future is a falsification of reality because it describes only a state and not a process.

I believe that there is no science which does not anticipate the future – which is not preceded by an imaginative flight into the future. It proves itself as a science by remaining honest, by recognizing its results even when they are contrary to expectation, without becoming discouraged or immediately abandoning an idea which *in that particular form* fails to correspond to reality. This is all the more true of a philosophy which is a philosophy of man, which begins with the present deformation of man and anticipates man whole and complete, and yet never abandons its scientific method.

'You cannot understand philosophy if you understand philosophy alone,' said Robert Havemann in his eleventh Lecture on Natural Science and View of the World.

Philosophy can only be understood and its wisdom appreciated on the basis of a comprehensive knowledge of reality itself. Modern materialism differs from all past philosophies precisely in that it does not construct 'out of its head' an absolute and unshakable system of all relationships and then expect science to supply the proofs of the philosophical system's correctness.[21]

I think Havemann does less than justice to 'all past philosophies' – the Greek natural philosophers, Aristotle, Descartes, Bacon, Kant and Hegel prove him mistaken – but he is right to accuse 'marxist philosophers' of a wrong attitude. The 'abstract dialectic' with which he reproaches them is indeed a dead one, and therefore not a dialectic at all; and the 'dialectical materialism' of the party schools is dogmatism which preserves only the petrified ingredients of marxist philosophy.

Such 'dialectical materialism', as Havemann points out, has played no creative or productive part in the development of modern theoretical or practical science during the last fifty years – or almost none. Nevertheless I believe that Havemann underrates the importance of philosophy.

The 'dialectic of nature' was never the most thoroughly thought out or scientifically founded part of marxist philosophy. Marx touched upon problems of natural science only occasionally and with considerable caution, concentrating his genius above all upon the problems of man and his historical development, the study of the laws of social dynamics, the critique of political economy and the scientific analysis of labour and capital. His methodology of social science and its consequences have had such a lasting effect on historical philosophy, national economy and sociology as a whole that no serious student in any of these fields can fail to take them into account. As a result, there are today many marxists (including some very good ones) outside the ranks of the world's communist parties while the communist parties include countless non-marxists. Marxist philosophy has crossed all political and ideological frontiers.

I know the objection that marxism, although it is a philosophy for the intellectual, is essentially a 'guide to action', a call to the class struggle, for the simple man. Any important philosophy is a guide to action, though generally indirectly and not as an imperative. Neither is marxism a *direct* guide to action. It is not a service manual, a set of instructions for use, a thesaurus of quotations for any given situation. It is – in world-historical terms – a guide to action not only for the working class, which Marx hoped would liberate the world by liberating itself, but also for all those who want to put an end to the alienation of man. The unique creative feature of marxism is not that it encourages the class struggle (the existence of classes and of the class struggle was discovered long before Marx) but that it introduces the consciousness of man's historical goal of self-realization into the class struggle.

In the process of rousing the working class to a revolutionary class consciousness and organizing it into a militant political movement, a certain sloganizing simplification of socialist ideas, principles and demands was unavoidable. Yet the political consciousness of an *avant-garde* was also being formed into a 'counter-ideology' against the dominant ideology, which included the false consciousness of the rulers and the ruled. The programmes of the social-democratic parties were an amalgam of scientific discoveries, utopian long-term aims, practical demands – and the remains of this false consciousness. Marx's criticism of the Gotha Programme was precisely a criticism of this false consciousness and the misty clouds of future 'ideologies' rising from it.

Philosophic and scientific discoveries appeal to the intellect of a minority, not the the masses. Impulse must pave the way for reason. The right thing is not always the simple one, and even the simple thing is difficult to do if it is to be done right. And so it is not marxism in its totality, as philosophy, science and the striving for a historical–utopian goal, which appeals to the masses and eventually seizes power. Only an intellectual *avant-garde* (emerging from the intelligentsia, the working class and other social strata) is capable of absorbing marxism as a whole and bringing it into harmony again and again with developing reality and scientific knowledge. But marxism enables this *avant-garde* to bring the ideas of socialism, political class consciousness, revolutionary aims to the masses and, together with the masses, to seize power.

Until now, no social system has succeeded in existing without *an ideology as a tool of intellectual repression*. Freud called this a 'Super-Ego', created to reconcile the ego with the dominant reality principle and to control the recalcitrant id by means of authority as represented by persons or institutions, moral pressures and intellectual confusion. The rule of the Soviets, and, later, of the communist party and state apparatus was and still is a system of repression, practised by a minority in the name of a majority which is fictitious but possible. (Doubtless this majority already exists in the Soviet Union but it is unconfirmed because no alternative choice has been offered.)

A fortress situation created a fortress ideology. This was probably inevitable but surely not in the absurd form of Stalinist dogmatism.

Lot's wife was turned into a pillar of salt when she stopped and looked back. Certain ideologues have a tendency, when looking back on the Stalin era, if not to turn into pillars of salt themselves, at least to see everything that happened – just because it happened – as petrified 'historical necessity'. An ideology justifying the Soviet system – threatened from outside, afflicted by terrible shortages within – was unavoidable, but not the ideological sanctioning of a self-lacerating terror whose aim was to preserve Stalin's rule against the majority at any price. That marxism was not utterly destroyed by the pressures of an ideology in which a 'thesis' required for tactical reasons took precedence over thought; and where facts, falsifications, and quotations were lumped together as 'proof' of the impregnable accuracy of the thesis; that marxism was not among the countless dead but is still alive today, this is evidence of its immense vitality.

Kolakowski wrote in 1956 that the development of marxism 'has transformed a science into a mythology, into soft matter from which the backbone of reason has been removed'.[22] A few pages further on he revised this excessively harsh judgement and recognized the special nature of marxism. A total transformation of thinking into ideology, he believes,

is impossible in practice. An ideology which is born of science cannot abandon its scientific façade, and this façade exerts its influence on the ideology. In this way traces of the scientific tradition appear in the ideology from time to time . . .[23]

What appears 'from time to time' are not merely traces, and it is not the façade but the scientific *foundations* of marxism which have remained, not intact, but at any rate capable of holding up the edifice; so that, although 'monolithic' ideology may collapse, the as yet incomplete structure of marxism does not. It was not so much the content of that ideology, adapted to the leader's tactical requirements by his own hand, which was monolithic, as its form. This today, that tomorrow, but always monolithic, always a profession of faith excluding the slightest possibility of doubt.

The 'monolithic' character of an ideology can preserve its power for a short while; in the long run it cannot be preserved, because uneven historical development creates contradictions, and thus a forcibly maintained ideology is bound to contain more and more false consciousness. How can there be a common 'monolithic'

ideology for Western Europe, Russia and China? A scientific
method can be held in common; a philosophy, a view of the future
perhaps; certainly not an ideology.

THE TRUTH AND THE 'CLASS VIEW'

In the fortress of rigid ideology we run the risk of mistrusting
everything that comes from 'the other camp' and of assuming
that any scientific discovery or new idea is a product of the devil's
kitchen of the enemy. The theoretical cover for this pernicious
error has been the dogma of the 'class character' of the truth – the
assertion that, from the 'class viewpoint', something can be true
for one class which is not true for another. In an article entitled
Marxism and Ideology, published first in the Italian communist
journal *Rinascità* and later in the journal of the Austrian communist party *Weg und Ziel*, I wrote:

We must finally overcome the fear which old-time fortress commanders had of venturing forth into the open. We must 'ideologically
coexist', that is to say we must know the real ideas of those who
think differently from ourselves and not just a selection of trimmed
quotations; we must try to project ourselves into their minds so as
to argue with them in an 'immanent' way and not from the outside,
just for the sake of winning; we must beware of mistaking condemna-
tory epithets, such as 'bourgeois, decadent, anti-marxist, revisionist,
dogmatic', for proofs of truth. Let us return to the simple categories
'correct' and 'false': for there is no such thing as a 'bourgeois' or
'proletarian', 'capitalist' or 'socialist' scientific finding: there are only
correct or false (or half-correct, doubtful, etc.) ones.[24]

These sentences, which do not seem to me to be in any way sensa-
tional, have been condemned as heresy by many communists.

I have been told, for example:

His proposition does not distinguish between the natural and the
social sciences. Yet it is obvious that a non-party, supra-party social
science in a class society is impossible. More than that: Lenin in his
article *Marxism and Revisionism* stresses that 'if geometric axioms had
a bearing on human interests, people would certainly try to refute
them. Theories of natural history which touched upon old ideological
prejudices have been and are . . . most bitterly opposed.'

What I lacked was 'insight into the class-conditioned nature of all ideas. We can return to the "simple categories" . . . only at the price of going back to the era before the ideology of marxism.'[25]

The method of such discussion consists in first quoting the person under attack as having said something he has not said, and then 'ideologically demolishing' the alleged statement. A quotation from Lenin quickly makes its appearance, misunderstood by the quoter almost before he has had time to consider it: 'If geometric axioms had a bearing on human interests, people would surely try to refute them.' Surely they would. Yet Galileo's findings were correct. He withdrew them because he was afraid of torture; but no Inquisition on earth was able to refute them. The earth turns, no matter who is its ruler; no class viewpoint can stop or accelerate the movement. There is in general no such thing as a 'non-party, supra-party social science'; yet the findings of social science are correct or false, whatever the viewpoint. Certainly it is more diffi-cult to establish the truth in the social sciences than in the natural sciences, not only because the former do not lend themselves to experimental or mathematical proof, but also because interests of many kinds influence the researcher himself. Such influences frequently stand in the way of establishing the truth; sometimes they assist; but any examination of social processes ceases to be scientific as soon as it abandons its search for the truth and looks only for the stuff that propaganda is made of.

The 'class viewpoint' can be a help or a hindrance in so far as new discoveries or insights correspond to or contradict the in-terests of a class. But nothing is ever *true* because it corresponds to the interests of a progressive class. A class is progressive when the truth corresponds to its interests, that is to say the interests of advancing mankind – sometimes not immediately, in the given situation. We must concede to the hard-boiled *Real*-politicians that domination and falsehood, success and deception, seizure of power and hypocrisy are readily compatible, and that the truth in most cases requires far-sightedness in order to become effective.

IDEOLOGY AND ART

Science is cognition: therefore it is not ideology.

Artistic cognition is different in its nature from scientific cogni-tion, but in so far as literature, music and the visual arts are *cognition of reality*, they also do not belong to the sphere of ideology.

Their means of expression – language, colour, rhythm, sound, structure, symmetry and asymmetry, harmony and disharmony – are not of ideological origin or nature and generally develop free from ideological influences. I say 'generally' because religions and other ideologies are always trying to influence, not only the content, but also the forms of art. Sometimes this has gone so far that certain musical instruments and tone sequences were prohibited and others prescribed.

When I maintain that the arts, by their nature, are *not ideology*, I do not mean that they are immune from ideology or wholly autonomous. Ideology usually endeavours to enlist the arts in its service, and works of art are frequently no more than ideology objectified and given sensory effect (it is not ideology, however, which determines the *quality* of a work of art). More frequently, works of art are the opposite: a triumph of reality over ideology.

The artist is not autonomous, not untouched by the dominant ideas, prejudices, value concepts – the ideology – of his time. His time moves, forms, develops him: but *as an artist* he does not experience that time through the filter of an ideology, i.e. not in falsified or distorted form, but is able to perceive the latent reality so that it grips him not as a *state* but as a *process*. His sensibility breaks through the crust of conditioning, of that which is accepted as 'normal' and sanctioned by an unchallengeable 'order'; in 'being-thus' he senses the possibility of 'being-otherwise', in the daily occurrence he discovers the exceptional, in the inconspicuous detail he finds access to the essential, to the hitherto obscured connection.

In the preface to his *Contribution to the Critique of Political Economy* Marx speaks of

the sum total of these relations of production . . . [as] the economic structure of society – the real foundation on which rise legal and political superstructures and to which correspond definite forms of social consciousness. . . . With the change of the economic foundation, the entire immense superstructure is more or less rapidly transformed. In considering such transformations, the distinction should always be made between the material transformation of the economic conditions of production, which can be determined with the precision of natural science, and the legal, political, religious, aesthetic, or philosophic – in short ideological forms in which men become conscious of this conflict and fight it out.[26]

So there you are, the orthodox 'superstructure pundits' tell us. Art forms are ideological forms, and they change – at greater or lesser speed – together with the superstructure. Apart from the fact that not every word of Marx's must absolutely be accepted as gospel, there are two things to be noted in connection with these fundamental principles of his philosophy of history. What determines the 'superstructure' is the sum total of the relations, resulting from the development of productive forces, between the rulers and the ruled, between classes and other social groups: of the *real* relations between human beings generally. (It need hardly be emphasized how much the 'superstructure' reacts back upon the 'foundation'.) Secondly, it is the 'ideological forms' in which men become conscious of the conflict between the new material and moral productive forces and the established social relations, and fight it out. What is meant here is not ideology as the sum of notions which serve a social group in organizing its values, not mystified consciousness, but ideological forms (i.e. intellectual forms, the forms which ideas take), in which the conflict between an outdated reality and one which is thrusting forward to become a new reality is fought out. In this conflict there have been and still are writers and artists who align themselves with the dying ideology; but generally, because their individual experience, as expressed, represents the totality of the condition and the conflict, they have been and are partisans of the new reality against the old. These 'dreamers', these 'fools', these slaves of the imagination are so much gripped by reality that in their work they frequently attack the very things which, as ideologues, they believe or think they believe. And even if their work has been conceived according to a false consciousness, they find it desperately hard to resist the temptation of reality; suddenly, reality emerges from the tattered remnants of an ideology: sometimes overpoweringly, as in Balzac, Dostoevsky or Tolstoy. Thus art may seem to be less articulate than philosophy or sociology; but it is only the language of art which is different, and it has the advantage of being less prone to ideological constructions. Its strength is not the formula but form; its capacity is not to create new laws but to prepare the ground for new laws by discovering man's new reality developing through conflict.

The more literature and the arts are engaged in the great conflicts of our time (directly or indirectly, consciously or unconsciously), the less should they become illustrations of an ideology. Ideologies not only mystify reality, they also cling to the vestiges of a reality that has long since vanished. The more rapidly reality advances, the more the socialist artist, swept forward in that advance, must correct the ideology of his own 'camp' as well as challenging the bourgeois world. No party or state leadership can lay down or prescribe what is reality; when it presumes to 'bring the ideological front into line with all the other sectors of our work',[27] it is plucking out its own eye which offends because it perceives what is as yet invisible to the *Real*-politicians and the ideologues.

And if we must use a military terminology, literature and art are not parts of a front which has to be brought into line with economic, political, administrative or inner-party activities: they are reconnaissance units sent into unknown territory, which often bring back unexpected or unwelcome reports. In fact it is best not to use such a terminology: not to deploy art and literature along fronts: and to refrain from instructing them in strategy or tactics.

The architectural concept of 'superstructure' should also be used sparingly in connection with art and literature, as being too static and lifeless. The tragedies of Aeschylus, Sophocles and Euripides were – in the broad, free sense of the word – 'superstructure' of the triumphant or, respectively, of the decaying Athenian democracy. In them, too, social conflicts were fought out in 'ideological form', and the rapidly changing situation was made visible in the change of philosophic principles – and even of formal elements, such as the role of the chorus. But if they were not very much more than ideological superstructure, how could they still be effective today? As superstructure of what? Through the medium of what ideology?

What is it in Hamlet that moves us? The fact that he is a mirror image of the Elizabethan age? The representative of what ideology? Dozens of interpretations contradict one another, and who is right? Goethe? Nietzsche? Brecht? Kott? Shakespeare, surely – but what is Shakespeare's ambiguous, enigmatic Hamlet who turns a different face towards each succeeding epoch? There is no denying that the Renaissance, the Reformation, commercial capital and a humanism which had become sceptical were all factors, among others, which created this intellectual in the midst of power and murder, voluptuousness and violence, revenge and betrayal. But today the effect of the play is undiminished, and its topicality intense. Yet what does the superstructure or the ideology of the Elizabethan age mean to the theatre audience? Hamlet is *our* Hamlet; his person, his *condition humaine* bursts through the confines of the historically conditioned here and now.

There is no such thing as bourgeois or proletarian, capitalist or socialist forms or means of expression in art. There is such a thing as a socialist way of thinking. This way of thinking determines the artist's attitude in crucial situations: but it does not prejudice his adherence to this or that movement in art, nor saddle him with a view of reality laid down by a sacred ideology.

Art which turns away from all social contents, tendencies and possibilities runs the risk of dying of malnutrition; but so does art which is viewed exclusively as the performance of a social mission. Resolutions and leading articles make a poor diet.

Freed from every tie, art dissolves into insubstantiality: robbed of all freedom, it becomes blind, deaf and mute.

The law of its freedom binds it with a gentle force to the social and the generally human. But only art itself, by a free decision, can effectively accept this bond.

ANTI-INTELLECTUALISM

The concept of the 'intellectual' is vague. Even when it began to come into use in the last third of the nineteenth century it was not so much a synonym for 'brain worker' as a defamatory collective noun for people who defended Dreyfus, sympathized with the proletariat or supported modern art. Anti-intellectualism was part of anti-rationalism, anti-marxism, anti-semitism and all reactionary movements and ideologies. In the jargon of the Nazis, which included 'workers with the fist and forehead' (as if people thought with their foreheads and worked with their fists), the intellectual was Germanized into '*Intelligenzbestie*' ('intelligence beast'). The Russian concept of the 'intelligentsia' was free from pejorative meaning. In most other countries, however, anti-intellectualism has taken root, assuming an aggressive character in times of crisis, and influencing – more in some places, less in others – even the working-class movement and the socialist world.

The *Grosse Brockhaus* dictionary of the German language, 1954 gives the following definition: '*Intellectual*: brain worker; also, one-sided person who lives by the intellect. . . . Intellectualism neglects the effect and value of the unconscious, of the forces of emotion and the will. . . . *Intelligence* . . . the predominance of the mind often causes other gifts and impulses to wither and leads to ideology and abstract intellectualism.'

Herders Staatslexikon, the Catholic German encyclopaedia, 1959, tells us that 'the odium of the troublemaker' attaches 'very easily' to intellectuals. The intelligentsia lives 'in a curious state of tension *vis-à-vis* democracy'. It 'creates a growing sense of insecurity and dissatisfaction by continually intensifying social and cultural criticism, and so preparing the ground for demagogic promises of salvation. . . .'

Billy Graham, the preacher, says it more clearly: 'In place of the Bible, we have substituted reason, rationalism, mind culture, science worship, the working power of government, Freudianism, humanism, naturalism, behaviourism, positivism, materialism and idealism.'[28]

Louis Bromfield says in his study 'The Triumph of the Egghead' that future dictionaries will contain something like the following definition: '*Egghead*: concept introduced into popular use by the Alsop brothers to mean "intellectual": a person of spurious intellectual pretensions, often a professor or the protégé of a professor. Fundamentally superficial. Over-emotional and feminine in reactions to any problem. . . . A doctrinaire supporter of Middle-European socialism. . . . A self-conscious prig, so given to examining all sides of a question that he becomes thoroughly addled and never gets any further while remaining always in the same spot. An anaemic bleeding heart.'[29] Eisenhower said at a public meeting in Los Angeles in 1954 that an intellectual is 'a man who takes more words than are necessary to tell more than he knows'. Hofstadter adds that this remark is perhaps a variation on that made by Charles E. Wilson, Eisenhower's Secretary of State: 'An egghead is a man who understands nothing of what he knows.'

Chancellor Erhard summed it all up in one word: *Pinscher* (terrier).

These eggheads and terriers are always being accused by more massive bipeds, who know nothing of what they are meant to be responsible for, of being 'troublemakers', of putting critical reason in the place of a faithful heart, of failing to be 'patriotic' and 'serving the people', and instead being 'undependable, pusillanimous and irresponsible'. In their 'abstract intellectualism', it is claimed, negative and destructive tendencies predominate – doubt, hairsplitting and a distaste for discipline. Their so-called knowledge ignores the tactical requirements of the moment, the loyalty of the simple follower, the unchanging devotion of the man in the street. The Austrian publicist Ernst Epler spoke as follows about the 'vacillations' of intellectuals in the discussion on marxism and ideology to which I have already referred:

> I feel that the argument concerning political vacillation strikes home. The fact is that at the time when our world movement and our party committed grave errors fraught with evil consequences, I never vacillated politically at all. And with this I reproach myself today. At the price of being rejected by comrades who have not succeeded in overcoming our past, I now propose, instead of immediately jumping to attention, to vacillate for a while whenever I am confronted with any new political problem. I propose to consider every argument and every counter-argument, regardless of where they come from, and to be ready to let my judgement be swayed by them.[30]

All holders of power, big or small, consider such an attitude typical of the intellectual and an alarming threat to good organization. The intellectual is constantly under suspicion of 'deviation': to the 'left' in the capitalist world: to the 'right' in the socialist. 'Left' implies the class struggle, the planning of the future, socialism, internationalism, and scepticism, 'Right' implies individual freedom, democratic criticism, free art, modernism, cosmopolitanism and scepticism. The ideal for those in power is an intellectual without deviations, a thinking machine who serves them by knowing his subject, who answers questions instead of asking them, who offers results without giving an example of how to think; in a word, whose thinking combines maximum accuracy with a minimum of depth. Are we entitled to describe such a thinking machine as an intellectual?

WHO IS AN INTELLECTUAL?

When I speak of intellectuals I do not mean all university or college graduates. I am not thinking of a sociological category, but rather of a moral and intellectual quality. It does not simply apply to 'brain workers' as opposed to 'manual workers'. A highly skilled manual worker needs much more brain than many a university graduate pen-pushing behind a desk. 'There is no human activity from which all intervention of the intellect can be excluded,'[31] said Antonio Gramsci, most of whose work, written in Mussolini's prisons, is still relatively unknown north of the Alps although Gramsci was, with Rosa Luxemburg and Lenin, the most important marxist thinker of his time. '*Homo sapiens* cannot be separated from *homo faber*.'[32] All human beings are intellectuals, Gramsci believed; but not all, living in society, are able to preserve and exercise the faculty.

We need to remind ourselves of the 'intellectual' present in almost every human being – undeveloped, withered as a result of neglect or stunted by the division of labour – not only in order to counter the academic mumbo-jumbo on the one hand and the manual worker's sense of inferiority, with its tendency towards anti-intellectualism, on the other hand: but also in order to remember that the goal of all social development and education is a society of men in whom thought and practice, intellectual and physical activity have fused into one. 'In the modern world,' claimed Gramsci, 'the technical education necessary for even the most primitive and unskilled industrial work must form the basis for the new type of intellectual.'[33]

Today this type is beginning to come into being; but at the same time we have become aware of the extreme difficulty of combining increased specialization of labour with a proper education of the mind and the emotions. Gramsci, who examined the social significance of the intellectual and the problems related to it more thoroughly and more objectively than any other marxist, spoke of the intellectuals' decisive role in the development of modern nations, and called them the 'connective tissue' of the nation. Every important social class produces its own 'organic' intellectuals, but depends also on the 'traditional' intellectuals – priests, philosophers, scholars, writers, doctors, etc. Every class which comes into power uses its intellectuals as 'officials of the superstructure', entrusts them with 'performing subordinate functions within the social hegemony and the political régime'.

But there is a scale of intellectual qualification apart from that of the hierarchy within the military, administrative and ideological power machines. 'The creative workers in the various sciences, philosophy, art, etc., should be placed at the highest point of the scale: the humble administrators and propagandists of an already existing and stored intellectual heritage, at the lowest.' In situations of extreme contradiction the difference between the highest and lowest, says Gramsci, is 'truly qualitative'.[34]

In our constant situation of extreme contradiction, the fundamental definition of the intellectual emerges precisely from this 'truly qualitative' difference of which Gramsci speaks.

The writer Paul Alexander Baran, whose work is commemorated in the *Monthly Review* of March 1965, drew a qualitative distinction between the intellectual and the 'intellect worker' in his study *The Commitment of the Intellectual*. He defines 'intellect workers' as 'technicians', whose work does not consist in setting aims but in working out the means of achieving them – not in envisaging the broad outlines but in concentrating on the small details. He adds: 'To avoid a possible misunderstanding: intellect workers can be (and sometimes are) intellectuals, and intellectuals are frequently intellect workers.' What distinguishes an intellectual, in his opinion, is his commitment to the ideals of humanity, the search for truth, and a ruthless criticism of everything that exists. 'It may be said,' Baran continues, 'that I am identifying being an intellectual with being a hero, that it is unreasonable to demand from people that they should withstand all the pressures of vested interests and brave all the dangers to their individual well-being for the sake of human advancement. I agree that it would be unreasonable to *demand* it. Nor do I.'[35]

This is a noble, perhaps too high-flown definition of the intellectual. But the initiative and the heroism of intellectuals 'at the highest point of the scale' are our greatest hope today.

IMPULSE AND ACTION

Every tendency towards good is opposed by a tendency towards evil. This inner contradiction is more then ever inherent in men and their work in our time. In both the major social systems, there is an unmistakable tendency for intellectuals to withdraw from the political sphere. The abdication of intellectuals as politically active critics of the existing order and as prophets of the future encourages the formation of power élites of the worst kind. Politics is increasingly regarded as an unfortunately still necessary trade, carried on by people who have not quite enough intellect to be scientists or enough talent to be writers or enough know-how to be technologists. Many believe that political rule is the prerogative of such mediocrities, and that they can be beaten only by their own methods, so that anyone who overthrows them will end up by resembling them.

But the retreat of the intellectual into technology and science, with their apparent freedom from value-judgements, is seldom final. Such an intellectual finds himself again and again in situations which make it clear that what he does, however free from value-judgements it may appear to be, in fact serves a certain system of values. He cannot escape his responsibilities. Anyone who has ever been gripped by a great idea can never completely escape its fascination. It is preserved like glowing ash in the very denial of the renegade.

The real problem arises from the fact that although the intellectuals who are the freest and most feared – the 'abstract' or 'unattached' intellectuals, the writers, scholars and students – are capable of providing a first impulse, they are not, if left to themselves, capable of taking or reversing important decisions. In an industrial society they need, on the one hand, the cooperation of self-aware, organized workers, and on the other hand the support of intellectuals inside the power apparatus. These 'organic' intellectuals of the ruling classes are no longer entirely the submissive 'officials of the superstructure' they are meant to be; some of them have become dissatisfied with carrying out the 'subordinate functions within the social hegemony and the political régime'. It is precisely the most highly qualified 'technicians' of the establishment who are the first to realize how inefficient and wasteful it is, how it is incapable of gauging the future or planning far ahead.

A confidential document issued by the British Employers' Confederation points out that 'staff workers' – supervisory employees, technicians and engineers, on whom capital relies – are becoming less dependable than in the past, and that their organization into trade unions would lead to increasingly serious problems for the employers, because staff unions are 'generally more articulate, more militant, and more effective than the manual workers' unions'.[36] The Establishment's possibilities of buying the specialists it needs – with money, prestige, far-reaching authority, the illusion of participating in the real running of the country – are enormous; yet the economic rulers distrust the staffs on whom they depend,

E

and many of these staffs may eventually decide to restrict the power of their greedy and power-hungry masters so as to avoid disaster, and to insist on structural changes so that production may not turn to destruction.

THE INTELLECTUAL IN THE SOCIALIST WORLD

The potential power of the intellectual in that part of the world which is struggling to build socialism is quite as great as in the capitalist world: indeed I would venture to say that in the long-term view it is greater.

The repressive administrative measures, infamous accusations, trials and condemnations of intractable intellectuals in socialist countries are not a proof of the contrary; rather, they are the negative consequence of the fact that intellectuals have to be taken seriously: their influence, particularly over young people, has to be recognized and requires careful watching.

The Czech psychiatrist and author Josef Nesvadba used to tell the following story: once when addressing a writers' symposium he was asked whether it was possible to emigrate behind the Iron Curtain. 'Most certainly!' said Nesvadba. 'But why on earth should you want to?' 'Because there at least you get put in prison because of what you write.' 'Oh, that's all finished now,' said Nesvadba. Whereupon his friend decided not to emigrate.

Many things have happened since that conversation to prove how wrong the Czech was in his ironic optimism.

> *They who once stood firm before machine-guns*
> *are afraid today of my guitar ...*

Why is Wolf Biermann's guitar, like those of many others, so feared? Because in the socialist world poems walk in the streets, novels reverberate in politics, films become the centres of thunder-storms. Goethe described Lord Byron's dramas as 'parliamentary speeches in disguise'. Many works of socialist literature are disguised parliamentary speeches in the same sense, unpublished leading articles, secret political manifestos. In struggles which are apparently about aesthetic questions, about the evaluation of a book, an author, or an artistic method, the fight is really over fundamental political issues.

THE STRUGGLE FOR KAFKA

In the summer of 1962, speaking at the World Peace Congress in Moscow, Jean-Paul Sartre spoke of the attempt 'to falsify the great works of literature with the help of officially controlled critics and quotations'. That was what had happened to Kafka.

In the West he is falsified and distorted; in the East he is passed over in silence. Conversely, we are all suffering from the wrong we are doing him: in the West and the East alike we distort him by our passionate prejudice, and nowhere do we derive any benefit from his true universality, that is to say from the value which he could have for everyone if he were allowed to mature in our minds and hearts in perfect freedom and, as Marx says in another context, 'without adulteration'.[37]

At about the same time an article of mine on Kafka was published by Peter Huchel, who was then the brilliant editor of the East German review *Sinn und Form*. In this article I wrote: 'We must preserve Kafka from canonisation, but we must also defend him against dogmatic bigots. . . . His work is incomparably more than the death cry of a historical epoch; it is world literature . . .'[38]

Like no other writer before him, Kafka depicted alienation in its most extreme forms, but he also fought desperately for a way out. . . . He stood midway between those who look backwards – for whom the present becomes reality only when it is past, when it has entered the store of fixed images and objects, the rubbish dump of the memory – and those who dream ahead, who feel the present as the beginning of the future and the abundance of as yet unformed possibilities . . .[39]

A conference on Kafka was being prepared in Prague. Violent outbursts against modern art by Khrushchev and Ilyitchev made it seem likely that the conference would never take place. But, for the first time, pronouncements from Moscow were being rejected – sometimes tacitly, sometimes explicitly – by many European communist parties. Eduard Goldstücker, a professor at Charles University in Prague who had been condemned to life imprisonment in the Slansky trial and rehabilitated after the Twentieth Congress, spoke at a mass meeting and attacked the ideas on art held in Moscow, whilst at the same time emphasizing the historical achievement of Khrushchev, 'the man to whom I am not the only one to owe freedom and life'. It was largely because of Goldstücker that the conference took place after all.

On 27 May 1963 communist scholars and writers from Czechoslovakia, the G.D.R., Poland, Hungary, Yugoslavia, France and Austria met at Liblice in order to discuss Kafka's work and revise the orthodox communist judgements already passed on it. But the discussion went far beyond that. The delegates from the G.D.R. denied Kafka's topical significance; they opposed to Kafka, the 'rootless', the 'lone intellectual', Thomas Mann with his 'profoundly social content', and they suggested that Kafka was 'out of place' in the socialist world. This did not pass unchallenged. Roger Garaudy, Eduard Goldstücker, Roman Karst, Jiři Hajek, myself and others stressed Kafka's topical significance not only in the capitalist but also in the socialist world. We pointed out that alienation had by no means been removed, either economically or politically, by the expropriation of landowners and industrialists.

For the first time, communists discussed in open debate not only 'decadence', 'realism' and 'the cultural heritage', but the problem of alienation within a socialism which was inadequate and had been distorted by a system of rule of which Stalin was the incarnation but not the sole cause.

The direct, thought not the most significant, result of this conference was that Kafka was published in the Soviet Union and finally also in the G.D.R. More important was the fact that with Kafka, the young Marx was, as it were, smuggled into a number of socialist countries. Many young people learned about the word 'alienation' for the first time. The discussion could no longer be arrested.

Alienation is not removed by a single revolutionary action, still less by the dust-covered files of the bureaucrats. After a revolution, the world of having and of the ruling order continues to live on in the world that is being newly made, not merely as a relic of the past but as something fed by the new machinery of power. The struggle for Kafka was successful. Other, similar, struggles fail. But those who are momentarily defeated do not despair of their historical superiority.

HISTORICAL SUPERIORITY

The 'organic' intellectuals of the new class within the socialist system, growing up in a society which has not yet overcome alienation, have many features in common with the technicians, administrators and bureaucrats in the bourgeois world. They all bear the stamp of modern industrial society with its mechanism and its intrinsic problems. On both sides, the 'technicians' directly connected with production are opposed to the power of amateurish overlords, be they private owners or the representatives of a state organization; they are against parasitism, whether public or private; but they are also suspicious of the 'dreamers', the 'unattached' intellectuals. On both sides, the technical and the traditional intelligentsia lack mutual understanding. Both power apparatuses would feel less secure if such understanding came about.

The 'traditional' intellectuals in both social systems, writers, scientists, teachers and students, resemble one another more than orthodox ideologues are prepared to admit; they are beginning to become aware of what they have in common; but the differences between them are more clearly recognizable than those between 'technicians'.

The quality of a country or a social system is not judged by the number of cars but by the number of educated men and women it produces. How high is the general level of education? How strong the incentive to go on studying? What social conditions are there to encourage higher education, to favour the constant renewal and extension of élites from all classes of the population, and to prevent these élites from becoming privileged castes? Although in most socialist countries teachers and doctors – i.e. those concerned with forming human beings rather than products – are underpaid, and in some socialist countries engineers are underpaid as well, education has to a large extent ceased to be a privilege and so the impetus towards education is increasing as learning ceases to be a social requirement and becomes an inner one. Although polytechnic education is still imperfect and in some respects questionable, although technical subjects outweigh the humanities, and one-sidedness and 'party-mindedness' are cultivated at the expense of intellectual breadth and freedom, the development and experiments in the educational systems of the socialist countries give grounds for high hopes. Unlike most students in the capitalist world, many of these young people (and some older ones) are convinced that they will one day be able to alter the undemocratic system of government and achieve socialist democracy and humanity. They believe in their potential power.

Very well, my opponents may say, young people in the socialist countries are more dynamic than ours. But when the standard of living begins to approach our level, when material demands become more numerous and more refined simply as a result of being satisfied, when there is more pleasure and more freedom, will this not have an emasculating effect?

Such things will happen. But we can assume that in a society based on common ownership, material consumption need not become as exaggerated as it has in societies based on profit. We can hope that every success in the struggle towards freedom will be an encouragement to fresh effort. The idea of socialism is not killed – does not have to be killed – by reality.

In the capitalist world social reality is no longer measured against an idea but only against success. We should not underestimate the meaning of the Declaration of Human Rights, the sense of universal justice, for American and European intellectuals, especially students. But in the socialist world what is taught to young people as 'Marxism–Leninism' constantly invites comparison with reality. Although 'Marxism–Leninism', the official ideology of socialist states, is to a large extent false consciousness, the ideas it contains, its critical method, the humanist utopia at its core – this has proved indestructible. In that syllabus there is dynamite.

In the capitalist world, businessmen and *Real*-politicians, those notorious possessors of common sense, need the intellectual as an expert but have not the capacity to control him. The intellectual superiority of the egghead frightens and angers the thickhead forced to depend on him. The attitude of many working-class officials in power, though similar, is rooted in a more profound contradiction. The idea of socialism, especially in its marxist form, does not stem from so-called 'simple' men but from highly educated intellectuals. Intellectuals have been the *avant-garde* of all great revolutions; but marxism, more than any other revolutionary philosophy, presupposes intellectual ability. Palmiro Togliatti once said to me in a conversation about a party official whom we both disliked: 'How can the man be a marxist if he isn't even abreast of bourgeois culture?' The remark should not be interpreted as intellectual arrogance. We must get rid of the double meanings of words. Institutionally, anyone who belongs to a marxist party passes for a marxist. But there are many marxists who do not belong to any party, and in every 'marxist' party there are plenty of people who are not marxists. Togliatti did not mean these but the 'braggarts' (as Lenin called them) who merely assimilate 'what is contained in communist books and pamphlets' and by this very one-sidedness 'prove incapable of combining the various branches of knowledge' in order to act 'in the way that communism demands'.[40] If such braggarts fail to enrich their minds with all the knowledge necessary for an educated modern person, yet claim to be regarded, not as rank-and-file communists, but as infallible marxists who brook no contradiction, then they need to be reminded of Togliatti's remark and Lenin's speech.

Both the official who has come to power in the name of marxism and the educated marxist intellectual whom he confronts appear to invoke the same authority. If the official is merely a tactician who separates practice from theory, he will be dimly aware that what challenges him is the critical spirit of marxism itself. When power stems from an idea, that idea will elevate it and threaten it at the same time. It is the idea, invoked by the state apparatus, which ensures the potential strength of the intellectual even when the apparatus seems momentarily to have defeated him.

THE SPIRIT OF CRITICISM

Every ruling system desires stability and hates criticism, unless it be 'constructive', i.e. not criticism at all but affirmation. Criticism of any single point is often interpreted as denial of the entire system, because dogmatic creeds will only tolerate an unconditional Yea or Nay. Yet the spirit of criticism inherent in marxism demands that marxism, too, should incessantly criticize itself. 'I am not a marxist,' said Marx – meaning that marxism denies itself when it ceases to question itself. The spirit of marxism must, in constant contradiction to the system, continue to be dynamic and encourage freedom of criticism, doubt, renewal.

The organization requires that all knowledge and ideas should be simplified and reduced until they become an ideology. But the marxist within the organization must never stop applying the critical method of marxism to everything. He must express doubts and expound new ideas. This leads again and again to conflict between the theoreticians (so called) and the practitioners, between marxist intellectuals and the apparatus. The combination of theoretician and practitioner within one person, appropriate to marxism as the 'philosophy of practice', is desirable but only rarely attained. The practitioners will always form the great majority and will resent the critical attitude of an intellectual *avant-garde* as what they call a disturbance factor. That is why we have the apparently paradoxical situation in which the adaptable non-marxist has an easier time in the socialist world than the marxist. Werner Hartke was a member of the Nazi party when the communist resistance fighter Robert Havemann was sentenced to death. Years later, Hartke as President of the Academy of Sciences of the German Democratic Republic demanded Havemann's expulsion on the grounds of 'behaviour unworthy of the Academy'. The demand was rejected in a secret ballot; Havemann was nevertheless expelled. Marxists in the socialist world are intellectual guerrillas – powerless when the apparatus steamrollers them, yet holders of potential power. 'We shall be an army again some day,' one of these indomitable *guerrilleros* said to me.

On 9 September 1965 *Pravda* published an article by Rumyantsev, the former editor-in-chief of *Izvestia*, saying:

In his last writings, Lenin enjoined us to produce the maximum number of people of whom it could be guaranteed 'that they do not accept a single word on trust and will not say a single word that goes against their conscience; that they will not be afraid to admit difficulties nor to fight for the achievement of the aim they have seriously set themselves', that is to say the building of a truly human, truly communist society.

This article with its unusual quotation from Lenin, its description of the marxist intellectual as a man who accepts nothing on trust, openly admits difficulties and says nothing that goes against his conscience, caused, justifiably, a considerable stir.

I do not wish to over-simplify the problem of the marxist intellectual in the socialist world. Every kind of 'guidance' of artistic or scientific thought, every kind of tutelage of the intellect by a party, is invidious. But the intellectual who supports socialism must ask himself:

How can I combine independence of thought with the discipline necessary for the conduct of the struggle?

How can I keep the spirit of criticism alive under all circumstances without causing consequences which I do not intend?

How, in other words, can I be an intellectual in a context which challenges my rights as an intellectual?

The intellectual who is on the side of socialism knows that no idea can be put into effect without organization. At the same time he knows that any organization is bound to deform the idea. Should he, as an intellectual, accept the risk of organization or, 'to save his soul', remain outside it? Should he recognize the disturbing division of labour: here the man who visualizes the future – there, the man who, by action, distorts the design? Here, the immaculate conscience of a critical mind – there, hands dirtied by the practice of politics? Should the intellectual who is for socialism leave the way open for pragmatism and crude practical common sense by withdrawing into total impotence, or should he try to relate his potential power to what exists?

There is no universal answer. Socialism, whether or not it is in power, has need of intellectuals both *intra* and *extra muros*. The intellectual not attached to any party has fewer difficulties to overcome when he criticizes or when he analyses the present or the past. The intellectual inside the party is forced to consider: how far can I go without being misunderstood by my friends, without causing harm instead of good? When must I refuse to listen to my inner censor – at the risk of becoming isolated? But without the existence of the intellectual *intra muros*, who is obliged to reason in this way, the potential effectiveness of the one working *extra muros* would be minimal. We who strive for a more humane world need each other, whether we are 'inside' or 'outside', and our intellectual coexistence – no, our cooperation – is indispensable.

Whenever intellectuals in the socialist world criticize the methods of their rulers or suggest structural changes in the sphere of economics, politics, or culture, the capitalist world pretends that this amounts to an anti-communist resistance. Dogmatic *Real*-politicians in their wonderland of rigid ideas, secret services and military power may believe this; but many of their experts are quite aware that the socialist world, despite inner crises, is a permanent one. The experts go on telling lies merely because it is their job to do so. Thus, there seems to exist a secret agreement between orthodox dogmatists on both sides. Extreme anti-communists would like communism to be so obdurate, intolerant, and closed to new ideas that they can go on representing it as the work of the devil. Communists who really correspond to this description would like the capitalist world to be so depraved, repulsive and empty of ideas that any coexistence with it must appear as a betrayal and a disgrace. That is why the reactionary forces on the one side are the abettors of the conservative forces on the other, and why any opposition by marxist intellectuals is invariably hailed as anti-communist from the outside, to the delight of those against whom that opposition is directed.

THE COMMON TASK

This makes it even more important to establish an alliance, across the frontiers and walls, between those of us who think and who for that reason are deeply troubled – an alliance of all who understand that we do not merely belong to antagonistic social systems but also live in *one world*, a world which a few madmen could blow up tomorrow. The objective interaction of the opposed systems is the novel feature (perhaps the most significant one) of our age. To recognize this subjectively and consciously to draw consequences from it is becoming the duty (again, perhaps the most significant one) of all intellectuals. We must learn to recognize that we share the responsibility for the development of 'the others' who live beyond our frontiers and outside our system. We must plan the world of tomorrow together with those who think differently from us. We must support one another: support all efforts by intellectuals in the capitalist world to fight the stupidity and brutality of their rulers: support all efforts by intellectuals in the socialist world to achieve greater freedom and humanity, the right to criticize and the right to democratic co-determination. We must support one another: we must criticize one another: we must meet in order to examine what already exists and think about what is to come. It does not seem to me utopian to expect more from this process than from the stumbling progress of the myopic *Real*-politicians.

The role of intellectuals in the formation of a nation, of which Gramsci spoke, is today becoming a decisive role in the forming of humanity. Technology, economics, the multitude of problems calling for joint solution, all point in the same direction. But we shall not arrive at this humanity automatically as a result of so-called 'progress' which is supposed to carry us along, motionless, as though on an historical conveyor-belt. We shall arrive only through the conscious cooperation of men and women whose reason and humanity can overcome national egoism and dogmatic prejudice.

There are two paradigmatic figures of the European intellectual: Doctor Abelard and Doctor Faustus. The former was castrated, the latter taken away by the devil. In both cases the rulers were of one mind with the illiterates: intelligence is worthy of castration or hell. It took Goethe to redeem Faust from the power of evil and to offer an alternative future for the intellectual.

The common task of all who have the courage and the right to call themselves intellectuals is no longer to remain the 'connective tissue of the nation', but to become the connective tissue of mankind. Their community of thought and struggle across all fronts can contribute more than any congress, any summit meeting, any balance of terror, any *Real*-political agreement, towards preventing the catastrophe: the catastrophe in which man is castrated and the world is taken away by the devil.

Notes

1. *Die Zeit*, Hamburg, 3 April 1964
2. C. Wright Mills, *The Causes of World War Three* (New York: Simon & Schuster, 1959)
3. Nazim Hikmet. Translated from the original manuscript
4. Norman Mailer, *Advertisements for Myself* (New York: Putnam, 1959; London: André Deutsch)
5. ibid
6. ibid
7. Frantz Fanon, *The Wretched of the Earth* (London: MacGibbon & Kee, 1965)
8. Franz Marek, *Philosophie der Weltrevolution* (Vienna: Europa Verlag, 1966)
9. Friedrich Hegel, *The Philosophy of Fine Art* (London: Bell, 1920)
10. Karl Marx, 'Theses on Feuerbach' in Marx and Engels, *The German Ideology* (New York: International Publishers, 1947)
11. Elias Canetti, *Tagebuch*, Vienna, December 1965. Report on a symposium on 'Our Century and its Novel', held under the auspices of the Austrian Society for Literature

12. Karl Marx, *The German Ideology*
13. ibid
14. Leszek Kolakowski, *Der Mensch ohne Alternative* (Munich: Piper, 1960)
15. Robert Musil, *The Man Without Qualities*, vol. II (London: Secker & Warburg, 1954)
16. Palmiro Togliatti, quoted from Roger Garaudy, 'Vom Bannfluch zum Dialog' in *Der Dialog oder Ändert sich das Varhaltnis zwischen Katholizismus und Kommunismus?* (Reinbek: Rowohlt, 1966)
17. ibid
18. ibid
19. ibid
20. Jean-Paul Sartre, *Marxismus und Existentialismus* (Reinbek: Rowohlt, 1964)
21. Robert Havemann, *Dialektik ohne Dogma?* (Reinbek: Rowohlt, 1964)
22. Leszek Kolakowski, *Der Mensch ohne Alternative*
23. ibid
24. Ernst Fischer on marxism and ideology, in *Rinascità*, Rome, February 1965. Monthly supplement, *Il Contemporaneo* no. 2. Also in *Weg und Ziel*, Vienna, May 1965
25. *Weg und Ziel*, Vienna, June 1965
26. Karl Marx, *A Contribution to the Critique of Political Economy: Author's Preface*, in *Marx on Economics*, Robert Freedman (ed.) (Harmondsworth: Penguin, 1962)
27. A. A. Zhdanov, *On Literature, Music and Philosophy* (London: Lawrence & Wishart, 1950)
28. Quoted in Richard Holfstadter, *Anti-Intellectualism in American Life* (New York: Knopf, 1963; London: Jonathan Cape)
29. Louis Bromfield, 'The Triumph of the Egghead', *The Freeman*, vol. III, December 1952. Quoted in Hofstadter, *Anti-Intellectualism in American Life*.
30. Ernst Epler, *Weg und Ziel*, Vienna, April 1966.
31. Antonio Gramsci, *Gli intellettuali e l'organizzazione della cultura* (Turin: Einaudi, 1949)
32. ibid
33. ibid
34. ibid
35. Paul A. Baran, 'The Commitment of the Intellectual', *Monthly Review*, March 1965
36. *The Times*, 26 October 1964
37. *Sinn und Form*, nos V and VI, 1962
38. ibid
39. ibid
40. V. I. Lenin, 'The Tasks of the Youth League', speech delivered at the Third All-Russian Congress of the Russian Young Communist League, 2 October 1920, collected works vol. 31 (London: Lawrence & Wishart, 1966)

Chapter 3

THE DEFORMATION
OF MAN

I. THE ALTERNATIVE

'*Je est un autre!*' Today Rimbaud's words have lost their power to shock.

In our industrialized, commercialized, bureaucratized world, the fact that 'I is another' has become a platitude.

The 'I', freed from the bonds of feudal order and rank, becomes conscious of itself, seeks refuge in anonymity, in being like everyone else. Man without an 'I' enjoys the pleasures of depersonalization. Incessantly occupied, he is wholly given up to irresponsible passivity. Adapted to the requirements of society – or, rather, of the power élite who manipulate society – he is the useful Everyman, the exchangeable Nobody. He has become so accustomed to the vacuum that it neither bores nor alarms him. He is what he has and what others think of him; and what they think of him depends on what he has. What he must have is success. What he yearns for is popularity. Great success gives him the right to scandalize the public; if he is less successful, he must learn how to give no offence to anyone.

The best recommendation for such creatures is: they don't make any difficulties. Their highest virtue is: they do not make themselves conspicuous. In the end, such a society produces only two human types: the conditioners and the conditioned – the active and the passive barbarians.[1]

This society of 'active and passive barbarians' is the result of technical, industrial, and political revolutions in which the bourgeoisie has been the determining force. It has reached its extreme in the United States; but the same tendency towards depersonalization, irresponsibility, loss of identity, and the decay of the 'I' is manifest in all countries with a highly developed modern civilization.

It seems to be a paradox: the more categorically the ego liberated itself from a system in which the super-ego was accepted as a divine order, the more its own definition became blurred. As consciousness increased, there developed a sense of being at the mercy of the unknown; as individuality increased, it became more doubtful. The unquestioning assertion 'I am' led to the anxious question 'Am I?' The proud 'I think, therefore I am', led to the anguished 'I suffer, therefore I must exist'. The end is Hamm's absurd 'I was always absent'. Such has been the rise and fall of the autonomous 'I', which had the audacity to want to 'posit' the world, to take possession of the world, and was finally possessed by it.

THE FLUID 'I'

Goethe's Faust, who was continually changing, never doubted that he was an indestructible self, identical with himself while becoming different, indestructible in a transient world, a man immortalizing himself by his deeds.

> Es kann die Spur von meinen Erdentagen
> nicht in Äonen untergehn . . .

(Whole aeons cannot efface the trace of my earthly days . . .)
Around the turn of the century Hugo von Hofmannsthal wrote:

> Dies ist ein Ding, das keiner voll aussinnt,
> und viel zu grauenhaft, als dass man klage:
> Dass alles gleitet and vorüberrinnt
> Und dass mein eignes Ich, durch nichts gehemmt,

Herüberglitt aus einem kleinen Kind
Mir wie ein Hund unheimlich stumm und fremd . . .[2]

(This is a thing that no one thinks out to the end, a thing too dreadful for complaint: that everything glides and flows past and that my own self, held back by nothing, came gliding here from a small child, terrifyingly dumb and strange to me, like a dog . . .)

And Marcel Proust:

These strange selves which were to bear each a different name, the possibility of their coming had, by reason of their indifference to the object of my love, always alarmed me. . . .

No doubt this self had maintained some contact with the old self, as a friend, unconcerned by a bereavement, speaks of it nevertheless, to those who come to the house, in a suitable tone of sorrow . . .

But it was into a new personality that I was tending to pass altogether. It is not because other people are dead that our affection for them grows faint, it is because we ourselves are dying. Albertine had no cause to rebuke her friend. The man who was usurping his name had merely inherited it. . . . My new self, while it grew up in the shadow of the old, had often heard the other speak of Albertine; through that other self, through the information that it gathered from it, it thought that it knew her . . .[3]

In a study on Proust, Samuel Beckett wrote:

Personality . . . whose permanent reality can only be understood, if at all, as retrospective hypothesis. The individual is formed by a continuous process of pouring from a vessel containing the sluggish, pale and single-coloured liquid of the future into another vessel containing the turbulent and, as a result of events undergone, many-coloured liquid of the past.[4]

WHAT IS I?
Arthur Adamov asked in 1938:

What exists? I know for a start that I exist. But who is I? What is I? All that I know of myself is that I suffer. And if I suffer it is because at the very root of myself there is mutilation and separation.

I am separated. I cannot name what I am separated from. But I am separated . . .

Once it was called God. Now it has no name . . .[5]

Investigating the decay of language, Eugene Ionesco formulates it thus:

The Smiths and the Martins cannot speak because they cannot think. They cannot think because nothing moves them. They have no more passions. They can no longer be themselves. They can 'become' someone else. Because they are not themselves, they can only be the others: the world of the impersonal. They are exchangeable . . .[6]

Thousands more could be added to these few quotations which illustrate the withering away of the self.

What has happened to the self? Whence this distortion, this evaporation? Why this flight into the anonymous, the amorphous, the insubstantial?

THE WORK OF MAN OUTGROWS MAN

Out of the gold leaf of sacred backgrounds, out of the hierarchy of purple cloaks and cassocks, coats of arms and guilds, the Self stepped forward, at first provocatively, like a scandal crying to high heaven: Abelard and Heloïse, Guillaume, Villon, Michelangelo, Leonardo. Personality was a privilege granted only to a few, something ambivalent, stemming from Lucifer and Satan. Their self was 'being-different', and this was confirmed by the pressure of the world around them.

In the Middle Ages, the identity of those who were not tempted by the sacrilege of freedom was guaranteed by the feudal system which assured relative security within society. The artisan in his productive and his private sphere was at one with himself. He was able to produce himself in the form of his work, to objectify himself without deconcretizing himself, to comprehend man as a whole, through his own work and the role allotted to him by the divine world order.

With the development of the productive forces, self-realization increased as part of the incessant conflict which is the essence of man and which drives him forward from work to work and crisis to crisis. It was limited at first to only a few privileged individuals. Then it began to regress. With the technical and industrial revolutions at the beginning of the nineteenth century, work began to outgrow man. Having developed from nature and learnt to create his own world as a super-nature – having become human through work – man was now becoming dehumanized by work. The division of labour necessary for the all-round development of man forced him to become desperately narrow. The very thing which had raised him above all living things now reduced him to a crippled slave. What had released him from the animal kingdom now forced him to labour as cattle could never be made to labour.

THE POWER OF OBJECTS

The accumulation of objects, which horrified Shelley long ago, has become so overwhelming in class society that man, surrounded by his possessions like the new tenant in Ionesco's play, can scarcely breathe or be himself. This is the *world of having*. Man himself becomes an object. He sells himself as a commodity for production or prostitution: as 'manpower', sexual vessel or compliant brain. In countries with the most developed production and consumption, horror at this objectification of man is beginning to turn into an acceptance of it as a natural condition.

As material poverty becomes less extreme, the worker's alienation from the product and process of his work, from others and from himself, increasingly becomes a double alienation: the work product returns, no longer recognizable as such but magically transformed in the shape of a commodity. The product which has made the prisoner's own work meaningless and turned him into a mere function, an operation, a fragment, is now offered back to him – in his role of consumer – as the image of a newly-to-be-acquired self. What you have not yet got and the other man already has – so the commodity addresses him – makes you different from him, therefore not fully yourself. Recognize yourself in me. Who are you? Nothing. Separated. From what? From me. Buy yourself a self, piece by piece, instalment by instalment. What you've got, you've got. What you've got, you are. Become what you can be. Unite yourself with me. I am you.

The magic

> *mirror, mirror on the wall,*
> *who is the fairest of them all?*

has grown insolent and large, has leapt out of its frame, gone into the streets, multiplied a thousand-fold. O city of the thousand mirrors, the thousand magic mirrors with a woman in front of every one! None is fairer than you if you buy me, take me, wear me. Buy me for I do not cost much. I'm cheap. I'm a gift. Don't you recognize me? I am you, your own self whom you've been looking for, your dream, your dress, your shoe. Buy me, the shadow of beauty, and you shall be the fairest of them all.

F

Consumer goods create the illusion of an earthly beyond, a paradise of self-gratification. The immediate world is one of material production and of labour performed, not creatively, but in 'the sweat of thy brow'. The man condemned to this work is welcomed, saved, redeemed in the world of consumer goods. Publicity can 'in its way create an equally magnificent image of a Buick as the Church once created the image of God',[7] writes Allan Kaprow in his study *The Future of Pop Art*.

The commercialized *unio mystica* is no longer with God but with the commodity. Communion is consuming.

MAN AND MACHINE

Not only industry, man too is being automated. The Romantics' terror of the Golem, the machine which, made of dead matter, walks as though alive in human form, gives place to admiration of technical achievement and a desire for its perfection. A cyberneticist told me that he got on better with his machines than with people. The common language which man and machine learn to speak is precise and unambiguous, not diffused in the twilight of emotions and concealments. 'I want to be a machine!' declares Andy Warhol, the Pop artist, and the journalist Lil Picard adds that the saying will 'go down in art history and acquire the same importance as Flaubert's "*Emma Bovary, c'est moi*" in the history of literature'.[8]

But the living spirit resists the metamorphosis which turns it, not into a laurel tree like Daphne fleeing from Apollo, but into an automaton, a machine fleeing from the self. The desire to be absorbed in the man-created world of technology, institutions and machines – in the same way as the religious once wanted to give themselves to God, and the Romantics to nature – always to a power greater than themselves – this desire is resisted by man's desire for freedom and his need to be something more than a mechanical part.

The accumulation of objects, the concentration of capital, the economic and political power of institutions and organizations, have led to an atomization, a breaking-down of the whole into monads whose coherence has nothing to do with any pre-established harmony, but is imposed from the outside. The industrial revolution, as Eric Hobsbawm remarks in his *The Age of Revolution*, brought a loneliness into the world which was given the name of freedom. The sense of loneliness, abandonment, loss of contact makes many people (especially if historically disillusioned) ready to surrender to the inhuman mechanism, in order, by adapting themselves, quietly, inconspicuously to secure a crumb of individual freedom, or else, by a consistent process of self-mutilation, to cease to be human beings outside the universal automatism.

Others, however, have not abandoned the struggle for liberation, for man's victory over the mechanical, his release from the object-bound, the fragmentary and the deformed towards a meaningful, creative whole. In the sculpture of the Russian artist Ernst Neizvestny it is precisely this interaction of man and machine, this process of undecided metamorphosis, this struggle between man and his works which is given profoundly impressive form. What will be the outcome: man-as-object or a humanized product? Or will the struggle continue without end? Are we still capable of becoming masters of the outside world in order to create another which will be still more difficult to master, and so to progress from alienation to its removal and thence to a new alienation? Or are we faced with a final decision? Nothing can make me believe it.

The development of modern art – whose manifold aspects this is not the place to discuss – seems to me to be governed by the same conflict between two fundamental tendencies: either to surrender in the face of objectification or to complete the secularization of art. The latter means shaking the public out of its receptive passivity and drawing it into the productive process of which the work of art is only the apparently completed outcome. It means recognizing art not as the reflection of an already formed reality but as transformation, change, new creation: not as a permanent, remote mirror-image, but as active reality.

THE DESTROYED CREAM CAKE
A report on the Wiesbaden 'Fluxus Festival' of 1962 tells us that Wolf Vostell

mostly spent his time effacing, destroying and changing objects as an artistic and philosophic activity. He destroyed tin soldiers as though they were people, defaced photographs of cars in magazines so that they looked as if they had been hit by a tornado; hurled transparent glass balls at a glass wall which separated him from the public, and finally uttered a violent cry and flung and smeared a cream cake over the glass . . .[10]

The emphatic destruction of a cream cake of which one has eaten too much becomes a symbolic act. In principle, one approves of the cake. The purpose of one's life is to enlarge the cake. But occasionally the cake can serve to satisfy one's aggressive instinct.

The aggressive instinct is used for the benefit of trade. The miser has become antiquated. He hoarded the imperishable. Modern industry demands a rapid turnover of goods. Consumption is destruction, the destructive consumer is the best. Bite, rip, smash the commodity with teeth, claws, knives, revolvers and bombs! Buy – in order to destroy – the cream cake, the car, the jet plane! Consume cities, continents, planets! Swallow the moon, devour Mars, drink up the Milky Way! Increase the speed of the turnover! Above all, let things wear out more quickly! If the globe flies apart in fragments, we can supply the new model.

Yet art fights back against the triumph of total consumption, against the aggression of prosperity. It wants to find a way out from a world where everything is used up and worn out; it wants to break out from immobility and isolation. What Fernand Léger said at the Wassiliev Gallery in 1914, a few months before the First World War, still applies:

If pictorial expression has changed, it is because modern life demanded it. Life for the creative man today is far more concentrated and intricate than it was for the people of earlier centuries. The picture presented is less static, the separate object obtrudes less. A landscape traversed by a car or an express train loses descriptive value but gains synthetic value: the railway-carriage or the car window, together with speed, have changed the previous appearance of things. Modern man absorbs a hundred times more impressions than the eighteenth-century artist, so much so that, for example, our language today is full of diminutives and abbreviations. All this results in the concentration of the modern picture, its diversity and the breaking up of its forms.[11]

More than fifty years have gone by. Technological discoveries have not only changed the previous appearance of things, they have also changed the things themselves and man too. Modern man, who absorbs a hundred times more impressions than his ancestors, is losing the ability to absorb them because of their sheer quantity. Impressions become superficial stimuli, selected by the opinion-forming monopolies. The senses are losing the ability to retain and process that which impresses them; the world is defaced and the world defaces man just as Vostell defaces his photographs.

An *infantilism of having* is developing; adults come to behave more and more like babies, who want to touch everything and who recognize as real only the palpable, the edible and the destructible. Unlike the child, however, for whom reality is always expanding, we reduce the reality principle to the single principle of having. We think we are making a choice when publicity has long decided which commodity is to choose which buyer. We think we are the takers, yet we have been taken over.

It is art and literature which most stubbornly resist these fetishes and phantoms which, according to the will of the controllers, are meant to represent 'reality'. The attempt to take over art and make it subservient to publicity and propaganda, the attempt to put a stop to the search of art for reality, has been only partially successful. Artists are still trying to discover the reality which exists behind the fetishes and phantoms of power, consumption and ideology: they are still trying to discover man and his alternative.

PARTISANSHIP AND CRITICISM

The most sensitive and thoughtful people in the capitalist world sense and recognize the increasing alienation. The sight of their deformed fellow-men makes them suffer; they long to see man whole. But many of them despair of the possibility of changing the situation, the more so as great masses of people have become accustomed to the condition of total alienation; they stifle their occasional disquiet by increased consumption, and see no reason to break out of the 'comfortable, convenient houses of bondage' (Herbert Marcuse). They want a correction here, an addition there, but they do not notice their own painless dehumanization. Why take the incalculable risk of altering a highly developed industrial society, where the worker does not go hungry and the outcasts, the wretched of the earth, are only an amorphous minority? It is terrible to see a society tacitly affirmed by those who, under an anaesthetic, are mutilated by it. Even more terrible is the conviction of many of those who suffer that no social change can counteract the deformation and create more favourable conditions for the 'whole man'.

One of the most important reasons, though not the sole reason, for this conviction is the fact that the communists have not yet, in the countries where they are in power, given an example of any development towards the *whole man* – indeed they have not even outlined his image in a convincing or persuasive way. Without such an example and such an image, however crude it may at first be, many people on whom the future depends will go on disbelieving in the future.

SOCIALISM AND THE YOUNGER GENERATION

It seems to me that the responsibility of those trying to build socialism has never been so great as now. The pre-conditions for tracing the image of the *whole man*, feature by feature, have been there ever since the so-called personality cult came to an end and the world turned towards coexistence. Although ideological distortions of every kind succeeded in obscuring marxist philosophy, marxist scientific method and the marxist utopian vision of the future, they did not succeed in destroying them. Young people, when they study 'Marxism–Leninism' as a set subject at school, can still detect the original idea behind the phrases of false consciousness and compare those ideas with the reality around them. Among these young people there are some who are against socialism, some who are indifferent or bored, some who think only of their careers; but the core consists of those who believe in the ideas of socialism and therefore cannot accept their social deformation. What they want is not a return to capitalism but a breakthrough to a truly socialist society, to the humanist world from the vision of which Marx set out and which supplies the radiant energy, not only of his early writings, but of his work as a whole.

MY IDEOLOGICAL CONFUSION

When, in a talk to students at Charles University in Prague in the autumn of 1963, I said: 'I don't think that the enthusiasm of young people can be aroused by a mass of figures – production figures or productivity figures. What young people want to hear is: what is going to be done about *man*?', my young audience burst into demonstrative applause. I added: 'I regard it as the decisive mission of the young generation to take up this struggle for the whole man. . . . Criticize us as harshly as you wish; we have made bad mistakes. But be always aware that you must do it better. It can't be done with criticism alone. . . . Take the shovel out of our hands – not to throw it away, but to build your world!'

A few months later, a newspaper in the German Democratic Republic (not in Czechoslovakia) retorted that my words about productivity and production figures were symptomatic of my anti-marxist philosophy. Marx, I was informed, had said: 'Being determines consciousness.' In my 'ideological confusion' I had failed to grasp that Being is expressed primarily by production and productivity figures. The choice between the capitalist and the socialist systems 'lies first and foremost in the main sphere of human activity, which is the sphere of material production. . . . As members of the S.E.D. and citizens of the G.D.R., we oppose Ernst Fischer's thesis because it is entirely contrary to the programme of the S.E.D. as laid down at the VIth Party Congress.'[12]

My doubts concerning the suggestive power of production and productivity figures are thus promoted to a 'thesis'. As the polemic progresses, the thesis becomes an 'appeal': 'It is an example of empty idealism when Fischer appeals to the students of Prague: Don't worry about production and productivity figures, worry about Man!' The 'empty idealism' becomes subversion, for: 'The question is not whether the young can be made enthusiastic about production figures. Our task, in which Ernst Fischer is trying to obstruct us, consists rather in making the entire youth of the socialist countries *still more* enthusiastic about such figures.' Finally the article concludes with the austere precept:

The construction of socialism and communism includes several tasks, but foremost and decisive among them is production – the creation of the material and technical basis. Fischer's line of opposing man to production within socialism contradicts the marxist conception of the foundation and the superstructure. But our party's slogan: 'work, learn and live the socialist way' sums up, in a scientifically precise and popular form, the dialectic of the relations between man and production under socialism.[13]

DIGRESSION ON MARXISM

I do not venture to guess what degree of popularity this slogan has achieved in the G.D.R. But I am alarmed by the lack of scientific precision displayed by my unnamed tutor in 'dialectical materialism'. It is not his person that I care about, but the decay of marxism which he represents.

The great historico-philosophical discovery of the relationship between productive forces, production relations and 'superstructure', which Karl Marx formulated in its briefest form in the celebrated preface to his *Contribution to the Critique of Political Economy*, cannot be applied mechanically.

It is not an ideological bed of Procrustes into which any historical situation can be fitted at the cost of its feet or even its head. For example, it would be by no means true to say that the G.D.R. had been created as a result of new productive forces breaking through the old production relations. The G.D.R. was not created as a result of its own revolution, but as a result of the Russian revolution which took place almost forty years earlier. The new production relations (expropriation of landowners, industrialists and bankers) came from the outside, as a result of the victory of the Soviet army. With them came a superstructure together with a well-ordered ideology to dominate it. Thus the foundation had to be built and consolidated from the superstructure down, and in many respects this made a topsy-turvy world with unusually difficult problems. Social being was determined by the consciousness of a small minority. Destroyed factories had to be re-started, new industries had to be built up, low productivity had to be raised, and, above all, the hostile, suspicious or, at best, sceptical masses had to be won over: and all this in a divided country where national consciousness had no reason to support social revolution as it had where the Soviet army had brought liberation from alien German rule.

Instead of speaking of these difficulties, my nameless tutor (and in this he is not alone) brandishes quotations which do not happen to fit the given situation in any way whatsoever.

If I polemicize against certain publications, doctrines or methods in the G.D.R., this polemic is not directed against the G.D.R. itself. I support this second German State which does not threaten its neighbours but contributes to the securing of peace in Europe, which has destroyed not only the power of the dangerous old ruling class but also the old system of educational privilege, which tolerates no anti-semitism of any kind and is making honest efforts to create a new social order on the basis of common ownership of the principal means of production. I desire nothing so much as that its economic achievements may be added to and surpassed by the development of democracy, freedom and humanity.

It would not be just 'empty idealism' but pure foolishness to overlook or, worse still, to dispute the necessity for increased production and higher productivity in the Soviet Union and the People's Democracies. Economic backwardness in those countries is not only morally depressing for the nations concerned: it is a serious disturbance factor in international development as a whole. It would be wise, in my opinion, not to talk so much of 'objective' causes (of which there are many), but rather to ask whether the 'superstructure' with all its rigid forms and dogmas has not impeded and is not still impeding the development of the 'foundation' and whether changes in the superstructure may not be needed in order to improve the 'foundation'.

THE CONTINUING ALIENATION

The productive relations which, in their totality, form the real foundation, the economic structure of society, are determined not only by who is the *de jure* owner of the means of production, but also by who is *de facto* in possession of them. The expropriation of capitalist properties and the nationalization of enterprises constitute a social revolution of the widest scope. Yet the fact that private ownership has been forced to yield to the state does not directly alter a great deal so far as the worker is concerned. The state may claim to be *his* state – a state of workers and peasants; but the question is, up to what point is it his? Does the worker identify himself with the bureaucrat? Does he regard him as his representative, as the representative of his class, as the will and power of that class? And up to what point? *Has alienation been removed?* Are not production relations being mystified as much as they were before, objectified, reduced to relations between objects, between apparatuses and institutions? Yet the demystification of production relations, so that they become grasped and felt as relations between human beings, is one of the essential definitions of socialism. Of course economic laws continue to exist even under socialism; objects still exercise power and there is still a 'realm of necessity'. But these laws are recognizable, and consciousness is becoming more and more able to extend and confirm man's power over objects and to limit the realm of necessity for the benefit of freedom.

Revolution means a break with alienation. The old power apparatuses are smashed. Classes confront each other without an intermediary. Men plan their own future and take decisions in each situation as it arises. The assertion that Soviet power is more democratic than any traditional democracy, which, applied to later conditions, became one of the formulae of false consciousness, was true of the revolutionary era.

Once the revolution has triumphed, the overthrown yet not finally vanquished past rises up again – not in its totality, but with alarming force – in the form of habit, prejudice and deformation, and in the form of a continuing *world of having*. And it is not only the *old* self-alienation which is carried over into the new society; a *new* alienation is created when power passes, by institutionalization and bureaucratization, from revolutionary organs into the hands of a central authority.

The first step towards overcoming this new alienation is to admit that it exists: that 'people's enterprise' or 'workers' and peasants' State' are magic names – but magic names which it is now objectively possible to make real. Alienation can be removed only to the extent that *self-administration, co-determination*, and hence *co-responsibility* at the places of production and, beyond them, in all spheres of social life are introduced. Consciousness can become effective only to the extent that it becomes *social* consciousness, i.e. a consciousness which is democratically controlled and therefore compelled continually to develop, undergo correction and renew itself. The governing officials are largely unaware of what people really think, of the true and false things which really fill their consciousness. What they *are* aware of is largely a matter of chance. The consciousness of the rulers is an amalgam of true and false consciousness. Therefore only the most far-reaching and comprehensive democratic interaction can create a progressive social consciousness.

The expropriation of capitalist properties is a pre-condition of socialism, but it is not socialism itself. Production relations become socialist only through unmanipulated democracy within enterprises and the economy in general, through the triumph of the democratic principle in all spheres of social life. The parliamentary forms of democracy – which are there not to be destroyed but to be expanded – have always been, and still are, political 'superstructure'. The extension of the democratic principle to the economy itself, genuine democracy in factories guaranteed by workers' committees, works councils, trades unions, and other organs directly responsible to the workers, can remove the division between 'superstructure' and foundation. All such democratic organs are component parts of the new economic structure. The new production relations can be relations between human beings – relations which are not arbitrary but are founded both on economic laws and on the democratic, humane principle of socialism which recognizes man not merely in his working capacity, as a 'trained force of nature', but as a complete whole.

THE SOCIALIST CONSCIOUSNESS

Talking to members of a workers' council at a factory in Warsaw in 1957, I put the following question to them: 'When central organs of the state or the party adopt a decision, what do you say? "They've decided . . ." or "We've decided . . ."?' At first there was silence. Then one of the men said: 'Nobody has ever asked us such a question before. But now that I think of it: in the first years after the Liberation, the workers used to say "We". Then until October 1956, we used to say "They". Now once more we are saying "We".' All the members of the workers' council confirmed the truth of this.

The relationship between workers and engineers had for many years been bad; the workers had refused to support the engineers' claims for better pay, saying that they themselves were also badly paid. After October 1956 the workers' council took over responsibility for the entire factory. At its first meeting it unanimously adopted a decision to raise the engineers' salaries. One of the workers explained this to me. The salaries, he said, were too low in relation to the workers' wages and were thus humiliating to the technical intelligentsia. The impressive feature of the story was that the arguments which the workers used were not solely economic but also psychological, considering the engineer in the new circumstances not only as an important factor in production but as a hitherto humiliated fellow human being. A socialist consciousness was being born on the basis of new production conditions, namely the genuine joint authority of workers and staff.

The creation of a new socialist consciousness is a central problem of socialism, as it comes gradually into being and becomes recognizable in rough outline despite many distortions and setbacks. In the Russian revolution, consciousness had soared ahead of being. It had come about differently from what Marx had expected (for good reason, in his own time): new productive forces had not smashed the old production relations in one of the most developed capitalist countries. Instead, revolution had occurred in a backward country as the result of war, wretchedness, the elemental demand of the people as a whole for peace and the demand of the peasants for land. The undeveloped productive forces had not called for socialism. But historical decisions do not follow the textbooks; they are the product of unprecedented and unrepeatable situations.

THE OCTOBER REVOLUTION

Russia's choice in the autumn of 1917 was not, as is often said, between bourgeois democracy and the dictatorship of the proletariat. The alternative to Soviet power was counter-revolution, military dictatorship, a régime which would have anticipated fascism. Although the Bolsheviks in October 1917 had large masses of workers and peasants behind them, the triumph of the socialist revolution in Russia was not a historical necessity but was due to Lenin's genius, the ideas of his party, and a unique concentration of audacity, intelligence and will power. This preponderance of subjective factors, the belief in the omnipotence of the will when combined with a high degree of consciousness, tipped the scales and brought about victory with all its unparalleled problems. This victory seemed almost impossible, and there were good grounds for the predictions by intelligent people in the West that Soviet power would collapse.

The almost impossible succeeded; but because it was almost impossible, the achievement itself was fraught with the danger of future deformations. These deformations *in nucleo* were an excessive belief in the power of the pure will (voluntarism), the neglect and violation of reality, the ossification of an *avant-garde* into a power apparatus which, because the Party had proved to be right in the most difficult situations, now claimed the inalienable privilege of being right all the time. So long as Lenin was alive, his sense of reality, his ruthless candour, his willing talent for learning from the masses, for correcting mistakes, for enriching consciousness by new experience, for always striving towards the difficult balance between organization and spontaneity, wish and ability, idea and practice in the changing process of social reality, all this constituted a safeguard – although not a total one – against the danger.

The Russian revolution not only shook the world: it also broadened and accelerated, to an undreamt-of extent, the overall process of social revolution and change. The oppressed and exploited peoples of Asia and Africa were encouraged by it and in its light saw a real opportunity of getting rid of the colonial system. The existence of the Soviet Union – the socialist alternative – forced capital to make far-reaching concessions to the workers and to recognize, reluctantly, the need for what is known as the 'Welfare State'. If today the worker in the highly developed industrial countries of the capitalist world is incomparably better off than his father and grandfather, this is thanks partly to the Russian workers whose standard of living is lower than his own. The almost superhuman efforts and sacrifices of the Russian people have until now been of less benefit to the Russians themselves than to the workers in the capitalist world, the majority of whom deny, and often even condemn, the October revolution whose beneficiaries they are. A Russian woman whose Western host tried to impress her with the wealth of goods in his country commented harshly: 'Our blood, our tears – that is the raw material for which you have still not thanked us.'

The situation is not without paradoxical features. The socialist revolution was forced, by its triumph in a backward country, to undertake tasks which capitalism in the more developed countries had more or less already resolved. Russia had to be industrialized. The ingrained *nichevo*,* the laziness, indifference and irresponsibility of centuries had to be overcome. A spirit of organization, discipline and working morale had to be inculcated – and all this with a handful of skilled workers and a vast mass of illiterate peasants. Concentration upon this 'initial accumulation of socialism' relegated some essential tasks of socialism to the background and distorted many of its features.

Marx assumed that socialism would first triumph in the technically and industrially developed countries, so that the material conditions for socialism would be already present. He described as 'one of the civilizing sides of capital' that it enforces surplus labour – which society needs under all circumstances – 'in a manner and under conditions which promote the development of the productive forces, of social conditions, and the creation of the elements for a new and higher formation better than did the preceding

* 'It doesn't matter'.

forms of slavery, serfdom, etc.' Capital creates 'the material requirements and the germ of conditions, which make it possible to combine this surplus labour in a higher form of society with a greater reduction of the time devoted to material labour. . . .'[14]

THE DEFORMATION OF COMMUNISM

The conditions under which the socialist revolution in Russia came about have not, initially, encouraged or allowed any development of human potential for its own sake. The fact that 'initially' has come to mean 'for half a century' does not diminish the greatness of the October revolution, but it does inject a little disappointment into our admiration and, retrospectively, a little sadness into our early dreams. Anyone has a right to criticize the Soviet Union and to believe that communism has been negated by its results to date. But we who, in spite of everything, affirm the ideas and the aims of communism are in duty bound to speak more than anyone else of the inadequacy of what has been achieved and of the deformation of men and conditions in the socialist world. I believe that efforts towards the achievement of socialism are in the interest of mankind as a whole. Yet we who affirm communism are the ones most directly concerned, because when we speak of communism we speak of a cause which is directly our own. Therefore if we conceal what should be disclosed, defend what needs to be attacked or shore up what requires pulling down, we are guilty of treason against our own selves. We must admit that the renewal of man through communism has not yet taken place. There does not yet exist a convincing communist image of man to set against the dehumanization of man through capital, through the *world of having*. Man is deformed both there and here.

It did not have to happen. It was inevitable that the revolution should be harsh, indeed cruel. Yet it would have been possible to preserve the marxist image of man, even if sometimes the vision of it was clouded. It would have been possible to achieve gradually the realization of its most essential features. Something which appeared not only in great personalities such as Lenin, Gramsci or Rosa Luxemburg but also in the many anonymous supporters of communism has been lost. To re-create it is the hope and the aim of many communists today.

To analyse all the historical conditions, events and personalities which have brought about the power and the deformation of communism would require the life's work of more than one man. Many historians, economists and psychologists of many schools would have to work together in order to arrive at anything like a comprehensive and objective finding. I venture only to suggest some of the factors which, in my view, have contributed to this deformation:

The historical failure of social democracy in 1914 and 1918.

The isolation of the victorious Russian revolution.

Russia's backwardness and the immense destruction, disorganization and desolation wrought by war, civil war, and foreign intervention.

The absence of economic foundations and democratic traditions.

The necessity to create an efficient heavy industry at any price, i.e. to sacrifice the present to the future.

Lenin's death at a time when the problem of socialist democracy, which had waited for an answer at his sickbed, could not brook further delay. (The Soviets had lost their revolutionary democratic spirit. A bureaucratic apparatus was establishing its hegemony over the young Soviet power. The principle of socialist democracy, whose development in Russia presented an exceptionally difficult problem, was interred with Lenin.)

The exercise of power, not by democratic organs, but by the party, after the opposition within the party had been liquidated by the party apparatus and later, after Kirov's assassination, by the police apparatus which cleverly manipulated the paranoid despot whose tool it was.

The whole set of phenomena subsumed under the name of Stalinism: 'The party is always right! Stalin is always right! Stalin is infallible!'; the replacement of discussion by defamation, by State prosecution, by judiciary murder; contempt for man, the people, the working class; the destruction of civil rights; the utter defencelessness of the individual; the arbitrariness and cruelty of officials subject to no form of control; the emergence of a pragmatism disguised in threadbare ideology; the supremacy of tactics over strategy and ideology; the inevitable hypocrisy which acted as a poison within the whole of Soviet society.

The congealing of Marxism into a closed, systematic, compulsory ideology which only one man was entitled to revise if he deemed this to be tactically necessary.

In listing these points, I am aware that they are not sufficient to explain the deformation of communism. Things which happened in the distant past may have played a part in later developments. Thus, for example, the fact that Marx, increasingly preoccupied by his *Critique of Political Economy*, failed to find time to develop the philosophical ideas contained in his early writings, the philosophy of practice and man, has, I believe, contributed to an excessive 'objectification' of marxism. The economism of social democracy, the simplication of materialism and above all of dialectics has turned the great philosophy of our time into a collection of sturdy doctrines, a compendium of knowledge useful in the workers' struggle. The young Marx's image of man became submerged under economic and political demands, under the immediate aims of the class struggle, under the mechanism of party organization. And I think that Lenin, in his unique struggle for a revolutionary party and a revolutionary guide for action, in his indispensable polemic against social-democratic illusions, underestimated bourgeois democracy; I believe that he rightly recognized its dictatorial tendencies and its formal character, but not its positive results and possibilities. It should be added that many of Lenin's judgements, inevitably over-harsh within their polemical context, were later taken out of that context and dogmatically misused, while his positive comments on bourgeois democracy remained unnoticed under Stalinism.

Finally I believe that a kind of moral relativism (exclusive proletarian morality, no ethical principles beyond class interest, etc.) has obscured the humanist aims of communism.

NO CONVINCING COMMUNIST IMAGE OF MAN

The communist image of man, which had to serve during the heroic struggle against tsarism, during the triumph of the revolution and during the creation of Soviet heavy industry, has become a cliché. The virtues required were the virtues of an extreme situation: courage, endurance, cool-headedness, dedication, discipline, self-sacrifice, ruthlessness towards oneself and others. Revolution and the immense, elemental effort of construction call for these soldierly virtues, as does war. But if the humane goal is not to be lost sight of, other virtues must join these and gradually supersede them. Brecht, who was not a great lover of mankind in his youth, spoke of 'friendliness' in his years of maturity. The word was never adopted in the official communist vocabulary. Words such as freedom, truth, humanity are admitted only conditionally, not as 'abstract' concepts but qualified by terms such as 'proletarian', 'socialist', 'class view', etc. Sincerity, tolerance, objectivity still remain tainted with revisionism and are generally regarded as something smuggled in by the class enemy. Despite all the talk, past and present, about 'the all-round development of man', the communist image of man is still that of the tough soldier of the revolution, 'carved out of different wood' from the rest of the human race, or else it remains something vague, indefinite and faceless. The unfriendly bureaucrat who, 'for the sake of the cause', treats human beings as mere component parts of that cause, acts the 'professional revolutionary' who has exchanged the barricades for a desk. At the same time, seriously meant attempts to draw a new communist image of man yield only a blurred cliché, a conglomerate of memories of the revolution and demands such as every state addresses to its young people (demands for keenness, patriotism, recognition of authority, constant preparedness to fight in defence of the fatherland, rejection of nihilistic tendencies, respect for the flag, the army, the country's glorious traditions, etc.). The result is only melodramatic phrases – 'the spiritual beauty of Soviet man' or 'the glowing enthusiasm, the effervescent happiness, the high moral superiority of the builders of socialism'.

HYPOCRISY

Such phrases are quite frequently offered in good faith, so that one feels, behind the embarrassing words, a genuine desire to find once more the human being lost in the fastness of economic statistics and unreliable production figures, to discover at last the yearned-for hero of a new age adorned with all the emblems of his virtues. But at the same time they are surrounded by a haze of still undispelled hypocrisy. Lenin described hypocrisy as the worst vice of the bourgeois world. It is superfluous to speak of the hypocrisy of those who, in the name of freedom, attack other countries by force of arms, who support dissolute, bloody and corrupt rulers against their own people in the name of civilization, who bomb towns and villages, schools and hospitals without being attacked or threatened, all in the name of humanity. The fact that the *world of having* is a world of hypocrisy does not justify hypocrisy in those who are fighting that world. The argument that 'the others are just as bad' is unworthy of socialists. If the socialist world were merely no worse than the capitalist one, what would be the point of the sacrifices made to create it?

Because I am convinced that it can be better, that in its intentions and its potential it is already better, I am not afraid of the charge of 'fouling my own nest'. Those concerned with cleaning out their nest are always reproached with fouling it.

Hypocrisy is as much a deformation of the communist image of man as the heritage of arbitrariness and cruelty which Stalin's régime left behind it. It differs in extent and structure from the hypocrisy of Tartuffe or of the businessmen of whom it was said: 'They say God and mean cotton.' If there were only the Tartuffes (and there are many of them), only the Orgons would be their victims, not the whole of society. Hypocrisy, the most pernicious and persistent of all the diseases brought on by Stalinism, affected not only those naturally susceptible to it but also many healthy organisms. More than that, it turned its instigators' self-deception into a social conspiracy and so into the worst impediment to the development of socialism. It split the world into two: into a world of sensory perception, visible, audible, palpable reality, and then into a super-world of dogmas, quotations, resolutions, guidelines, thought-clichés and empty words.

Both worlds exist. If they fail to coincide, this is dismissed as the difference between pure being and blurred illusion, between the predestined order and accidental deviation, between the here and the beyond. But because there must be only *one* world, the higher life decrees that the lower must not be as it is; what *is* must approximate as closely as possible to what should be. If the contrast becomes too flagrant, this is either the work of saboteurs or an illusion of the senses. The police, or the report of some appropriate commission, then corrects the inadmissible truth accordingly.

The fact that such hypocrisy has been able to spread so wide and deep among people, to the point of splitting their consciousness between the private and the social self, is not only due to the exigencies of a régime which must always be right; its sources also lie elsewhere.

The Austrian biologist Kammerer, passionately convinced of the hereditary transmission of acquired characteristics, wanted to offer experimental proof of this. When none of his experiments confirmed his theory, he began to correct nature. Accused of fraud, he took his own life, without entertaining the smallest doubt of the correctness of his ideas. What nature had denied him would, he hoped, be vouchsafed one day to a luckier experimenter.

A Soviet miner in the thirties, questioned by a British workers' delegation about his wages, named a high figure. The interpreter, surprised, went back to ask him later: 'Do you really earn that much?' 'Of course not, just a third of what I said.' 'Why did you lie to the English comrades, then?' 'I want them to hurry up and make a revolution.'

Neither the biologist nor the miner was a hypocrite. But attitudes such as theirs have encouraged hypocrisy.

A unique revolution had taken place. Yet all the sacrifices of a backward country could not lead immediately to the workers' being better off than in the capitalist countries. Did this mean that the principles for which superhuman efforts had been made and were continuing to be made were wrong? And if they were right, and it was simply a case of reality proving obdurate, why not correct the results by propaganda? Was it not simply a 'white lie' if achievements were a little exaggerated, the positive features emphasized, the negative ones hushed up or at least presented as less important and as the inevitable by-products of a revolution with world-wide historical implications? Lenin thought otherwise. Although his declaration that the dictatorship of the proletariat – the Soviets – was a hundred times more democratic than the most advanced bourgeois democracy was truer of an idea than of the actual phenomenon, truer of tendencies than of facts, he still thought it necessary to talk about the evils, the irregularities and the mistakes – to tell the truth.

TACTICS AS THE MASTER OF THEORY
Not until Stalin came into power did hypocrisy really begin to flourish: the evergreen growth of hypocrisy that conceals and strangles, embellishes and devours the bare trunk. Simultaneously 'Marxism–Leninism' was set up as the unchallengeable ideology, the definitive doctrinal system. Both developments were connected, even if indirectly. Stalin had to be proved the sole legitimate successor of Marx, Engels and Lenin: the preserver and executor of their teachings. And so whatever seemed to confirm Stalin's practice in their works was especially selected, emphasized and canonized. Thus theory became more and more the handmaiden of

tactics in order to justify whatever was happening at any given time. Science was required to serve, not the principle of reality, but the fulfilment of wishes.

Stalin, who was always right as a matter of principle, had also always to be right in practice. The formula that no fortress could withstand the Bolsheviks (a formula which was the quintessence of voluntarism) led to an obligation to achieve victory at any price. Lenin had not concealed defeats; for example, he had spoken of strategic withdrawal at the time of the New Economic Policy (N.E.P.). Under Stalin there had to be nothing but victories. If a fortress failed to yield it was treason, and traitors had to be executed. If it still did not fall even then, it ceased to be called a fortress, and disappeared as though under a magic spell; grass grew over it, a garden of roses, a flourishing collective farm. Who can fail to see it? Who is not overjoyed? Who does not thank Stalin? Hypocrisy became an obligation.

As already suggested, such hypocrisy – especially in its early stages – was a highly complicated social phenomenon. There were genuine great successes and genuine great and small hypocrites, careerists, sycophants; an increasing national pride and a tendency to overlook suffering and injustice; a relationship of the masses to Stalin which reached the proportions of idolatry, and a rising fear with its roots in blood and incense. The borderline between faith and hypocrisy, admiration and Byzantine worship, conscious deception and false consciousness, was blurred. Is it wise to arouse the wrath of a god who is always victorious, who annihilates his enemies and who promises in the greyness of today a radiant day-after-tomorrow, is it wise to arouse his wrath by bringing him bad news? Things are moving forward after all, and if it so happens that something does not work at this particular point, in this particular field, is it wise to set one's seal and signature to the betrayal of an immutable principle by mere reality? Since a fact is only born when it is written down in black and white, is it wise to promote the non-event of an accident to the status of a fact? The god who is always victorious needs new victories: he also needs deputies who know how to be victorious by following his directives; and if they send bad news, then they are useless and incapable, perhaps even saboteurs.

FALSE CONSCIOUSNESS

Hypocrisy and false consciousness are interlinked. The laws which reality has to obey are laid down in holy writ, in dogmas the doubting of which means the first step towards defection, towards rebellion against the god, towards alliance with the class enemy, the first step towards the tribunal and the scaffold. But since reality is incessantly changing, since only one man is empowered to make changes in the fixed laws, and since these latter changes are determined by tactics, an ever-thickening tissue of false consciousness disguises the ideas, discoveries and methods of marxism as received in a simplified form. The spider that weaves the web is nourished on falsified facts, and hypocrisy, which supplies this nourishment of unreal reality, besides winning praise and medals, finds in the same false consciousness its own moral justification and confirmation. Hypocrisy has the function of obliterating the contradiction between reality and false consciousness, of fictitiously removing that contradiction; and false consciousness furnishes hypocrisy with a good conscience and the credentials of social indispensability.

The *doubling of the world* is virtually complete. But since Marxism–Leninism differs from religion by the fact that its promise is an earthly one, a realist utopia and not an unimaginable existence after death – since the object of Marxism–Leninism is to change the here-and-now, and therefore it stands and falls by the here-and-now – this double world cannot be a permanent condition. If the contradiction between what should be and what is, between word and deed, ideology and reality, becomes too great, hypocrisy loses its last trace of innocence, blind faith and self-deception. What is left is total demoralization, the acceptance of hypocrisy as a convention, an opportunist devaluation of all words and concepts, an adjustment of language in the socialist world, accepted either without resistance or with a gesture of contempt.

But at the same time there is a growing resolve among people of integrity, both inside and outside the party, those who believe in progress, to overcome this *doubling of the world*, to oppose the phrases to the reality, to see the world as it is and once more to try to change it not verbally but in fact, to bring it closer to the aim of a socialist humanity.

The administrators in their remote world know or at least suspect that something is wrong. But false consciousness, bureaucratic routine, the nature of the party with its fetishes, its doctrines and its forms of thinking and organization, have so spell-bound most of them that they have become monuments to their own past. I have often been struck by the spell which holds many an official in its power, so that when he steps out of the profane outside world into the sanctuary of the committee-room he ceases to be a man and is magically turned into the medium of an invisible superhuman force. Only a little while ago you spoke with him as one speaks with human beings about the conditions and demands of vulgar reality and often you had the impression that to a considerable extent you were in agreement. But at the precise moment when the official takes the place corresponding to his rank in the super-world of the ruling organization, he ceases to be what he was only a minute ago, and some mystical substance takes possession of him, alters his appearance, his voice and his opinion. Risen from the here-and-now into the beyond, he is now able to condemn in principle what only a moment ago, in private conversation, he recognized as justified and necessary.

THE BREAK WITH FALSE CONSCIOUSNESS

The productive forces which are throttled by the system of bureaucratic centralism begin to make themselves felt. Economic backwardness can no longer be concealed by false reports, statistics, lies. The productive forces are not affected by appeals to a non-existent enthusiasm for production figures, nor by a reshuffle of ministers, nor by hastily offered palliatives. Appeals to 'catch up and overtake' the industry and agriculture of the West are in vain. Technical and organizational measures can temporarily lead to partial economic success; but the pre-condition of steady improvement and consistent growth is a break with false consciousness.

Such a break, if it is merely simulated, only made half-heartedly and not even half-heartedly admitted but presented as the necessary adjustment of previous policy, can endanger the future of socialism. False consciousness cannot be eradicated merely by replacing optimistic lies by truthful information, putting economic experts in the place of amateurs, recognizing the principle of profitability, etc.

So long as man is obscured by objects, is regarded merely as an object among objects, raw material for official reports, a smoothly functioning component of society, an instrument which will demonstrate the correctness of theses and dogmas by its behaviour, false consciousness is bound to continue. A merely partial correction of false consciousness can easily lead to technocratic economism with an antiquated ideology superimposed upon it. To overcome the false consciousness it is necessary to have a true socialist consciousness which recognizes reality and aims at that totality of social relations which favours, to the greatest possible extent, the realization of *the whole man*.

There is a struggle going on between the *Real*-politicians who have grown up in a world of false consciousness, in a magic circle of unreality, and the rebels, despised and feared as idealists, for whom socialism is more than a matter of material 'catching up and overtaking'. For the latter, socialism represents the alternative to the enslavement of man by material products: the alternative to his being seduced and persuaded by monolithic power-centres into ideological hypocrisy or passive acceptance. Socialism for them represents a world where there is a real chance of gradually freeing man from the distortions he has suffered. This struggle to discover reality behind the fetishes and the objects, to create a new consciousness, to let consciousness and being creatively interact, has more chance of success in the socialist countries than elsewhere.

THE POWER OF THE MIND

In the capitalist world, not only the rulers but also many writers are convinced of the importance of literature, agreeing with Robbe-Grillet when he says: '*L'artiste ne met rien au-dessus de son travail, et il s'aperçoit vite qu'il ne peut créer que pour rien . . .*'[15] (The artist puts nothing above his work, and he soon realizes that he can only create for the sake of nothing.) What was scandalous yesterday is good business today; provocation becomes an aperitif, the slap in the face is a means of obtaining pleasure, the outrageous gesture is a best-seller. Literary success renders any further consequences unnecessary. Literature changes itself but not the world.

In the Soviet Union and the People's Democracies, on the other hand, both rulers and authors believe in the power of literature. Leading officials used to believe that they could exercise additional power over the people by means of plays and novels dealing with production matters. They laid on a supply of positive heroes on paper, a de-realization of reality which was neither Socialist nor Realist. Yet they were mistaken. The successes were ephemeral. Even the tedium of such literature could not dull the popular contempt for its insincerity. The only result was that people on whom the reading habit had been imposed from above dropped the dreary compulsory reading matter in favour of books of their own choice. Despite the ridiculously small edition in which it appeared, *Not By Bread Alone* was read a thousand times more in the Soviet Union than any book by Kochetov, who combined all the virtues of party-mindedness, vehement anti-revisionism and bureaucratic optimism. The literature of protest against all the Kochetovs has become a power in the land. Its only resources are men and women of talent and courage. Its strength does not lie in organization but in solidarity. It cannot dismiss any official or overthrow any minister, it cannot change the régime by any direct action, but it is changing the thinking of men, or at least contributing to such change. Its works are victories of reality over false consciousness. Its function is that of preparing a future worthy of man, even when it does not speak about it. Its mere presence and difference from what is officially encouraged or expected is enough. From the unpolitical poem to undisguised social criticism, it is not a repudiation of socialism but its anticipation, it is the spirit of freedom which refuses to be satisfied with economic reform but doggedly continues to ask: 'And what about man?'

This spirit is beginning to become aware of its power. It denies the resignation which will have us believe that artists create for the sake of nothing at all. It does not pretend (like Zhdanov and the cultural officials who are his successors and imitators) that literature can directly and without many forms of mediation intervene in the process of social change; it does not take itself for a labour team with specialized social duties; yet it is convinced that it is helping to create something: the man of tomorrow. It knows that every autonomous work of art is an act of liberation.

WHAT IS MAN TO DO WITH HIMSELF?

And when freedom comes, what will people do with it? [asks my well-disposed conversational partner from the bourgeois world]. Won't the impetus be exhausted as soon as the goal is attained? Won't concrete freedom, there as here, consist in a choice between different cars, holiday resorts and consumer goods of every kind?

Won't man in a free socialist world be confronted with nothingness exactly like man in every world where material poverty no longer disguises the real needs of man, his fear, his loneliness, the meaninglessness of his existence? All right, so he will be free, materially secure, with shorter working hours and more leisure – and then? How will he be different from us? What will he do with himself?

What does a man do with himself when he begins to be a man? The question is by no means absurd, but the answer is supplied, not by science, but by utopia. When freedom comes at last – that freedom for which not only writers are fighting in the socialist countries – will it spell the end of mental restlessness, the satiation of the mind?

First, freedom never comes, it only draws closer, beckoning us on. Freedom, so valiantly fought for, does not begin and end with the relaxation of restrictions, foreign travel, the possibility of reading and listening, writing and painting as you wish without having to fear reprisals; it is more intense and richer in content than that. The fight for freedom is a fight not only against the external compulsions imposed on men but also against the interior deformation which they suffer. The liberation of man, for writers in the socialist world (and not for them alone), is more than individual security based on guaranteed rights. It is a total process of gradual liberation from the world of objects, from the domination of things, institutions, prejudices, a development which reveals the new, as yet unattained, goal beyond each goal that has been achieved and removes the dream of free and perfect man ever further into infinity.

In the world to which the cold war has attached the epithet 'free', freedom is linked with having. 'Much money, much freedom', said Goethe of Byron. The apologists of capitalism accept it as dogma that freedom of ownership is the pre-condition of all freedom. The freedom for which the emancipated in the socialist countries strive is not linked with having; it presupposes the public ownership of the essential means of production. One of the aims of this struggle for freedom is to prevent social ownership from producing new forms of unfreedom through the domination of a new privileged stratum. It is precisely this interdependence of the struggle for freedom with all the problems, aims and tasks of socialist society which seems to justify the hope that the freedom achieved in the socialist world will not be self-sufficient and turned only towards the passing moment and the nothingness beyond it, but that it will be creative, forever active, restless and questing.

THE SELF-REALIZATION OF MAN

In his work, man created himself.

In his dreams, he flew ahead of himself.

Hegel in the *Phenomenology of Mind* spoke of this self-creation. The great thing about the phenomenology, says Marx in his critique of Hegelian dialectic, is

that Hegel conceives the self-creation of man as a process, his objectification as loss of the object, as alienation and as transcendence of this alienation; that he thus grasps the essence of *labour* and comprehends objective man – true, because real, man – as the outcome of man's *own labour*. The *real*, active orientation of man to himself as a species being, or his manifestation as a real species being (i.e. as a human being), is only possible by his really bringing out of himself all the *powers* that are his as the *species* man – something which in turn is only possible through the totality of man's actions, as the result of history – is only possible by man's treating these generic powers as objects: and this, to begin with, is again only possible in the form of estrangement.[16]

Until now, man (or, more precisely, men privileged as a result of their positions in society, their intelligence, or their talent and energy) has been more or less able to keep pace with his own works, to transcend the alienation of the exterior world which he has created, to reabsorb it into himself as an intellectual and spiritual extension and enrichment of himself, to become *more human* by means of it. Again and again, change, either revolutionary or gradual, has been necessary to advance this unity between man and his works, which has amounted to a human self-realization not only of a small élite but of increasingly large minorities of the human race. Through this creative process, says Erich Fromm, 'man makes a reality of his own nature; he returns to his own nature, which in theological language is nothing other than the return to God'.[17]

It seems to me that this idea of man's 'return' goes back too much to romanticism and mythology. Man in his self-realization does not *return* to his nature, which is as yet unformed although it is being conditioned by work, by consciousness and anticipation of the future: rather, he advances towards himself through the realization of his own potential. Alienation is neither falling away from God (original sin) nor loss of the world spirit which then comes back into its own; rather, the nature of man as a species is the realistic possibility of becoming humanity, the *whole man*. Humanity, which until now has not succeeded in raising itself from the unconscious condition of a species to that of a conscious community felt by every man, does not return to itself, it is not an original state from which man has fallen: it is a future, it is the great potential founded in the nature of man. The dehumanization of man is a fall from his future, not from his past.

The world-historical situation in which we find ourselves is monstrous and alarming because the works of man are outgrowing man at an unprecedented rate and to an unprecedented extent. The newly created and rapidly expanding outside world has not yet been mastered intellectually or spiritually in any of the existing social systems: it has not yet been reabsorbed into the inner world of man. Erich Fromm may be exaggerating when he writes:

Man today is faced with a decisive choice – not between capitalism and communism, but between a robot's existence (either communist or capitalist variety) and a humanist–democratic socialism. Most facts seem to indicate that he will choose a robot's existence, and this, in the long run, means sickness and annihilation. And yet all these facts are not strong enough to destroy our faith in the possibilities of reason, the good will and the inner health of man. So long as we can still think in alternatives, we are not lost. So long as we consult and plan with one another, we may hope . . .[18]

In setting our course towards the whole man we must not, however, proceed from false premises, but must constantly re-examine the way towards our utopian goal on the basis of technical progress (in the broadest sense of the word).

THE PROBLEM OF DIVISION OF LABOUR

Developments in technology, science and methods of work have made it impossible for men to fulfil themselves as whole men in the field of material production which is socially necessary. The fanatics of production figures have a vested interest in idealizing manual work and those who practise it. From the historical role of the working class they deduce that the industrial worker is the exemplary human type which, more than any other, approximates to the whole man. In fact, the industrial worker can only overcome his one-sidedness, his deformation and the fragmentary nature of his being to the extent that he transcends the frontiers of material production. It is precisely this recognition – the recognition that the self-realization of man takes place principally outside and beyond the sphere of socially necessary production – which arouses the anger of the typical bureaucrat. Nothing alarms such a bureaucrat more than the transformations of a 'simple' man into a man rendered more critical, more articulate and more difficult to please by knowledge, education, more complex needs and a more exacting intellect. He can produce any number of quotations to support his notion that the whole man is the one who can put his hand to any job, the rolling mill today, agriculture tomorrow, the chemical laboratory the day after. (The man he vaguely imagines to be the whole man is himself, the party official, who can take over any administrative department at any time, who is master of every subject even if he does not grasp it, teaching the peasant how to harvest beets, the writer how to write, and the mathematician how to do multiplication tables.)

Marx and Engels assumed, in their time and not without reason, that a future classless society would overcome the division of labour (which, while developing man's capacities, also fragments them and alienates man from his work and from himself) and would produce a new type of man active in all branches of production, familiar with every work process and thus fully able to realize himself. Since then the development of modern productive forces, the increasing specialization and the high degree of technical knowledge necessary for every part of every field of production have made it extremely unlikely that any society, of whatever kind, will succeed in doing away with the division of labour.

But the nature of the division of labour is changing.

Division of labour has led to the formation of social groups such as town and country (whose separation the young Marx described as 'the great divorce of material and intellectual labour') and also to the division into classes – the ruling and the ruled, the exploited and the exploiters, those who own and govern the means of production and those who have themselves been reduced to a mere means of production.

The separation between town and country, the 'imbecility of country life', is already disappearing in the highly industrialized countries of the capitalist world; the peasant class is dying out, the peasant is being transformed into an agricultural technician, into a man of modern civilization.

The historical function of socialism is to end the division into classes, and finally to end class society itself. The essential means of production, which bestow social power and make it possible to rule over men, are ceasing to be private property.

CREATIVE LABOUR

It is as though Marx had anticipated modern automation when he wrote that the development of the productive forces of labour was being driven so far forward that the possession and maintenance of the general wealth requires

only a *short working time* for society as a whole, and also that working society has a *scientific* attitude to the process of its progressive reproduction . . . in other words, *work done by man which could be left to be done by objects* has ceased.

Work carried beyond the limits of natural necessity creates

the *material* elements for the development of the rich personality, as many-sided in its production as in its consumption, whose labour therefore appears *no longer as labour* but as the full development of activity itself, in which natural necessity in its immediate form has disappeared, because historical necessity has replaced natural necessity.[19]

'Really free labour', such as musical composition, could be made possible in material production only by

1. its social character being posited, 2. by its being *scientific* in character and at the same time general labour, not the expenditure of effort by man as a *natural force trained in a particular way*, but as the subject which appears in the production process not in merely natural form but as an *activity* regulating all natural forces.[20]

Thus the elimination of work *as work*, the endowing of work with the character of a creative activity such as distinguishes the work of the scientific researcher and the artist, presupposes not only a social context but also the possibility that the worker's attitude towards material production can be that of a controlling agent. Today, the man at the control panel knows what takes place when he presses a button; yet the *how*, the interactions, the total process is beyond him. In a socialist society no cost will be spared to make him familiar with this total process. He will know what he is doing, but even such understood labour is by no means yet creative labour. I do not share the optimism of many technologists who believe that material production will be the sphere in which man can creatively realize himself. He will, to a greater extent than now, have the possibility of inventing, of participating in team-work for the improvement of equipment and the testing of new methods: that is to say he will be involved in activity which, compared with 'manual' work, is creative; but does this make him qualitatively something different from a specialist whose skill has increased? Is it not a mistake to expect the perfection of man to come from the perfection of technology? Are we not advancing along the wrong path? What is changed on this earth by the fact that we know what the back of the moon looks like? Does the astronaut belong to a higher category of man? Has the aeroplane caught up with the dream of flying – still less, overtaken it?

Unquestionably, creative work is being done in the great 're-search factories', such as those at Geneva or Dubna. Robert Jungk speaks of the constant renewal, improvement and expansion of the instruments and adds:

I wonder whether in this network of creative men and the machines they have developed the sense of alienation is still as strong as that felt in other, ordinary, 'workshops'. The 'network' of a laboratory is connected, through its best minds, to a global network of research and technology. It 'supplies' new research results and models of technical construction to the larger network and in exchange receives informa-tion about the work of other partial networks. Thus a vast, living, pulsating structure extending over the entire globe is created, gradually breaking down private, national and ideological divisions and revealing them as arbitrary.[21]

Thus, in both social systems, an expanding élite of researchers, engineers, technicians and highly skilled workers, although they cannot eliminate the division of labour, can nevertheless work creatively towards a common goal, and this goal can be set so far ahead that it appears entirely removed from vulgar utilitarian-ism. Yet the governments which supply the funds want nuclear physics to produce concrete results, not cosmic insights. When it is a matter of cancer rather than war, the flow of credits is less lavish.

Can automation by itself eliminate the division of labour? Can

it make men become truly man? The humanizing effect of technology depends not upon machines but upon men.

Lenin cautiously put his hopes in the role of the trades unions.

Trades unions . . . which only very slowly, in the course of years and
years, can and will develop into broader industrial unions with less
of the craft union about them (embracing entire industries, and not
only crafts, trades and occupations), and later proceed, through these
industrial unions, to eliminate the division of labour among people,
to educate and school people, give them *all-round development and an
all-round training*, so that they *are able to do everything*.[22]

The trade unions in the Soviet Union and the People's Democracies have not developed in the way Lenin expected. They
have degenerated into administrative machines. Nor does it seem
to me correct to define the whole man as the man 'who is able to
do everything'. As I have already pointed out, certain officials consider themselves to be such production 'aces' because, being able
to *direct* all kinds of work, they are convinced that they can also *do*
it. The whole man, the hope and aim of every progressive movement, is not simply a man experienced and competent in all
branches of production, the sum of all capabilities and skills. The
whole man must be a creative man.

It was Leonardo da Vinci who, in many respects, sketched the
human image of the future that we dream of – and who also put it
into practice. Yet nothing suggests that a future society is going to
produce genius *en masse*. And even genius cannot begin to absorb
the total body of knowledge available today, let alone take part
creatively in all spheres of science, technology and the arts.
Specialization (as concentration, as a defence against amateurishness and dilettantism) is one of the pre-conditions of creative work.
No man who has not learned to be thorough can disguise his lack
of substantial skill by a pretence of all-round capability. The central
problem is increasingly that of uniting specialized knowledge in one
or several spheres with a general education, that is to say with an
understanding of social, historical, cultural and intellectual connections, the interaction between the sciences, the intellectual disci-
plines and the multiplicity of the arts.

THE REALM OF FREEDOM

There was no other way of developing the manifold capacities of Man
[wrote Friedrich Schiller], than by placing them in opposition to each

other. This antagonism of powers is the great instrument of culture, but it is only the instrument; for as long as it persists, we are only on the way towards culture. . . . But can Man really be destined to neglect himself for any end whatever?[23]

In order not to neglect but to find himself, man must transcend the limits of material production.

Marx, who envisaged the possibility of an end of labour *as labour*, wrote later:

Just as the savage must wrestle with nature in order to satisfy his wants, in order to maintain his life and reproduce it, so civilized man has to do it, and he must do it in all forms of society and under all possible modes of production. With this development the realm of natural necessity expands, because his wants increase; but at the same time the forces of production increase, by which these wants are satisfied. The freedom in this field cannot consist of anything else but of the fact that socialized man, the associated producers, regulate their interchange with nature rationally, bring it under their control, instead of being ruled by it as by some blind power; that they accomplish their task with the least expenditure of energy and under conditions most adequate to their human nature and most worthy of it. But it always remains a realm of necessity. Beyond it begins that development of human power which is its own end, the true realm of freedom, which, however, can flourish only upon that realm of necessity as its basis. The shortening of the working day is its fundamental premise.[24]

The human development of forces which is its own purpose begins in the 'realm of freedom' beyond material production, that realm where man 'has no need either to encroach upon another's freedom in order to assert his own, or to display gracefulness at the cost of dignity'.[25] Capitalist society tries to reduce this realm of freedom, in which the dignity of man reveals itself in grace, to mere 'leisure time'. In this way the realm of freedom can be manipulated and subjugated to the needs of production which is the prop of capitalist society. It is not only a matter of stuffing the expanding leisure hours with goods. Leisure carries an inherent threat to capitalist society. Men released from the necessity of work must be given no time to find themselves. They must only *have* and *consume*. Once escaped from the apparatus, if they began to discover themselves as independent beings, they would become aware of the parasitic, anti-human nature of their rulers and institutions; they would begin to rebel – from the premise of an anticipated 'realm of freedom' – against the antiquated social forms around them.

The more powerfully and obstinately the apparatus fights against the autonomy of man, the more feverishly it endeavours to bind, control and deform man through false needs, false satisfactions and false consciousness.

THE WAGER FOR FAUST'S SOUL

The borderline between the 'realm of necessity' and the 'realm of freedom' will not remain fixed, since the problems of technology are linked with those of science and both are linked with man's desire for knowledge, for total understanding, for the infinite. The wager for Faust's soul is on. Will he, out of his enormous alienation after the conquest of the planets, the splitting of the atomic nucleus, the production of immeasurable energy, find his way back to himself, to the interior of the world of man? Will Mephistopheles subjugate him completely within his own works, so that the immortal element in him is lost?

In this great wager, this decisive contest, the responsibility of the countries concerned with building socialism is very great. There, too, Mephistopheles is at work, trying to misuse the Faustian urge in order to achieve concentration of power, to falsify the 'realm of freedom' beyond material production and to make of it a subordinate province to the 'realm of necessity'. Increased material production is necessary; but unless the realm of freedom is expanded at the same time, freedom from incessant control, from the communal reading of dreary leading articles, from staged discussions, from constant social interference in the most private and intimate aspects of life, Mephistopheles may triumph there too. The system which will win both the competition between social systems and the wager for Faust's soul is not the one that produces a larger quantity of goods, but the one that offers more freedom, grace, dignity, creative content and autonomous humanity.

Neither *homo faber* nor *homo sapiens*, neither working man nor thinking, speculating, searching man, nor a combination of both, is the whole man. *Homo ludens*, playing man, is also essential, for 'Man plays only when he is in the full sense of the word a man, and he is only wholly Man when he is playing'.[26] And *homo amator* is equally indispensable, man capable of loving, worthy of loving, versed in loving, capable of becoming one with the 'other', man

H

who produces humanity through sensual, spiritual, artistic communion and becomes aware of his own infinity. In that way he takes possession of the world, not as *having* but as *being*.

Only when we, both in the East and in the West, become aware of our own deformation do we reach the starting point from which we may overcome it.

Literature, made by men for men, has many and varying functions. To deny it any function is absurd: how can it, unless it has a function, find a public? To prescribe this or that function for literature is a failure of understanding, for literature by decree is literature without life. In the modern, bureaucratically centralized industrial world whose agents and victims we are, there would appear to be two elements of decisive importance: criticism and vision: ruthless, fetish-destroying criticism of the social reality on both sides, and a vision courageous enough to create an image of man with all the marks of the abyss from which he comes and all the features of the future of which he dreams, in his fear and his greatness, his vulnerability and his revolt, his absurdity and his gift of bestowing meaning, his power to create and distort inexhaustible possibilities.

If we believed man to be perfect, there would be nothing to keep us from despair.

To see man as deformed is to measure him against what he can become: man unscathed, man without distortion, man whole.

II. THE ABSURD GARDEN PARTY

From the mass of Czech and Slovak books, films and plays whose theme is alienation in the socialist world, I want to select *The Garden Party*,[27] a comedy by the young Czech playwright Václav Havel. While working as a stage hand, Havel became familiar with a world composed of scraps of text, half-completed characters, misplaced scenery, purposeless light effects, a world both highly coloured and indistinct, the fragmentary world of rehearsals, an absurd world. Yet is so-called normal, sane life, outside the rehearsal, any less absurd? Is it not more absurd?

In the kaleidoscope of the stage, in the midst of incessant metamorphosis, there is nevertheless the constant aim of transforming a manuscript into the magic reality of the theatre. In normal life there is neither author nor producer; no one knows what is being rehearsed, and no one can foresee what the final result will be. Word and gesture, speech and action fail to agree; war is planned in the name of peace, murder is re-christened freedom. Actors slap each other's faces while extolling mutual understanding. The empty phrase becomes action: the cliché becomes an event: nothing is as unreal as man: nothing so real as spectres. Is it not justified to put such absurdity, in normal life disguised by reassuring convention and routine, on the stage and to show the startled public that the world which the theatre of the absurd presents is in fact its own? The theatre of the absurd is not a joke perpetrated by snobs: it is an attempt to give artistic form to an essential aspect of our age.

THE NATURE OF THE ABSURD

This is not the place to speak of the innumerable ancestors of the 'theatre of the absurd' – the fool and the clown, Aristophanes and Shakespeare, Rabelais and Swift, Tieck and Grabbe, Nestroy and Lewis Carroll. I would refer the reader to Martin Esslin's book *The Theatre of the Absurd*,[28] which supplies some of the material for this chapter.

Let us remember that, side by side with the conflicts of tragedy and the contradictions of comedy, the apparent nonsense of the absurd has had a place in art for thousands of years. The world is already seen as absurd in the Eleusinian mysteries, with their ambivalent attitude towards the gods, their sudden switching from pious prayer to coarse abuse, their falling from the sublime to the ridiculous, their shifts from the cosmos to chaos where mud and beasts and God flow amorphously into one another. The absurd is that which runs counter to reason. We push an attitude *ad absurdum* when, by immanent criticism, by consistent exaggeration, by revealing its irrational nature, we push it to the point where it already is, that is to say to its true self, which pretends not to be itself but its opposite.

When the absurd in art is as much discussed as it is today, it means that the world is out of joint and all meaning has become questionable. Whether *the world* has a meaning is a religious or metaphysical question. The realistic, human counter-question is whether it is possible to give a meaning to *the world of man*. When a religious man loses his belief in God, the world becomes absurd. A man without religious beliefs is seized by a sense of total absurdity when he cannot see a future, and by a sense of partial absurdity when that which exists no longer agrees with what it claims to be, when word and deed, programme and practice deny one another.

In his study on Marcel Proust written in 1931, when he was twenty-four, Samuel Beckett wrote that the breakdown of love and friendship as a result of human 'isolation' has the dignity of tragedy,

whereas the attempt to communicate where no communication is possible is merely a monkey-like vulgarity or something horribly comic, like the madness of someone carrying on a conversation with pieces of furniture. . . . There is no communication because there are no means of communication.[29]

Eugène Ionesco, too, is convinced of the impossibility of human communication. (Not that I would dream of equating this crude virtuoso of theatrical devices with Beckett, who is a great poet.)

Kenneth Tynan, then dramatic critic of *The Observer*, attacked Ionesco in 1958 in the following terms: 'Here was a writer ready to declare that words were meaningless and that all communication between human beings was impossible.'[30]

Ionesco retorted that society itself separates human beings from one another. Therefore the language of society has to be destroyed, for it 'is nothing but clichés, empty formulas and slogans'.

Arthur Adamov, one of the creators of the modern theatre of the absurd, wrote in 1946: 'Modern man comes always to the same conclusion: behind its visible appearances, life hides a meaning that is eternally inaccessible to penetration by the spirit that seeks for its discovery.'[31]

Is then the absurd, the incomprehensibility or the senselessness of the world, an unchangeable condition of life, or is it the expression of a society which has become senseless? In a guest lecture delivered to the Austrian Society for Literature the Czech writer Jiří Hajek replied to this question in the following words:

Absurdity is not an immutably given fact. Communication between men is not impossible in principle; Havel, for instance, reveals in his plays the socially conditioned deformation of language: a language which has ceased to be a means of communication and has become an instrument for mimicry, serving to protect us from reality and our responsibilities.[32]

ALIENATED LANGUAGE

'Speechlessness' in an alienated world where it is difficult, if not impossible, to communicate with others, to partake of them, to be gripped by them as by fellow human beings, is a fundamental motif of modern literature. Some elements of both the tragic and the absurd cannot, I believe, be completely removed by any social change because they derive from the very nature of man, who must always remain incomplete. But they can be modified to a great extent by social factors, so that, in a world worthy of man, the absurd would no longer be the human condition, but could be exorcized by insight and laughter. Some writers of the absurd see the absurd as an unchangeable *condition humaine*, others see it as subject to social change; what both kinds of writers have in common is an overpowering experience of the discrepancy between word and reality, a sense of shock at the misuse of language which no longer clarifies but obscures and is no longer a means of communication but of alienation.

The self-alienation of man in language which has been alienated from him is obvious. We should not blame the inadequacy of language but the cool insolence of those who abuse it. And if language is imprecise, as pedants tell us, it resembles therein the blossoming tree, the dense forest and the heart of man; the things which are more precise than language are death, the mathematical formula and the precision machine.

In our industrial world which has become so wide and so empty, in this world of industry stuffed full with goods of every kind for commerce and consuming, the wealth of language which ripened in less advanced times has become outdated, useless, inadequate to the needs of information. The fact that it was once not merely an instrument of information but also a means of expression, the promise of a not yet objectified collective, has been forgotten. The increasing barbarization, simplification and specialization of language has created an inarticulate jargon (consonants disappear in a mess of inflated vowels, the howl of the pack is allied with current abbreviations). This is the jargon of officials and parties, experts and secret societies. It is no longer the people who speak, nor its educated men, but the ideal consumer whose only aim is to amass as many goods as possible with the smallest possible vocabulary – and why not, since his objects, his motor car, his suit, his tape recorder, speak for him? In literature some try to come to terms with language by means of a puritanical economy, others by a wild extravagance, a maximum of foreign words, archaisms, technical terms, invented words, in order to compensate for the inner decay. The writers of the absurd take speakers at their word. They catch language in the act, so that we see the emptiness where once there was the object.

PROVERB AND PHRASE

In a relatively simple world peasants and artisans express their experience in proverbs which are passed down from generation to generation. The same situations recur again and again; for each of them there are appropriate reflexes, prescriptions, proverbs, which generally correspond to reality. Word and world agree. Everything is expressible.

In a no longer stable society people who keep repeating the same proverbs or turns of phrase become comic figures. The old proverbs have been overtaken by a new social reality. When language lags behind reality it shows how its speakers have been left behind too.

The adage as a relic of a world that has already disappeared is the regular device of farce writers; but in a later transformation it becomes the *phrase*, which de-realizes reality and dehumanizes man. The more language and consciousness are outstripped by the progress of the world, new objects, technical discoveries, unimaginable productive forces, mysterious institutions, the greater the need for the final, simplifying cliché. The phrase, the cliché, creates the illusion of a stable world, a world not out of joint. It offers shelter from alarming knowledge, from decision and responsibility.

In the cliché past conditions are preserved in a form they never had.

I am convinced [wrote Karl Kraus], that happenings no longer happen; instead, the clichés operate spontaneously. Or, if things should nevertheless happen without being frightened off by the clichés, these happenings will stop when the clichés have been smashed. A rot has set in, and the phrase has started it.[33]

In the conflict between the world of appearances, which is regarded as real, and the darkened condition of being, the self loses its identity and is replaced by a closed system of phrases. The daily newspaper, the radio, the television screen deliver into the home what one is supposed to consider real at any given time; and the self required at that particular time, the convenient and useful self, is composed of such stuff as dreams are made of – not in free association, but for a well-designed purpose. The theatre of the absurd, though it may include different approaches, shows in a variety of ways how the clichés of a de-realized and dehumanized world 'operate spontaneously', how through the loss of language which expresses what *is*, man himself, as a rational being, becomes lost.

HUGO BLUDEK LEAVES HOME

In his comedy, Václav Havel shows how Hugo Bludek, a young man who wants to make a career, makes that career and on the way loses nothing but his self, his human identity.

The happy home of the Bludeks is ruled by the precept that 'the middle classes are the backbone of the nation'. The hero of the family is Uncle Jaros; he wanted to become a goldsmith and has become one; he has been guided by undeviating diligence, ambition, and a multitude of proverbs of grotesque ineptitude and unfailing effectiveness. He belongs to the past, when banality had not yet become intimate or all-pervading and when the cliché still retained, half blurred, some traces of originality.

Hugo plays chess with himself, a habit which does not betray a striking personality but is somewhat original, since you can decide who has won: me or myself. The legendary Uncle Jaros, the man who became what he wanted to become, has always been held up to him as an example. At last Hugo sets out, bored, to become *something*, not a goldsmith or a pilot or an engineer but *something* remunerative and respectable.

His father gives his last golden advice: 'My dear son! He who knows where the bee wears its sting is too tall for his trousers. Whosoever shall knock on Uncle Jaros's door, it shall be opened unto him. Your point of view is what your life is founded on. Do you think someone else can have your point of view for you?'

'Yes, Dad!'

And so Hugo takes his leave. He enters the kingdom where you get on only if you haven't got a point of view because it's someone else – the boss – who has one for you.

An official organization – the Closing Down Department, whose functions are infinitely vague (as though the officials in Kafka's *Castle* had joined the service of the State), is giving a garden party. Here Hugo meets not only the Closing Down Department's secretaries but also a prominent personality from the Opening Up Department. The garden party, drearily over-organized and inexorably optimistic (for its purpose is to 'provide a platform for a healthy, human, yet disciplined sociability among all officials'), gives Hugo the chance to acquire all the phrases which the kingdom of bureaucracy decrees to be reality at that particular moment. The Opening Up Department's Mr Plzak, who insists with a blackmailer's perseverance that the show must go on, is Hugo's great master in systematic absurdity.

THE APPARATUS

It is a period of cautious thawing of attitudes, and so Plzak's mouth overflows with what his desk drawers are full of:

You know, I'm not a bit fond of those old mummies who bury their heads in the sand when they're faced with problems such as, let's say, the life of the senses. Isn't love, goddamn it, a necessary thing if you only know how to lay your hands on it the right way? Laying your hands on something, that's part of working with human beings, isn't it? They've got a good old saying for it where I come from: Lay your hands on something and you've got something in hand . . .

. . . Our duty today is to discuss things and we mustn't be put off by contrary views . . .

Art, now, there's a thing we've got to consider. The colleagues from the Culture Department know jolly well why they're drafting a directive on artistic experiment. It's going to come into force as from the second quarter, did you know that?

Hugo is a quick learner. He abandons himself voluptuously to the phrase, the liberation from the self, the joy of depersonalization. What a saving of energy, no longer to have to struggle to preserve your individuality! Now at last everything can be concentrated on belonging to the organization and so achieving success: *getting on.*

The Opening Up Department is to be closed down. Not organization alone, reorganization too is the bureaucrat's delight. An office is divided into two; two offices are amalgamated; desks are transferred from the first floor to the third or from the third to the first. Sections exchange their numbers, their names, their chiefs; files are re-registered, posts refilled, rules revised. The self-satisfaction of the bureaucratic apparatus demands a great expenditure of time and effort.

Hugo joins in with a will. Because his phraseology is faultless, the bureaucrats accept him as one of themselves, and because he is arrogant, insolent and appears to be equipped with secret powers, he is regarded as a 'responsible cadre', a 'higher official'. For none of the cogs within the apparatus, no official, chief of section or divisional head ever knows quite clearly how great his power is at any given moment; he fears his colleagues, his secretary, the office messenger, for any one of them may be a spy from the governing authority, the State police or some vague superior body in the background. Any one of them may be carrying his sentence, already signed, in his pocket. In such an atmosphere a man like Hugo who wants to be nothing other than a man who has achieved success and who, just as Kafka's Gregor Samsa was transformed into an insect, has transformed himself into a phraseology, is invincible.

With his cold insolence and his tumbling *prestissimo* of phrases, Hugo succeeds in getting both the Closing Down Department and the Opening Up Department closed down and is himself appointed to form a Central Opening Up and Closing Down Commission.

THE LOST SELF

The Bludek family wait eagerly for Hugo's arrival. Their son has done better than Uncle Jaros because he has not aimed at a particular profession but at success itself, unproductive, abstract, absurd success in a world of ghostly de-realization. He never comes. He no longer exists. Instead there enters an interchangeable, faceless bureaucrat. No one recognizes him. He is a stranger to his parents as to himself, no longer a man, only a function, one who no longer has any being in a world of the still faintly living.

'I was always absent!' says Hamm in Beckett's *Endgame*. Hugo, who has cast off not only his own self but also every remnant of conscience, is less radical. He develops the comfortable philosophy that one should avoid being either really present or really absent at any time; it is better to be always in a state of indeterminacy between being and non-being, adapted to any given situation.

Me? Who am I? You know, I don't like questions like that, don't like them at all, they're so one-sided. Is that a question you can ask so simply? . . . You've got to understand that people who today understand nothing except today are merely a new edition of people who yesterday understood nothing except yesterday. Of course we've learnt that even today we've got to have an idea of what things were like yesterday, because nobody knows if it isn't by any chance going to come back tomorrow. . . . We're all a bit of what we were yesterday and a bit of what we are today and a bit of neither. . . . So it's just a question of more Being and less Not-Being at one time and more Not-Being and less Being at another – or else if you *are* too much you'll soon stop being altogether, and if you've got the knack of *not being* in certain situations and up to a certain extent, then in another situation you can *be* more . . .

Václav Havel makes bureaucracy absurd. But his courageous and intelligent satire is not merely parochial; it crosses frontiers and translates itself as though spontaneously into the languages of other nations and the phraseologies of other social systems. Hugo also represents the man whose standpoint is where the boss happens to be standing, the man who is something of what he was yesterday and something of what he will be tomorrow, but never so distinctly that he couldn't deny it at the drop of a hat.

Alienation, depersonalization, loss of identity, de-realization of reality, dehumanization of the world by bureaucratic managers and administrators – all these are central problems of all modern industrial societies, not only of capitalist society. The absurd is not an invention of absurd writers. Party critics are wrong to believe that a play such as *The Garden Party* is a negation of socialism or *Endgame* a negation of man. They are a negation of the negation of man and his ideas.

III. THE LOST MIRROR IMAGE

The problem of identity, of its reduction and loss, is a central theme of modern literature. There hardly exists another writer who has expressed the loss of the self – the self which, fleeing from itself, becomes 'the other', an object, a non-self to itself – with such urgency as Samuel Beckett.

In his preface to *Dreams*, August Strindberg wrote:

The characters are doubled or divided, they evaporate or condense, flow apart or agglomerate. But there stands a consciousness above them all; it is the consciousness of the dreamer. . . . He does not judge, he does not acquit, he is merely an arbiter. . .

In Strindberg's overheated naturalism the *characters* have melted away in order finally to resolidify as *figures*: the father, the mother, the gentleman, the lady, the son, the daughter. Later, Kafka was to reduce the very names of the figures to initials, and in Beckett's *Play* there are only W_1, W_2, M (woman one, woman two, man), whilst in his *Film*, acted by Buster Keaton, there exist only the fleeing O (object) and the pursuing E (eye). The splitting of the characters, their doubling or evaporation, all this has progressed to the point of extremity; Beckett says: 'What does "to walk" mean here? what does "away" mean here?' And something similar happens to the arbitrating consciousness of the narrator, which no longer 'stands above them all' but becomes indefinite, blurred and diffuse in its turn.

In the last book of Beckett's trilogy consisting of the novels *Molloy*, *Malone Dies*, and *The Unnameable*[34] the mutilated carcase of a man, stuck in a deep jug whose rim reaches to his mouth, utters these words:

'Where now? Who now? When now? Unquestioning. I, say I. Unbelieving.'

'I shall not say I again, ever again, it's too farcical. I shall put in its place, whenever I hear it, the third person, if I think of it.'

'But, my dear man, come, be reasonable, look, this is you, look at this photograph, and here's your file, no convictions, I assure you, come now, make an effort, at your age, to have no identity, it's a scandal, I assure you, look at this photograph. . . .'

So long as a stable world ordered into classes and castes assigns to each person his role in the great play of life, the 'I' is both bound and protected, predetermined within its limitations, but of a relatively solid structure. After the annihilation of the feudal order, in the capitalist world of free competition, man finds himself alone. The formation of the 'free' personality takes place simultaneously with a process of depersonalization. Man ceases to be what he *is* and comes to be what he *has*. Having overpowers being. In a world of having, a man's work becomes an alienation which it is impossible to transcend.

Having lost his own self in the process of exteriorization through work, he looks for his inner self in the mirror. Individual conscience has to take the place of caste rules. The age of self-reflection, of sentimentality, of the personal journal, is part of the industrial revolution. The image of the mirror is a double reflection: it reflects a man's success, i.e. what he stands for in the eyes of others: and it also reflects himself within his own individual conscience, however much that conscience may be conditioned by circumstance, convention and prejudice.

This increasing splitting of the personality gave a new and terrifying significance to the old *doppelgänger* motif. In pre-capitalist society the double had been a figure of comedy; in the age of romanticism, under the initial shock of the industrial revolution, he became a poignant symbol. Man was no longer at home within himself. He became 'another' in his own eyes, an object of – what?

The 'I', once it has come into being, can no longer escape from itself. In its flight it pursues itself, divides itself into the pursued and the pursuer. Baudelaire and Nietzsche anticipated the theme of Beckett's *Film*.

Baudelaire:

> *Je suis la plaie et le couteau!*
> *Je suis le soufflet et la joue!*
> *Je suis les membres et la roue*
> *Et la victime et le bourreau!*
>
> (*Les Fleurs du Mal*)

(I am the wound and the knife! I am the slap and the cheek! I am the limbs and the wheel, the victim and the executioner!)

Nietzsche:

> *Jetzt –*
> *von dir selbst erjagt,*
> *deine eigene Beute,*
> *in dich selbst eingebohrt . . .*
> *. . . zwischen hundert Spiegeln*
> *vor dir selber falsch,*
> *zwischen hundert Erinnerungen*
> *ungewiss,*
> *an jeder Wunde müd,*
> *an jedem Froste kalt,*
> *in eignen Stricken erwürgt,*
> Selbstkenner!
> Selbsthenker!
>
> (*Dionysos-Dithyramben*)

(Now – hunted by yourself, your own prey, piercing yourself . . . between a hundred mirrors, false in front of yourself – between a hundred memories uncertain, tired from every wound, freezing from every frost, strangled in your own ropes, *self-knower*! *self-executioner*!)

In *Film* (1967), O, the 'I' reduced to an object, flees from the eye, from self-perception, from responsibility. O escapes into a room. A rocking-chair tempts him. Yet eyes stare at him, dog and cat, goldfish and parrot, window, mirror, the eye of God from a picture pinned to the wall. O draws the curtain across the window through which the outside world stares at him, covers the mirror from which the *doppelgänger* stares at him, drives away the cat and the dog, spreads his coat over the parrot and the goldfish – those eyes through which nature stares at him – pulls the eye of God down from the wall, tears it to pieces and tramples it under his feet. At last he is no longer seen: he is alone with himself in the darkened room. With whom? Who is that – himself? What self? He takes a handful of photographs from his pocket, and stares at himself, the child, the boy, the young man he once was. Is he identical with what he was? Is he accountable to what he no longer is? He tears up the photographs and, freed from every 'I', sinks back into the rocking-chair. But now the eye pierces through his sleep, his *own* eye, and eye to eye with himself he collapses: self-knower! self-executioner!

Samuel Beckett is a poet beyond all political engagement. An eminently political author, the communist Louis Aragon, offers us a political variation on the theme of being confronted with one's own mirror image, of being hunted to earth by one's own eye.

Anthoine, the famous realist author, is forced to discover that he has lost his mirror image. The mirror image – the *other* that he once was – assumes human form under the name of Alfred and demands a reckoning. At the end, Alfred sees no other solution but that of killing the alienated creature that he has become, the realist author Anthoine. Yet it is not Anthoine who is killed; Alfred dies from loss of blood, and Anthoine remains somewhere, without mirror image but between a hundred mirrors, uncertain in the midst of a hundred memories.

It is not my intention here to analyse Aragon's important novel.[35] I speak only of the problem of identity, of the lost mirror image and the realist 'mirroring' of reality. At first, the loss of the mirror image was for Anthoine an almost happy experience. What he believed he saw in the mirror was no longer his own face but social reality. Yet was it? Was it not distorted, deformed, falsified by 'party-mindedness'? And what is *real*? Memory intervenes, with all its painful associations.

THE KILLER

1937. In a café in the rue Montorgueil, Anthoine meets his friend Michel, a Russian who has been suddenly recalled to Moscow from Spain.

Do you remember the men sitting behind me in the rue Montorgueil, a little to the side, so that I was able to see them without completely turning round. . . . It proved too much for Michel, he broke off in the middle of his story and said: this type, no, really, this type. . . . I've never seen a type like that . . .

I had seen him, but only just, from the side. I turned. . . . A sort of colossus, the face pale lead in colour, low forehead, a mastiff's jaws. It's always the same, his clothes always stand out sharply from those of his companions, an open collar above the animal neck, sleeves rolled up on the gross arms, and under the table the dog, the growling Alsatian wolfhound . . .

Have you ever come across anything like him before, types like that one over there. . . . What is it? What is it for? Look at his hands . . .!

But Anthoine has already come across the type before. Was it not at Gorky's funeral?

There, yes it was there that I saw them, types like that, perhaps not exactly the same model . . . but Michel did not like conversations of that kind. Of course, in all countries of the world, the police. . . . Certainly, a horrible type. . . . They had had their great day on the boulevards, the Champs-Elysées, in 1934, those types there . . .

A great day against the workers of Paris who had gone out into the streets to defend freedom. But not only then, not only in Paris . . .

The type in the restaurant was certainly horrible. And now I understood Michel. . . . There must be something badly wrong with society if it allowed such a specimen of inhumanity to appear in places frequented by normal people. It is as if a single shoulder thrust had toppled the dividing walls, and suddenly you become aware of beings who are capable of anything, who exist not only in nightmares, although usually they are kept hidden from civilization. . . . A killer! said Michel . . .

And how was it in Moscow? Gorky? The funeral? The trials?

I cast my mind back over all those things, in the rue Montorgueil, and thought of the difficulty of being a realist writer. A realist writer cannot describe things just as they happen. He must, of necessity, arrange them. And there are some things which can't be told in a novel. Mind you, the killer in the rue Montorgueil could have become a character in a novel. In the course of time I've seen so many things which at first had no deeper meaning. When they reveal themselves, afterwards, you feel a little foolish; it's awkward to see yourself as a witness of something you failed to understand at the time. Like the funeral . . .

Rue Montorgueil. Michel talked only about Spain. In his country a trial had just ended, not like the others, very quick, because the military . . . Tukhachevsky, the generals. Among them Eidemann, who had sat on my left in 1934, at the dinner at Gorky's . . . and Uborevich. . . . Remember, said Michel, things present themselves so quickly . . . then try to explain them! . . . Michel did not know any details about the death of the generals. They had been shot immediately after the sentences, twenty-four hours after the marshal's arrest . . .

The killer was leaning across the table, shaking the hand of the fellow sitting opposite with his enormous hand, a friendly gesture no doubt . . .

The images become confused, flow into one another. There was the funeral. Gorky was being carried to his grave.

The funeral . . . from the standpoint of realism one ought to describe the guard of honour, the uniforms, the mounted militia, groups of people in the crowd, the expression of the *simple man*, the people's sorrow. That is what one should do, isn't it? without dragging in vague and highly subjective impressions from heaven knows where. We had already joined the funeral cortège, in front of us the government, a few ranks of soldiers, and just in front of them Stalin's *simple* tunic, Zhdanov's tall figure, Molotov . . .

And again the rue Montorgueil.

You're very pessimistic, Michel. . . . I, pessimistic? and he laughed and said, you write and write and write about things as you see them, then the meaning changes; you can't publish truth with the commentary of what follows, that's the servitude of realism, one of its great difficulties, that's where we come up against its limitations . . . it may be that many years have to pass before the truth can be published . . . after upheavals, wars, the death of contemporaries. . . . Suddenly, all at once, his face became clouded, doubtless because of the killer . . .

that type over there, he makes me shiver. . . . The funeral cortège set off. . . . And then, on my left (Fougère and Louppol were on my right) there were two or three people, jostling me, talking very loudly, perhaps because they had identified me as a foreigner and a foreigner understands better if you yell, that's a well-known fact isn't it? They were speaking among themselves, but for my benefit, quite evidently. The fellow directly next to me became a little familiar. He pushed me with his elbow. One of those loud-mouthed fellows (I thought of him when Michel showed me his 'killer') . . .

Where are the limits of realism? The demon of analogy has nothing to do with it, that much is certain. . . . No, that isn't dialectical, that isn't realism. In any case I did not put this question to myself then, I would have thought analogies of that kind inconceivable, because, I thought, the *form* can't be the same if the *content* is different. . . . And that a man who has a dirty mug of a face . . . does it reveal an ideology . . . or very nearly. . . . Besides, even today I think it is inconceivable. Like certain facts in physics or mathematics, which I accept because people who know have told me that it is so, but of which I cannot have a picture, things which I cannot imagine. And anyway, even those who know these things cannot imagine them . . .

In the funeral cortège, the men on his left, the killers, were trying, loud-mouthed and coarse, to provoke the foreigner, the suspect foreigner, trying to encourage him to say something against the Soviet leaders. Finally he broke from the ranks and made off as quickly as he could . . .

STALIN IS ALWAYS RIGHT!
In Spain, things were coming to an end. Michel was in Paris, abruptly recalled to Moscow.

He was so sad. That was understandable – Spain. . . . But look, Michel, that isn't over, it can change again. It isn't the same as Abyssinia. . . . He shook his head. Not quite the same, no. . . . He embraced us. He went. Not yet. He was already shutting the door behind him, he opened it again to come back into our small entrance hall: Fougère . . . Anthoine . . . before I go, I'd like just to tell you something. . . . He did not want to come back into the flat, only a word. All right. He was going back to his country. He did not know what awaited him there. But perhaps it would be a long time before he came back to Paris, and so. . . . Hard things can happen in the world. Whatever happens, whatever might happen to him, remember, you two . . . remember, the last words you will have heard from me . . . remember, *Stalin is always right* . . .

Michel was going to his death. In December he made one more speech to some writers. The next day Mihail Koltsov, Editor-in-Chief of *Pravda*, was arrested and ceased to exist. They say he died in 1942. He was rehabilitated in 1954. After the death of the man who was always right.

What do you want then? What should I see in the mirror? This empty world, like a room abandoned in haste, the book on the floor, tattered, tattered. . . . All the dead, the unknown, friends for all time or for a day, all those who died, with their faith upon their lips. Do you remember the screams in Lyons which used to come from the cellar of the Hotel Terminus? And the corpses in the place Bellecour. . . . And others, before they were shot, when they had so little time, so little room on their lips for a last word, barely room for a cry meant for their country, and they hurled the challenge in the hang-man's face: Stalin . . . how bitter, how bitter it all is, I am thinking of you, Michel, who should have had a future, together with all those who dreamed of a just life, justice in heaven as on earth.

What disorder, dear God, what disorder! Not only I have lost my image. A whole century can no longer find the connection between its soul and what it sees. And there are millions of us, lost children of the immense conflict . . .

WHERE ARE THE FRONTIERS OF REALISM?
Thus the problem of realism transcends the frontiers of aesthetics and becomes a problem of attitude towards reality. You see in the mirror what is visible, here and now, the fragment of reality, from your standpoint. But what if everything is shaken and overthrown, what if the visible no longer agrees with the soul, the world with the self, what if this convention collapses? What if the lost mirror image, the vanished self, returns as an accusing *doppelgänger*, and if it insists that I is not 'another' and no one can take away its responsibility, no God nor emperor nor tribune? And if it asks: Where is right? Sent from Moscow to Madrid in order to fight for freedom, suddenly recalled to Moscow, not killed in the Spanish war of liberation but perishing miserably in the Soviet Union, an 'agent of the class enemy'. The fist of the killer, the mercenary of power, across the frontiers, across the world. But it's only *form*, a similarity of form, what matters is the *content* and the content is fundamentally different. Where are the frontiers of realism? How far does the law of dialectics go? In the context of world history, the content is fundamentally different, but for countless people the

I

form became the fist which hit them, the *content*, therefore, the final, deadly content, of their existence. The form reacts upon the content as the means does upon the end, and the outcome is apalling deformation.

The *doppelgänger* refuses to be put off: What do you say about reality when the screams from the cellars grow louder than the singer's voice? What is your guideline? What is valid? 'Stalin is always right! The Party is always right!' And if it is no longer right? Who decides? Where is the arbiter? And where is the mirror image? And what about reality? In what way do you perceive it? As a socialist, I know, you reflect it correctly, truthfully, for your standpoint is the 'class standpoint' and you are guided by 'party-mindedness' which can never go wrong. But who says that the standpoint from which you survey the world is really the class standpoint? The party, naturally, the leadership of the party. Be party-minded and you won't go wrong. And so they produced a *realistic* counterfeit of Stalin as a radiant father figure, and the difficulties in Soviet industry and agriculture were *realistically* portrayed as the devil's work of saboteurs, subversionists and spies, and the accused in the Moscow trials and later in Budapest, Sofia, Prague, *realistically* described as traitors and criminals ever since childhood, and the world *realistically* presented as a struggle between gigantic espionage machines, as a monstrous thriller.

The almost inconceivable thing is that most of us communists, mature men endowed with reason and power of judgement, have, within the tremendous conflict of the self, seen reality in these terms or have believed that we were seeing it like this. Here the individual self, the apparently autonomous self conditioned by background and childhood and therefore suppressed as 'petty-bourgeois – individualist' – there the self fused with the 'others', against the world of having which was increasingly assuming the features of Hitler, the self formed from the molten mass of the community, strengthened by 'party-mindedness' and 'class standpoint', renouncing subjectivity for the sake of the cause.

THE ARBITER

Aragon speaks with great admiration of Stevenson's novel *Dr Jekyll and Mr Hyde*, the novel of the split personality, of the good self and its evil *doppelgänger*. But such a splitting into a good and an evil self is too mechanical, the limits are indefinite, the one flows and veers into the other. Dr Jekyll and Mr Hyde are no longer distinguishable from one another.

In us, men of this time, good and evil no longer require incarnation under symbolical aspects, they coexist within the same man as an alternative of the soul, and the man over there hates war and yet, in all righteousness, performs the gestures of one who unleashes it.

Yet who is to decide what is right and what is wrong? Christian Fustel-Schmidt enters the novel, not a marxist, as the author emphasizes, and yet as it were the third person of the two double selves, Alfred and Anthoine. Christian's magic mirror has three parts, three faces of man, a dialectical trinity.

What Stevenson did not see, nor you, nor anyone else, is the third person, the arbiter between good and evil, who sleeps from time to time and then evil prevails over good, or the other way round. The mediator. The third, inner reincarnation of man. The indifferent one, don't you see? The indifferent one . . .

This triple self is reminiscent, in its formation, of the ego, the id and the super-ego, yet it does not correspond to the structure outlined by Freud; every self in Aragon's novel is rooted in the unconscious and strives for a consciousness of its own, whether true or false. The arbiter who has been lost is not the super-ego, the imperious father of conventions and institutions; on the contrary, his task is to arbitrate between the super-ego – which has become questionable – and the ego which accuses it (and which is not identical with the id), between good which has become transformed into evil and evil which suddenly has assumed the features of goodness, to arbitrate between them conscientiously and rationally; and what is involved is more than Hegel's recognition of the function of evil in world history: it is a decision which is not dogmatic but which must be arrived at afresh in every new situation, a decision capable of restoring the identity of the self.

This third self, this impartial arbiter, is – so I believe – the truly human element in man, it is the *intention of humanism*. The standpoint of a class, a party, a fighting community can never be the final instance; in each case it is necessary to ask whether and to what extent it is in agreement with the humanization and self-realization of man. The principle that 'everything is good which is useful to the German people' – or a party or some other group – is as challengeable as the dictum that 'what's good for General Motors is good for America'. Yet how are we to find again this third self, this arbiter, who has not, it is true, fallen quite silent but who speaks so softly that, surrounded by so much noise, we must go deep into ourselves to hear his voice? Aragon dispenses no ready-made formula, for a writer is a diagnostician, not a pharmacist. He describes a conflict which goes straight through each one of us, straight through the world and affects all those whose self is also 'another', dedicated to a common cause.

The great difficulty in the development of realism stems from the fact that, in order to make its rules valid, it is not the novelist's mind but the world itself which will have to change. The curious thing is that the very people who want to change the world have seen fit to begin the operation with the novelist's mind. . . . We are living at a time when, although one would like to believe the contrary, everywhere in the world the practice of putting the cart before the horse is more prevalent than ever before. It would be perfectly right and just if the writers were to accuse the politicians of having totally failed to organize the production of positive men, whom they require as models for their novels. . . . Yet the contrary takes place, and the politicians accuse the novelists because they fail to supply the people with heroes for their emulation. Is it not topsy-turvy?

You make noble statements. You get worked up. You criticize. And you're quite right to do so, it's our job to be right. We've been right so many times that we forget all the times when we've been wrong. No, I'm being unfair: in recent years we've been allowing ourselves the luxury of guilt, we scratch our wounds, our intellectual wounds of course. But there are others which scratch off only slowly. Or worse: which refuse to scratch off at all – do what you will, they won't scratch off . . .

We have been right so many times! O this task of being right, always right, officials of infallibility! Let us, then, begin to speak of the times when we have been wrong, let us try to give an account of ourselves to our lost mirror image! And may the answer no longer swagger ahead, exclamation mark held high, with the silent march of inadmissible questions trailing behind! A start has been made at a few congresses of communists, of catholics, of protestants – but only a start, and what resistance there is to it!

In this dark world, the spiritual unrest which has seized hold of many communists, catholics and protestants in reaction against orthodoxy, self-complacency and intolerance, and their readiness to admit errors and to try to change what has gone wrong, offers great encouragement. Only the most resolute 'positive heroes', only the doctrinaires, the bureaucrats, the professional optimists know nothing of the despair Aragon speaks of: yet we are determined not to remain caught in it. We marxists, all too often arrogant in our mistakes, infallible in our false judgements, intolerant when we are right and when we are wrong, we are not acquitting ourselves of being identical with those we once were; but we hope that we have learned a few lessons, and we are still looking for the future in search of which we once set out. Missed opportunities, shattered illusions, broken mirrors – yet our desire to give meaning to our world remains intact. We shall continue.

Notes

1. Erich Fromm, *Der moderne Mensch und seine Zukunft* (Frankfurt: Europäische Verlagsanstalt, 1906)
2. Hugo von Hofmannsthal, *Die Gedichte und kleinen Dramen* (Leipzig: Insel, 1918)
3. Marcel Proust, *The Sweet Cheat Gone*, translated by C. K. Scott-Moncrieff (London: Chatto & Windus, 1947)
4. Samuel Beckett, *Proust* (New York: Grove Press, 1957)
5. Arthur Adamov, *L'aveu* (Paris: Sagittaire, 1946)
6. Eugène Ionesco, 'Die Tragödie der Sprache', *Argumente und Argumente* (Neuwied: Luchterhand, 1964)
7. Allan Kaprow, 'Die Zukunft der Pop Art', in Jürgen Becker and Wolf Vostell, *Happenings* (Reinbek: Rowohlt, 1965)
8. ibid
9. E. J. Hobsbawm, *The Age of Revolution 1789–1848* (London: Weidenfeld & Nicolson, 1962)
10. Jürgen Becker and Wolf Vostell, *Happenings*
11. Robert L. Delevoy, *Léger* (Geneva: Skira, 1962)
12. *Sonntag*, no. 16, April 1964
13. ibid
14. Karl Marx, *Capital*, vol. III, F. Engels (ed.) (London: Allen & Unwin)
15. Alain Robbe-Grillet, speech at symposium on the novel, Vienna, 1965
16. Karl Marx, *Economic and Philosophical Manuscripts* (London: Lawrence & Wishart)
17. Erich Fromm, *Das Menschenbild bei Marx* (Stuttgart: Europäische Verlagsanstalt, 1963)
18. Erich Fromm, *Der moderne Mensch und seine Zukunft*

19. Karl Marx, *Grundrisse der Kritik der Politischen Ökonomie*, rough draft, 1857–8 (Moscow: Foreign Languages Publishing House, 1939)
20. ibid
21. Robert Jungk, *Die grosse Maschine* (Berne: Scherz, 1966)
22. V. I. Lenin, ' "Left-Wing" Communism – an Infantile Disorder', collected works vol. 31 (London: Lawrence & Wishart, 1966)
23. Friedrich Schiller, *On the Aesthetic Education of Man, in a Series of Letters*, translated by R. Snell (London: Routledge & Kegan Paul, 1954) letter 6
24. Karl Marx, *Capital*, vol. III, F. Engels (ed.)
25. Friedrich Schiller, *On the Aesthetic Education of Man*, letter 27
26. ibid, letter 15
27. Václav Havel, *Das Gartenfest* (Reinbek: Rowohlt, 1964)
28. Martin Esslin, *The Theatre of the Absurd* (London: Eyre & Spottiswoode, 1962)
29. Samuel Beckett, *Proust*, quoted in Esslin, *The Theatre of the Absurd*
30. Kenneth Tynan, 'Ionesco: Man of Destiny?', quoted in Esslin, *The Theatre of the Absurd*
31. Arthur Adamov, 'Une fin et un commencement', quoted in Esslin, *The Theatre of the Absurd*
32. Jiři Hajek, MS.
33. Karl Kraus, *Pro Domo et Mundo*, collected works vol. III (Munich: Kosel, 1955)
34. Samuel Beckett, *The Unnameable* (New York: Grove Press, 1958)
35. Louis Aragon, *La Mise à Mort* (Paris: Gallimard, 1965)

Chapter 4

THE PROBLEM OF DECADENCE

Marc Chagall spoke in May 1963 of the moral crisis in art which, he believed, was characteristic of our time.

In July 1963, Louis Aragon published Chagall's statement in *Les Lettres Françaises*, adding in a brief but significant introduction:

It appears important to us to acquaint our readers with a text with which they may or may not agree, but which has to be accepted as a fact, and, since it comes from one of the greatest painters of our time, as a fact of some weight. Never before, perhaps, has the moral crisis among artists been reflected with such intensity . . .

We believe in the permanence of human genius and we cannot envisage an end-game. There will always – and this is not a matter of schools or fashions – be a world view, forms of expression of human greatness, worthy of what that greatness once was, capable of gripping and inspiring us. That is our unshakeable conviction, and the art of Marc Chagall brilliantly refutes any notion of a fatal decadence in art . . .[1]

A 'SHRINKING PROCESS'

Chagall said: 'Painting re-creates nature,' and also: 'Our whole inner world is a reality; it is perhaps much more real even than the visible world. If you call fantastic or unreal everything that seems illogical, you prove only that you do not understand nature.'[2] Nature is incomparably more than that which can be photographed, and reality is more than the outside world. The artist must be able to be amazed and astonished if he is to re-create nature, de-natured and debased by the process of seeing which has become mere routine; he must be able to perceive reality as the visible and the invisible, the tangible and the not-yet-grasped, the comprehended and the dimly sensed, the present, the remembered and the anticipated, against a background of infinity.

Chagall, whose art is full of suggestive power, a dream fabric of memory, the Russian village, Chassidism, childhood, Bible and *kabbala*, the milk-yielding cow in the sky, people floating in the ether, direct experience, true naïvety, love of paradox and genuine popular feeling – the term is often abused, but it applies to Chagall – spoke with deep concern of a 'shrinking process' in painting since the French revolution.

Impressionism, he said, had opened a window.

A rainbow began to shine on the horizon of our world. This new world had different, more intense colours, but it was also, it seems to me, a narrower world than, for example, Courbet's naturalistic one.

Likewise, Courbet's naturalism was narrower than Delacroix's world of Romanticism; and Delacroix's world, in its turn, was narrower and more declamatory than the neo-classical world of David and Ingres.

Let me stop there.

After Impressionism came the Cubist world which led us into the hidden geometry of things.

Later, the abstract painters led us into a world of the smallest elements and of matter itself . . .

Thus one has the impression of being engaged in a shrinking process . . .

Perhaps I, too, have been mistaken many times? I have painted pictures upside down. In my pictures people floated in the air, and I cut off their heads and cut up their bodies into pieces. This I did in the name of a different perspective, a different composition and a different sense of form.

And our world became, for us, more and more a little world in which we, little creatures, were clinging to the little elements of our nature until the moment when we came close to the smallest elements of that nature – to the atom . . .

During recent years I have often spoken of a kind of chemistry, of an authentic colour of matter, as of a thermometer of authenticity . . .

A moral crisis in art, Chagall said, is always a crisis of colour, of matter, of word and melody, a crisis, as it were, of chemical composition. The true chemistry of man and of art consists of

elements of love and a certain naturalness which corresponds to nature, a nature which tolerates no evil, no hatred, no indifference . . .

If we are moved to the depths of our soul by, for instance, the Bible, it is above all because the Bible is, by its chemistry, the greatest work of art in the world; because it conceals within itself the highest ideal of life on our planet.

Let another chemical genius appear, and humanity will follow him for a new conception of the world, another radiance of life . . .[3]

ART AND RELIGION

Until (and including) the Renaissance, says Chagall, art reflected the religious spirit, or at least reflected the religious feeling of its epoch. With the disappearance of religious feeling, the art of the nineteenth and twentieth centuries became a dull reflection of scientific discoveries.

A few revolutionaries wanted to introduce a new order scientifically into the economic and social life of our time. But in the course of years all scientific theories come to contradict one another.

Changes in the social order, as well as in art, are perhaps more assured if they come out of our souls and not only from our heads . . .

Are there no revolutionary methods other than those we have experienced?

Is there no basis for art other than decorative art which seeks only to please, or the art of experiment, or the art without mercy which sets out to terrify us?

It is childish to repeat the truth which has been known for so long: the world in all its domains can save itself only through love. Without love it will gradually die . . .[4]

The great painter's statements, important as they are, tend in many respects to over-simplify when he develops the idea of the 'authentic' basic colour which determines the 'chemistry' of an age, explains the revolution in art as conditioned by a change in the basic colour (Cimabue, Giotto, Masaccio), ascribes the decay of the chemical substance to the decay of religious feeling, and advocates religion – whether it be the Bible or a new conception of universal love – as a means of overcoming the present moral and aesthetic crisis.

A shrinking process, a narrowing of the world in the art of the nineteenth and twentieth centuries, can hardly be denied. I believe, however, that Chagall overlooks certain very powerful counter-tendencies, even though he speaks of the discovery of new possibilities and means of expression. ('With the appearance of impressionism, a rainbow began to shine on the horizon of our world!') So far as subject-matter is concerned, man has been to a large extent swallowed up by objects; at the same time, however, art has been able to take possession of these objects and extract from them a new beauty and meaning. And as for the world of art becoming continually smaller, turning more and more to the smallest elements, to the atom, science too has turned its attention increasingly, with instruments and methods of ever greater precision, to the study of the atom and finally succeeded in splitting the atom, thus releasing undreamed-of energies for good or evil. Modern science has made the invisible visible. Ernst Mach, not so very long ago, said that no one had ever seen an atom and no one would ever see what did not exist. A short time afterwards it became possible to make the existence of the atom visible. The accomplishments of science could not but find their reflection in art. 'Art does not reproduce the visible,' said Paul Klee, 'art makes visible.' In the nineteenth and twentieth centuries, art made visible what had previously been invisible in nature and especially in the human soul, and what it made visible was unexpected and overwhelming.

Chagall sees the development in art as a progressive process of decadence ever since the disappearance of religious feeling. It cannot be denied that the breakdown of the old order based on religion led to alarming consequences in literature and art. The *loss of myth*, until then a rich source of nourishment for the arts, threatened to set off a shrinking process. Ever since Romanticism, artists and poets have been struggling for a revival of the old religious myths or, with an incomparably wider perspective, for the development of a new, secularized mythology rooted in the world of man, not in the beyond. These efforts, which must eventually decide the future of art, will be discussed in another context; for the present, let us just mention them in passing.

The question which directly presents itself is this: If we recognize the crisis of which Chagall speaks, is there nothing to it but decay, shrinking and decadence? Is there no counter-force, no total process which negates the disintegration and in which the forces of the new are predominant?

DECADENCE IN ANCIENT ART

In order to answer this question it is necessary to compare modern with ancient decadence. The decay of the ancient world, of the Roman Empire, was hopeless and inexorable. A society which had been in movement for centuries – the struggle between aristocrats and plebeians contributing largely to this dynamism – began to grow rigid after the triumph of the Caesars. The power of the old peasantry was broken, the struggles for the *ager publicus* came to an end with the victory of large estate ownership and an unproductive slave economy. A parasitic urban proletariat was no longer fighting for land but for bread and circuses. The Caesar with his financial bureaucratic and military power apparatus became the agent of the property-owners. Yet ownership did not produce dynamic capital but idleness and extravagance. All attempts to constitute a new, productive peasantry and to develop the urban trades failed to yield any adequate result. There was no class which was interested in the development of new productive forces, no counter-force with a concept of far-reaching social change; vicious-tempered idlers, mutinous soldiers and menacing barbarians have nothing in common with such a force. Even the most competent rulers of the late Roman Empire were historically on the defensive, endeavouring to conserve rather than to advance towards new goals. There was only the possibility of looking back to a republican past that had gone beyond recall, or forward to an unattainable Christian beyond; but there was no hope of changing the world as it existed. The individual could draw moral postulates from pagan or Christian philosophy, but not social perspectives. Thus the inexorable decadence of the late ancient world was caused by the absence of progressive social forces which, by identifying their specific interests with the general interest, might have set and striven for a new social aim, and also by the total desocialization of the individual resulting from that absence.

Analysing a text by the late Roman historian Ammianus Marcellinus in his admirable book *Mimesis*, Erich Auerbach describes how 'the distorted, gory and spectral reality' of the decaying Roman Empire pervaded language itself with sombre magnificence and hollow brilliance. The oppressive quality of Ammianus's world, which often resembles a bad dream, is not so much that it is full of terrible things as that a counterweight is completely lacking.

Striking only in the sensory, resigned and as it were paralyzed despite its stubborn rhetorical passion, his manner of writing history nowhere displays anything redeeming, nowhere anything that points to a better future, nowhere a figure or an act about which stirs the refreshing atmosphere of a greater freedom, a greater humanity. It had begun, of course, in Tacitus, though by no means to the same extent. And the cause of it is doubtless the hopelessly defensive situation in which antique civilization found itself more and more deeply enmeshed. No longer able to generate new hope and new life from within, it had to restrict itself to measures which at best could only check decline and preserve the *status quo*; but these measures too grow more and more senile, their execution more and more arduous.[5]

There are similar phenomena in all periods of decadence: a ghostly sombreness and rigidity, a preponderance of the grotesque, the garish and the horrific, a tendency towards masks and grimaces, reality as a nightmare without sense or aim, a sense of the sequence of events being accidental instead of casual, the growing gap between society and the individual, the retreat from a world felt to be chaotic into a narrow, private, inner life, into contempt of reality and apocalyptic vision. Yet modern decadence differs profoundly from that of the ancient world.

THE MODERN COUNTER-FORCES

While the decadence of the world of chivalry, of the system of guilds and estates, of absolutism, or of bourgeois capitalist society is, in many of its individual features, related to that of the late ancient world, it nevertheless differs profoundly from it because the productive forces are always in a state of development; there is always an emergent new class with new social aims, and thus the situation is never without hope. Today, not only the rising working class but the totality of the economic and intellectual productive forces at work prevent a decay as crippling as that of the unproductive Roman Empire. The stagnation of bourgeois capitalist society is different from that of late Roman society; by the mere existence of socialist counter-forces it is obliged, through all its crises, to avoid a continuing stagnation in the development of its productive forces. It cannot fall into complete rigidity. This constant movement and the impulse of the continually changing power relationships modifies the nature of the decadence, the counter-forces pervade the process of decadence itself, so that it is never a hopeless wasting away but a continually alternating rise and fall.

This reciprocal action, this dynamism which does not tolerate a halt, also marks the development of art movements and individual artists. Within impressionism, for example, side by side with the disintegration of the image, the loss of structure, the veiling of reality by a flickering surface, the counter-tendency made itself felt, and suddenly there was Cézanne with his solidity and strength, his victory over the disintegration of the image. And after him came cubism, which was also an end but still more a new beginning, a new foundation concealed among the fragments of the old.

The schematic notion that art and literature within bourgeois society, which is historically approaching its end, are sinking more and more into the darkness, does not correspond to the reality. At a time when Germany had fallen into the barbarian decadence of national-socialist politics, philosophy, and art, there was a flowering of literature and of the art of the film in the United States, where monopoly capitalism was no less developed. The characteristic feature of our time is the speed with which situations change, the interaction – as well as the opposing action – of all world-political forces, the presence of a *total process* in spite of, indeed because of, the struggle between the social systems.

The French revolution, recognized by everyone – together with the industrial revolution in England – as a turning point, is seen by many as the beginning of decadence. Bourgeois society is viewed as progressive decadence, as the decay of the Middle Ages, as a vicious atomization of the world. It was, and still is, all that; but it also meant the coming into being of tremendous economic and intellectual productive forces, that is to say not only specialization, alienation and degeneration, but also the expansion of the world, the socialization of labour, the *possibility* of a world of plenty as well as of apocalyptic doom.

As a result of the revolution of October 1917 capitalism was overthrown at first in a sixth, and later in a third of the world. Seriously threatened in another third, it is nevertheless showing an astonishing vitality. The revolution at first stunned and then rallied the bourgeoisie. The tremendous shock administered to the world had, to some extent, the effect of shock therapy. Fear stupefies, but it also teaches. The writing on the wall confused many minds; some stronger minds, however, have translated it into current language. The enemies of socialism have quietly gone to work taking over much of what they most vociferously condemn. The State supervises the economy, planning is cautiously introduced, expansion and full employment are cautiously adopted as objectives, economic growth is encouraged by State initiative, workers' claims are given more attention than before. Thus the effects of revolution reach deep into the world of its opponents, and this indirect success, this gradual influencing of the antagonist, is one of its most essential results. The competition between social systems is turning into a stimulus of overall development.

The late ancient world knew nothing of this kind. Anyone who overlooks this dialectic of the modern world, this advance by means of contrasts, this productive contradiction, is bound to simplify the problem of decadence.

ALIENATION

In the age of industrial and technical revolution, the release and mastering of hitherto unimagined natural forces, the complete change in production methods as a result of technical discoveries, the expansion and enrichment of the world, at first encouraged a kind of Promethean consciousness. Prometheus, with Lucifer beside him, became the favourite mythical figure. Soon, however, the image darkened; Prometheus was seen chained to the Caucasian rock, his flesh torn by vultures (this is how Géricault and others represent him), Lucifer became Satan, the fallen angel, damned and despairing in his arrogant loneliness. Man's enchantment at the fabulous growth of his works was replaced by horror at seeing the creation outgrow the creator. The objects he had produced turned against him, assumed a ghostly life of their own, became mysterious, uncontrollable, 'demonic'. In the midst of increasing division of labour, specialization and rational production methods, man in the bourgeois age faced his own work *as a stranger*, alienated from his own work, his own product, his institutions and his own self. That which had been accomplished through the force of reason suddenly appeared to obey irrational, incomprehensible laws; the feeling of belonging to a whole, to a community, was lost; enmeshed in *object connections*, man became fragmented and no longer understood the *sense connections*.

Writers and artists felt this alienation most intensely. The commissioning art patron, the whole direct relationship between the producer and the consumer of art, disappeared with the old social order. Everything became a commodity, including the work of art; everything, including the public, was turned into an anonymous, unpredictable *market*. The artist or writer, once part of a whole, now became a fragment like everyone else, trying, surrounded by the unknown, to fit fragments together into a whole. Romanticism was the passionate protest against this fragmentation, objectification and alienation, the first intellectual revolution against the bourgeois world from within the bourgeois world. Friedrich Schiller, an opponent of the German Romantic school yet a participator in the general Romantic movement, wrote in the sixth of his letters *On the Aesthetic Education of Man*:

. . . the whole now gave place to an ingenious piece of machinery, in which out of the botching together of a vast number of lifeless parts a collective mechanical life results . . . enjoyment was separated from labour, means from ends, effort from reward. Eternally chained to only one single little fragment of the whole, Man himself grew to be only a fragment; with the monotonous noise of the wheel he drives everlastingly in his ears, he never develops the harmony of his being, and instead of imprinting humanity upon his nature he becomes merely the imprint of his occupation, of his science. But even the meagre fragmentary association which still links the individual members to the whole does not depend on forms which present themselves spontaneously (for how could such an artificial and clandestine piece of mechanism be entrusted to their freedom?) but is assigned to them with scrupulous exactness by a formula in which their free intelligence is restricted. The lifeless letter takes the place of the living understanding, and a practised memory is a surer guide than genius and feeling.[6]

We have heard this complaint about the loss of the whole, about the atomization, mechanization, dehumanization of existence, about the power of objects subjugating man, the power of death subjugating life, since the days of Rousseau. The price man paid for the unfolding of tremendous productive forces was the wholeness of his nature. The ideal of the whole man, originating in the ancient world, had been revived during the Renaissance. Its pre-condition has always been, and still is, the *possibility of leisure* and freedom from specialization. Discussing Montaigne's Renaissance concept of the whole man, Erich Auerbach writes:

Montaigne's social and economic circumstances made it easy for him to develop and preserve his whole self. His needs were met halfway by his period, which had not yet fully developed for the upper classes of society the duty, the technique, and the ethos of specialized work, but on the contrary, under the influence of the oligarchic civilization of antiquity, strove for the most general and most human culture of the individual.[7]

Yet it was precisely in the absence of the circumstances necessary for the whole man that the ancient world died of a dragging decadence; and it is precisely the pre-conditions for a dynamic development of productive forces, supplying a constantly effective antidote to decadence, which destroyed the wholeness of man. Man was threatened with becoming an object unto himself, or at least a reflection of the objects with which he was faced, the deeds he performed, the few rigid qualities which he evolved in their simplest form.

The artist of the Romantic age, proudly and fearfully conscious of his loneliness as a mark of being one of the damned and the chosen, hated the consistent utilitarianism of bourgeois society, the spirit which allowed only that which was useful to be of value. Charles Dickens wrote in *Hard Times*:

You saw nothing in Coketown but what was severely workful. If the members of a religious persuasion built a chapel there – as the members of eighteen religious persuasions had done – they made it a pious warehouse of red brick. . . . The jail might have been the infirmary, the infirmary might have been the jail, the town hall might have been either, or both, or anything else, for anything that appeared to the contrary in the graces of their construction. Fact, fact, fact, everywhere in the material aspect of the town; fact, fact, fact, everywhere in the immaterial . . .[8]

The hatred of this utilitarianism was common to almost all artists and writers of the period following the great industrial and political revolutions of the bourgeoisie. Society was no longer the 'home' of man (poor and narrow though it might be), but an alien land, the jungle, the struggle of all against all, the end which justifies the means, utility as the value which devours all others. It was as though the Egyptian papyrus which tells of the man risen from the dead had become a reality darkened with coal-dust and competition: 'Whomsoever he encounters on his way he devours. . . . He has taken the hearts away from the gods. . . . He has swallowed up the understanding of every god . . .'

The dynamism of utility overthrew the old hierarchy of values. Religion, the central constellation, began to pale. God was forced to abdicate in favour of 'reason'. But crises and catastrophes of every kind, everything that an enlightened century had to offer in the way of dirt and slums, humiliation and decay, alcoholism and mass epidemics, hunger and hatred, shook the belief in the power – and even in the right – of reason. The increasing rate of development in all spheres of science, technology and production meant that, while details were known with absolute precision, the view of the whole was lost. The most heterogeneous ideas, prejudices, ways of life and thought jostled one another, striving for domination yet adaptable, autocratic yet eclectic, mutually opposed yet interwoven with one another: liberalism, nationalism, cosmopolitanism, positivism, individualism, socialism, the fatherland and the international, freedom and prosperity, democracy and ambitions towards world rule, *sacro egoismo* and the greatest happiness of the greatest number, nation and humanity. The perspective of religion had a vanishing point: God. How could God be transposed into the material world of the here-and-now? All the philosophic, political, economic, moral views – not merely contradictory to one another but actually overthrowing one another – assumed authoritative postures as though they were new religions, yet undermined the old idea that something absolute existed or could exist. The great world-historical gain – the fact that no permanent ice cover of dogma can form on so turbulent a stream, that even if such a cover does form it cannot arrest the invisible movement below, that after a short while the floes must melt and disappear – this invaluable mutability was overshadowed by anxiety, confusion, and suspicion of reason, even of consciousness itself.

K

The relativism which has increased ever since the time of Romanticism, the uncertainty and instability of all values, is of course a sign of the decadence, decay and disintegration of the old, stable order. The disintegration is alarming, problematic, full of dangers, yet it is precisely by being disturbed that the content of life undergoes enrichment; narrow horizons are widened, space and time expanded, every continent, every age is drawn into the common pool of knowledge and experience. This has led to a chaotic confusion of the most primitive and the subtlest things – primeval fetish and internal combustion engine, jungle and metropolis – and also to a gradual or spasmodic interpenetration of heterogeneous phenomena, a progressive unification of the world. Development within a closed and limited system had been relatively predictable and capable of being taken in at a glance; in an open world exposed on all sides to the interaction of social forces, development becomes unaccountable and impossible to gauge. The cost of progress is so great that progress itself seems continually endangered. The secularization of God, the earthly value to which all action must relate if it is to have meaning, can only be humanity. Yet humanity – *humanitas* – has always been, and still is, only a hope and an ideal, not yet a reality.

In such a situation, art could no longer be in agreement with the principle and system of the society within which it had to exist and to assert itself; it turned to criticism, protest, revolt. The fundamental disagreement of art and literature with social reality, the negation of the conditions which it undertook to represent, was an entirely new phenomenon. The critical spirit resulting from the loss of social stability was not prepared to recognize aesthetic laws which banished the plebeian, the common, the base from the sphere of art or admitted it only in the form of comedy. Fielding, Smollett, Richardson, Diderot, Lessing, the poets of the *Sturm und Drang* had already begun to consider 'ordinary' people and everyday conditions worthy of serious artistic treatment. Romanticism broke down the remaining walls; all classes of people, down to the declassed, the wretched and the outcast, everything ugly, horrific, grotesque and distorted, was drawn into the scope of the arts. There was no longer any reality that was considered 'untouchable'. On the contrary: the forbidden became the favourite subject matter of an art in revolt.

THE REVOLT OF UGLINESS

Goya, the plebeian risen to the position of a court favourite, was the first major artist to attack, with the savage and aggressive ugliness of his *Caprichos*, the classic canon of Beauty which Winckelmann had established on the basis of inaccurate knowledge and false ideas concerning the ancient world. The rediscovery of ugliness, not degraded to a mere matter for farce but as a subject matter of sombre dignity and greatness, the 'satanism' of the Romantics, was a weapon to be used in literature and art against the bourgeois world. This tendency towards the 'satanic' (Blake, Byron, Shelley, Stendhal, Balzac, Kleist, Arnim, Hoffmann, etc.,) the artists' enjoyment of the horrific and the ugly, was seen by many as a symptom of degeneration and decline. Goethe, despite the fact that he was influenced by Winckelmann and repelled by Dante's 'revolting, often loathsome greatness' (*Annals* 1821), saw much more clearly how this 'degeneration' meant a breakthrough towards new possibilities. Pointing to the new literary tendencies in France, he said to Eckermann:

They begin to declare tedious the representations of noble sentiments and deeds, and attempt to treat of all sorts of abominations. Instead of the beautiful subjects from Grecian mythology, there are devils, witches, and vampires, and the lofty heroes of antiquity must give place to jugglers and galley slaves . . .

This 'chase after outward means of effect' was 'the greatest injury that can befall a talent, although literature in general will gain by this tendency of the moment'.

Eckermann, as much a stranger to dialectics as many of our own contemporary critics of art and literature, who are never weary of condemning the 'vicousness' of modern art, replied with astonishment: 'But how can an attempt that destroys individual talents be favourable to literature in general?'

And Goethe:

The extremes and excrescences I have described will gradually disappear; but at last this great advantage will remain – besides a freer form, richer and more diversified subjects will have been attained, and *no object of the broadest world and the most manifold life will be any longer excluded as unpoetical.* . . .[9]

Not only the ugly, the horrific and the grotesque, but also every category of what had previously been forbidden, the pathological, aberrant and deformed, became an 'art-worthy' subject for Romanticism and for modern realism which was closely linked to it. To all the pedants who are prepared to approve of this only if the artist takes no pleasure in ugliness and critically condemns it ('I begot all my children without sexual pleasure,' a German pastor once told me), we must retort that, although it is possible to beget children without pleasure, a work of art produced without the artist's identifying himself with his 'negative' characters in the process of creation can only be a moral tract. Such pedants should further consider that it was the rejected and the humiliated, the prostitutes and the criminals, all the colourful, terrible and sympathy-provoking figures on the periphery of society, and not factory workers, who were the incarnation of protest in the eyes of writers rebelling against the bourgeois world. Factory workers were slow to be discovered by literature and art; the forbidden, outlawed and outcast, the 'other', the 'No' flung at the bourgeois world, had to be discovered first, as a pre-condition. And even then, the industrial proletariat (appearing for the first time in Stendhal's *Lucien Leuwen*) was first seen by writers as the Lucifer of the suburbs, the sombre avenger, destroyer and annihilator. This is how Rimbaud saw the proletarian:

> ... *C'est la Crapule,*
> *Sire. Ça bave aux murs, ça monte, ça pullule:*
> – *Puisqu'ils ne mangent pas, Sire, ce sont des gueux!*

(That, Sire, is the Scum! It licks round the walls, it rises, it seethes: – because they don't eat, Sire, they're beggars!)[10]

> *Le Poète prendra le sanglot des Infâmes,*
> *La haine des Forçats, la clameur des Maudits,*
> *Et ses rayons d'amour flagelleront les Femmes.*
> *Ses strophes bondiront: Voilà! voilà! bandits!*

(The Poet will take the sobs of the Infamous, the hate of the Galley-slaves, the clamour of the Damned; and the beams of his love will scourge Womankind. His verses will leap out: There's for you! There! Villains!)[11]

The proletariat was not seen as differentiated into individuals but as an elemental social force. Even in Zola, who created a vast number of proletarian characters and for whom the proletariat was certainly more than a faceless mass, the individuals are always fused into a productive or destructive elemental force. In order to depict those mines, those tenements, those black landscapes and desperate demonstrations without sentimentality or moralization, writers and artists had first to undergo the experience of discovering the ugly, the forbidden and the concealed. 'Decadence', fascinated by ugliness, cleared the way for a realistic, as distinct from idealizing, portrayal of proletarian life and unrest.

EXPERIENCE, NOT ILLUSTRATION

For the visual arts, the loss of a given set of religious subjects (or at any rate subjects regarded as sublime) represented a greater difficulty than for literature. It is true that the secularization of subject-matter had already begun earlier, in a variety of ways, with Rubens, Bruegel, Vermeer, Chardin, Hogarth, and Goya, to name only a few. Yet the historical subject cannot compete, so far as direct effectiveness is concerned, with the religious one. Annunciation, crucifixion, and ascension do not admit of the question whether such a thing has ever really happened; the mythical element blots out the historical. Yet every painting which claims to represent a historical event is not a copy of that event but a fiction. It is at this point that the significance of subject begins to diminish in favour of that of form.

As early as Delacroix, it is not so much the subject as the manner of representation that we remember: not what the picture *tells* but what it *is*. The subject is overpowered by structure and movement, by the rhythm of the forms and the luminosity of the colours. Here, as in Byron, Géricault, Stendhal, Balzac, we feel the new *myth of passion*, Romanticism's defiant answer to bourgeois respectability. Thus, for example, in the image of the Goddess of Liberty, her breasts bare, the tricolour held high, advancing at the head of the fighters on the barricades (and, even earlier, in *The Raft of the Medusa*), there is an attempt – pointing towards the future – to transform history into myth. Such paintings are not meant to create the illusion that it was really so, for it cannot have been so; the intention, rather, is to convey an experience, revolutionary or otherwise, to the viewer by means of expression and form, rhythm and colour. It is less and less a matter of depicting events, more and more of conveying experience. This function of visual art is well able to hold its own against photography and the film.

And so, when Chagall laments the narrowing of the world in the development of art, he is right to the extent that it has become increasingly difficult to find a standpoint from which the new age could be depicted *in its totality*. There was, there is no longer any *whole*, 'God-willed' and capable of being surveyed at a single glance, as in the religious Middle Ages. Everything has become a rapidly progressing *process*, hardly any longer to be grasped in its totality, yet able still to be experienced through concentration upon the detail or the fragment. This revolution has encouraged resignation, withdrawal into fragmentariness, despairing subjectivism in art. But on the other hand, what expansion, what enrichment, what deepening of experienced reality made visible through art!

In the visual arts Delacroix was the last artist capable of creating the illusion of totality by violent, theatrical effects, of presenting historical (or fictional) events as though he had been present like an all-knowing but invisible god. But the greatness of his works does not reside in their subjects or themes. The continued attempts to tell stories, or narrate history in paintings – by the French academic painters, the Düsseldorf school in Germany, etc. – led to a flat triviality, an insipid imitativeness, a decline which denies art as art. When a museum guide speaks only of the 'content' of a picture ('Here, you see, is Prince So-and-So, and this petition being handed to him by burghers and peasants had a text that went thus-and-thus, and the scene shown here played such-and-such a role in the history of our country . . .') – when, in other words, a work of art has become no more than an illustration, a showpiece in a panopticon – it is a sure sign of a dying art divesting itself of its own true nature.

True modern art shunned such self-exteriorization in an empty outside world. Caspar David Friedrich, for a long time thrust aside by the Düsseldorf school with its theatrical naturalism, accused as early as 1834 by the academicians of 'having in effect destroyed nature', said emphatically: 'The painter should not merely paint what he sees in front of himself, but also what he sees within himself. But if he sees nothing within himself, let him abstain also from painting what he sees in front of him.' Many more recent artists have endorsed this position. Thus, Cézanne to Gasquet:

The landscape is reflected within me, becomes human, becomes conceivable. I objectify it, convey it, retain it in my picture. . . . My painting, the landscape, both outside myself, but the one chaotic, ephemeral, confused, without logical existence, outside all reason, the other permanent, accessible to feeling, ordered into categories, participating in the mode, the drama of ideas. . . .

Or Picasso: 'A painter paints to get rid of his sensations and visions.' Or Max Ernst: 'The painter's task is to observe and externalize what he sees inside himself.'

FROM STENDHAL TO PROUST

In literature the extreme concentration upon the inner world of man began with Stendhal, although the external world continued to be closely and critically observed. In *The Life of Henri Brulard* Stendhal speaks again and again of the surge of memories. Landscapes play 'like the bow of a violin' upon his soul. Bells and drums bring back pictures of his childhood. It is in the shadow of sensations that facts become visible, like ruins.

I beg the reader, if I should ever find one, to remember that I lay claim to the truth only in regard to *my own sensations*; where facts are concerned, my memory has always been short.

He does not, he emphasizes, describe things in themselves, 'but only their effect upon myself'. And finally the frequently recurring comparison with the fragmentary fresco:

I see images and recall the impression they made on my heart, but am in the dark concerning their causes and meanings. It is exactly like the frescoes in the Campo Santo in Pisa, where you can clearly see an arm, while the piece next to it, which represented the head, has dropped off. I can see a sequence of extremely clear pictures, but with no expression other than that of how they affected me. More than that: I see this expression solely by remembering the effect it had on me.

While striving for absolute truthfulness, Stendhal does not conceal the subjectivity with which he transforms feeling into fact and conjures up reality out of images stored in his memory. Thus we see how clearly the inventor of the modern novel sketched out the method which Marcel Proust was later to develop to perfection.

Both authors were, above all, masters of psychological insight, but both were also incomparably more than that: discoverers of the complex interrelationships, inaccessible to any crude method, between the outer and the inner world of man. Proust is capable of expressing what is almost inexpressible. His ability to experience the inner and the outer world in their most subtle interconnection as a unity which is never fixed, always in process of becoming – more precisely, to be at home in the indefinite border country in which they merge into another – goes beyond psychology.

Human reality is an amalgam of the outer and the inner world. The inner world includes social elements such as language, custom, habit, environment, ideology, the aura of objects. The existential self with its elemental urges connected with the womb, birth and death, cosmic dread and the desire to absorb 'the other', to swallow up the outer world, to get *beside oneself*, is embedded in the social self, from which it receives order and colour; and, rooted in both domains, the unique, unrepeatable individual self, the self which, given the necessary conditions, is capable of free decision. The aim of both Stendhal and Proust was to make this totality visible and not merely to reflect the outer world.

Through the constant, intangible alternations of outer and inner world, of things seen and things remembered, of experience and reflection, reality becomes as real as it only rarely is. It acquires the mode of the surreal. Elements of surrealism are anticipated.

The discovery of Romanticism that reality is interwoven with dreams becomes, in Proust, a fusion in time. The imperceptible rise and fall of the time level holds remembered being in dreamlike suspension. Today, which once was tomorrow, sinks back into yesterday. The reality of memory is constantly changed by the process of remembering, which always adds a drop of the here-and-now; it is never at a standstill, but in deep and gentle motion. It is a process and a trial. That which is conjured up is immediately questioned, that which seems certain becomes doubtful, the doubtful is proved, the proved is seen to be unprovable. Such contemplation and experience from different points of time and view yield an abundance of new, hitherto undreamt-of dimensions. The fixed standpoint of the narrator placed above men and events has been abandoned. The narrator stands in the midst of it all, he is neither all-knowing nor sovereign, yet he gains – as when one unexpectedly enters a hall of mirrors – through the multiplicity of reflections a new possibility, reminiscent of cubism, of seeing objects and men from many aspects at the same time.

Just as the physicists, using new methods of precise observation, explored the atom as a microcosm, revealing unexpected aspects of the macrocosm, so great writers made it their task to uncover the molecular movements of the human soul. What they revealed was an almost frightening wealth of complexities, fields of force, contradictions. The extraordinary precision and subtlety of Proust's work was, of course, connected with the author's specific characteristics, the fact that he was the son of a rich Jewish family, a sick man and a homosexual, obviously predestined for such sensibility; the delicate nuances of his transitions from the outer to the inner world must appear alien and irrelevant to many who have to work hard for a living; yet to dismiss his work as 'decadent' would be patently absurd.

There is no doubt that an artist or writer who concentrates exclusively upon the difficult, the inexpressible aspects of the inner life must become isolated, pulled down too deep into the realm of shadows; yet Odysseus brings discoveries to light from underground which point with a quiet force towards the future, while artificial attempts by artists of inadequate gifts to depict men solely as the representatives of social forces and counter-forces vanish with the day whose demands they illustrate. The deeper, subtler, richer image of man which we owe to writers like Proust contradicts the 'narrowing' and 'impoverishment' which are supposed to be symptomatic of decadence.

BEING AND SEEMING

While trying to depict all aspects of the reality of the bourgeois world, artists became aware that it was a world which concealed itself, withdrawing from view into the shadow of appearances. They felt more and more clearly the contradiction between what claims to be real and the way in which objects envelop and swallow up man. A widening gap between being and seeming, between reality and the conventional phrase, lie or hypocrisy, is characteristic of decay and decadence. The words are still there, expressing great aims and demands, but no one any longer believes in them; the word is a sentry whom they forgot to relieve, while behind it the temple of liberty it once guarded has been replaced by a prison or a warehouse. What is said has lost none of its vowels or consonants but only its content; the meaning has been exchanged. The deed denies the word. The language of the past provides a screen for contemporary swindles. This contradiction, symptomatic of decline, assumed intolerable proportions during the years before the First World War.

There was a smell of ruins [I once wrote in a study on Hanns Eisler], and this smell, mixed with the respectable one of a well-soaped civilization that had been washed in many waters, stank in the nostrils of the young. The classics were compulsory reading. Rulers sold nations on the market, yet Goethe was on their lips. Financial deals were clinched in the shadow of quotations from Schiller. The starry sky above and the laws of morality within us were as dear to the stock exchange as to the general staffs and the universities. . . . Rebelling against this lying attitude of a world that had grown catastrophic, many of the younger artists rejected what they had inherited from their fathers: the masterpieces of the classics which had been debased to a thesaurus of quotations and put into circulation like I.O.U.s that could never be honoured . . .[13]

LATE AND EARLY COMERS

Before I attempt to speak of the characteristic features of decadence, it is necessary to ask the question: should not the concept of decadence, so often misinterpreted and misused, be abandoned altogether?

Since phenomena such as decay, decline and decadence undoubtedly exist, I would plead for retaining the concept, although it should be used circumspectly and not for the purposes of propaganda. We must note first of all that new movements in art rarely come about in a smooth transition from old to new, but often in contradiction and revolt, breaking with what has preceded them; that they develop, reach a climax and begin to decline, and innovators who arise out of that decline suddenly cease to belong to it, inspired by a new artistic principle (e.g. Cézanne), or else opposition begins to form within the original movement with the aim of overthrowing the old principle (e.g. expressionism). These revolutions in art have a connection with social change, which is sometimes almost direct but, more frequently, is mediated in a variety of complex ways. In no case is it only the rise or decay of social classes which is 'reflected' in tendencies within literature and art; periods of artistic flowering and decay may exist *within* a class or a system, especially since it is always an epoch *as a whole* which acts upon the artist.

To speak of the decay or decadence of a movement, tendency or school in the arts seems to me appropriate when art within that movement has *become* that which it should have *overcome*, that is to say a negation of itself through empty phrases, clichés, routine, hypocrisy, apology, or fetishism. Thus the faded late-comers of an epoch deserve to be described as decadent, as distinct from the early-comers who – often in a confused and confusing manner, disturbingly, yet sometimes with a great integrity – are the heralds of a new era.

The academic painters of the Second Empire, who endeavoured to imitate Delacroix with great facility but little power, were such 'late-comers'. For instance, the painter of historical canvases Paul Delaroche with his cold and insipid theatrical effects; or Ernest Meissonier, whose elegant battle canvases looked as if Mars had had his hair curled by Venus. They were popular, but less so than other painters in whose hands Delacroix's passion was debased to lasciviousness and the radiance of his nudes into mere glamour. Alexandre Cabanet, Jules Lefebvre, Paul Baudry and others painted courtesans as heroines, as allegorical figures entitled 'Truth', 'Freedom', or 'Happiness', created an Olympian *demi-monde*, a sentimental and pathetic nation of harlots which well befitted the régime of Napoleon III and which Offenbach exposed to ridicule in his satirical operettas.

Not all imitative art is decadent. It may not be academic, but may represent a noble, though hopeless, attempt to cling to vanishing forms of greatness, to resist decay. However, elements of something new are always mixed in with imitativeness of this elevated kind, and this is what distinguishes it from the vulgar variety wrapped up in hypocritical phrases and bedecked with medals.

Impressionism was one of the great revolts against the decadence of an official art. It was a breaking out of the dusty studio into the open air, into the modern world of technology and the great cities. But it was also a flight away from them. It was freshness, liveliness, spontaneity, a paean to everyday life – and at the same time the abandonment of the 'grand' subject, of rigid outline and strict structure. For a long time I was inclined to see in this devaluation of the subject, this eclipse of the 'what' by the 'how', a symptom of decadence, and I put forward this view in my book *The Necessity of Art*. Today I believe that I was wrong: not only because great religious and historical subjects had forfeited their genuine pathos in the bourgeois age, but also because in this devaluation of the subject we can recognize a certain rejection of 'ideology' as false consciousness. The 'ordinary' was dipped in colour and radiance. Are battles, coronations, historical events really so much more significant than the 'little' subjects 'seen under a light', the light discovered by impressionism? In contrast to Lefebvre and Bouguereau in Paris, Makart in Vienna, Piloty and his school in Berlin, impressionism did not represent decay but a fresh start towards new possibilities. It is true, however, that the tendency towards complete dissolution of the image in colour and light carried within it a danger of decay. But a counter-tendency, a desire for severity, solidity, coherence, for line and structure, began to stir within impressionism. Degas first transcended the limits of impressionism with his dense compositions of figures in movement. But it was Cézanne, with his solidly-made *The Railway Cutting*, painted at a very early date (1867), who became the herald of a new art no longer dedicated to the 'impression', to the shimmering, brief moment.

BOASTFUL DECADENCE

The visual arts of the bourgeois age reflect a long-drawn-out struggle between conspicuous consumption and unlimited productivity, between parasitic extravagance and austere construction, bloated magniloquence and incisive frankness, ornament and essence. Flamboyant consumption, the boastful, swaggering, extravagant quality of clothes and dwellings, paintings and monuments is, to my mind, a sign of decadence. The apotheosis of philistinism (Gabriele d'Annunzio, Bouguereau, Makart), hysteria as a substitute for passion (Oscar Wilde's *Salome*, Franz von Stuck's *Die Sünde*), coquettish immorality, idealization of the *demi-monde* in contrast to Toulouse-Lautrec's cool view of it, the pomp of massive architecture for prestige (the Reichstag building in Berlin, the monument to Vittorio Emanuele in Rome, later the monument to the Battle of Leipzig in that city) all belong together: all are forms of a parasitic and monumental hypocrisy.

But at the same time protests in literature and art against such exhalations of concentrated capital and imperialist expansion, against the over-satiation and insatiability of the ruling stratum, became more and more violent. What had begun with impressionism was continued by movements which in many respects contradicted one another: naturalism, cubism, surrealism, futurism, expressionism. All these contributed to an art of protest against the bourgeois world, although by no means all were immune from infection by that world.

National socialism outlawed this art of protest as 'degenerate' and 'decadent'; but it is precisely the 'German Art' celebrated and promoted by the Nazis which, in the light of world-historical and art-historical developments, has been proved to be hopelessly decadent.

Our healthy, unspoilt people will no longer tolerate an art which is remote from life and contrary to nature. . . . This degenerate art is destruction, stemming from destructive Marxism, that mortal enemy of everything that is natural and folk-like. . . . We shall from now on wage a merciless mopping-up campaign against the last elements of disintegration in our culture!

Thus Adolf Hitler opening the 'Degenerate Art' exhibition in 1937. The German people were called upon to sit in 'mystic judgement' upon the 'vandals of art', upon Kollwitz and Barlach, Dix and Lehmbruck, Grosz and Beckmann, Klee and Kandinsky, Nolde and Schmidt-Rotluff, Becker-Modersohn and Kokoschka. The exhibition aimed, according to the catalogue, at 'unmasking the degeneration of art as Art Bolshevism in the full sense of the word'. The verdict was pronounced: 'The artists ought to be tied up next to their pictures, so that every German could spit in their faces.'

The day before, the 'First Great German Art Exhibition' had been opened opposite, in the new House of German Culture. It was a hotch-potch of brutality and idyllic sentimentalism, 'German tectonics' and heel-clicking subservience, heroically heaving chests and abject conventionalism, hearts full of sunshine and brains full of sand. 'The people,' said Goebbels, 'want to see and enjoy the beautiful and the sublime. . . . A world of wonder shall open here before their astounded eyes. . . .' The 'popular and militant' German art mustered for the exhibition was 'a movement towards the organization of optimism'.

Art as deception, as 'organization of optimism' in a society whose rulers are organizing catastrophe, can only be the servant of false consciousness and empty phrases and hypocrisy: of decadence in the name of greater efficiency.

A visitor who, in conversation with me, implied that Picasso had certainly painted some praiseworthy peace-doves but had unfortunately failed to find the path to Socialist Realism, challenged me with the following question: 'Since you do not consider that Picasso, Beckmann, Zadkine are decadent, what then do you think *is* decadent?'

I opened a folder, took out a bundle of different reproductions and showed him the head of a youth.

'But isn't that an antique head?'

'There was decadence in the antique, too, but this rubbish here has been knocked together out of academic classicism, down-at-heel Gothic and the mentality of the S.S. Look how unclean, how ludicrously violent all the forms are: the neck, straining as though it were carrying the globe instead of an empty shell of a head, the coy disorder of the hair, the sickly cruelty of the mouth – an underdeveloped superman? And the same type here, half German soldier, half St George, the dragon-killer as a hybrid of superficial naturalism and swaggering allegory; this one is called "I Care For Germany" and had the place it deserved in the Adolf-Hitler-Shrine at Pasewalk. And that one there . . .'

'But what's decadent about that? Labour, the horny hand. . . . Was that by a Nazi too? A pity!'

'This is a study for a monument to labour on the Reich Autobahn, made by the Reich sculptor, Josef Thorak. For me this is a perfect example of decadence, of truly degenerate art. Look at the inconceivable dilation of the muscles, those lumps of flesh, this frenzied activity; and goodness knows what these giants from a provincial ballet company are supposed to be doing on the Autobahn.'

'They're dragging a block of stone.'

'Realism, then, but without reality. Was the Reich Autobahn built without machines merely so that Josef Thorak could cook up this muscle stew to supply more German Art?'

'Is that how you see it? I don't know. . . . But why decadent?'

'It's a kind of emptiness with its mouth full of words, a hollowness trying to appear massive, the heroic as ornament, the sublime as routine – when ghostly, unreal spooks like this are taken for reality, we are, I think, entitled to speak of decadence. Or do you believe that Nazi art was a victory over Western, capitalist, cosmopolitan decadence, and Hitler the renewer of German national culture?'

'All the same,' said my visitor, 'we too demand from art that it should have beauty, *joie de vivre*, optimism. Some artists believe that there is a contradiction between truth and beauty. This contradiction, which is typical of the world of monopoly capital, has been resolved in our country. As for the Nazis, they had no right to reject expressionism and encourage the art of beauty. Their beauty was a lie.'

'Can a work of art celebrating a lie be beautiful?'

'Your arguments are ambiguous,' said my visitor. 'You want to disguise the real nature of decadence, which is an expression of monopoly capital and imperialism.'

'Was not Hitler's Germany the extreme form of monopoly capital and imperialism, and if that is so, and if I understand you right, was not his art the quintessence of decadent art?'

'Wasn't it you who said that art is not ideology – although influenced by it? And now suddenly you admit that the art of the Nazis . . .'

'Hitler's régime did not tolerate spontaneous art. It burned what it did not accept. So, apart from a forbidden, persecuted, exiled art, all that remained was the official art made to order. Such an art was indeed a reflection of the ruling ideology, that is to say of the superstructure of an anti-human power. And so it was decadent.'

WAS GENGHIS KHAN DECADENT?

The fascist glorification of the inhuman, the setting up of a 'standard image' without warmth, without tolerance, without respect for human beings different from oneself, an image in which harshness, cruelty and ruthlessness predominate – this must be defined as a symptom of decadence. But is this so under all circumstances? Is it so when someone who has been attacked defends himself? When, in defending his human rights, he does not shrink from using inhuman means?

Hatred, even against degradation
Distorts the features;
Anger, even against injustice,
Makes the voice hoarse.[14]

For the inhuman to be felt as decadent, there has to be a sense of contrast between civilization and barbarism, outward morality and brutal practice. In *Within a Budding Grove* Proust speaks of the contrast between the writer Bergotte's work and his private life, adding: '. . . this contrast had never before been so striking as it was in Bergotte's time, because . . . in proportion as society grew more corrupt, our notions of morality were increasingly exalted.' This contrast between refinement and corruption, between higher standards of education and forms of living and a diminishing sense of responsibility, between richer material and intellectual possibilities and a consciousness not commensurate with these, encourages phenomena of decadence. As society becomes relatively more humanized through improved standards of living, wages, housing, education, hygiene and social welfare, there is also a greater degree of objectification of life, moral and spiritual corruption, concentration of power and relative dehumanization.

Genghis Khan was not decadent, any more than was the savage who tied his prisoner to the stake. But the stake in the midst of civilization becomes a sure symptom of decadence.

It has not been my intention here to analyse the entire phenomenon of decadence, which allows of many interpretations because it lacks definition; I have merely tried to disclose decadence where it has pretensions to health, uprightness and dignity, bearing in mind the fact that it should not be thought of as an absolute but always relatively, in relation to a complex process.

We must distinguish between the decline or rise of mankind as a whole, the decline or rise of classes, nations and social systems, and the decline or rise of the arts (or of a particular branch of the arts) within classes, nations and social systems (outside influences and stimuli being constantly taken into account). All these things interact with one another, condition and interpenetrate one another in a multitude of ways, forming a continual reciprocal process, without ever becoming a rigid mechanism. This in itself provides many possibilities of applying and misusing the concept of 'decadence', and makes it necessary to concretize it in every particular case.

How can our epoch, which is more than a *fin-de-siècle*, more than a transition to new social systems, perhaps a revolution of unforeseeable scope – how can our epoch of endings and beginnings, of cannibalistic civilizations and civilized cannibalism, of dehumanization and previously unimagined possibilities of true humanity, preserve itself from decadence? Decadence, poison and ferment, refinement and brutalization, death urge and desire for the ultimate metamorphosis, interweaves that which is ending with that which is beginning, so closely that we cannot distinguish the black thread from the gold, still less assert that only the gold thread is good for the fabric while the black threatens to destroy it.

Chagall's diagnosis is brilliant and problematic. The 'shrinking process' from God (or whatever name we may give to the infinite and to the meaning of life related to it) down to the neutrino, the smallest particle of matter which has to be tracked down by the biggest machines, is alarming not only to Chagall. Yet this 'narrowing' is at the same time a broadening of our knowledge of the world, and the scientists of all nations who unite in the hunt for the neutrino imply a certain possibility of humanity, at least as a 'work team'. Perhaps the thing which all mankind holds in common – the secularized myth of man and his inexhaustibility, the spirit stirring silently under the rubble of stupidity, greed and lust for power – will after all prove the stronger. Down there, in the stubborn darkness of the searching generations, the 'chemistry' of which Chagall speaks may be at work to discover the 'fundamental colour' of a new epoch. It may be that this 'fundamental colour', about to come into being, merely requires a new form of vision, and that many of those who have been so vehemently accused of decadence – from Rimbaud to Kafka, from Cézanne to Picasso – have had an essential share in preparing it.

Notes

1. Louis Aragon, *Les Lettres Françaises*, Paris, July 1963
2. Marc Chagall, *Les Lettres Françaises*, Paris, July 1963
3. ibid
4. ibid

L

Letters, translated by R. Snell (London: Routledge & Kegan Paul, 1954) letter 6

7. Erich Auerbach, *Mimesis* op. cit.
8. Charles Dickens, *Hard Times*, quoted in E. J. Hobsbawm, *The Age of Revolution 1789–1848* (London: Weidenfeld & Nicolson, 1962)
9. *Conversations of Goethe with Eckermann*, translated by John Oxenford (London: Dent, 1930)
10. *Rimbaud: Selected Verse*, translated by Oliver Bernard (Harmondsworth: Penguin, 1962)
11. ibid
12. Ernst Fischer, 'Hanns Eisler und die Literatur', *Sinn und Form*, Berlin. special edition, 1964
13. Bertolt Brecht, 'To Our Successors', from John Willett, *The Theatre of Bertolt Brecht* (London: Methuen, 1959)

Chapter 5

IN PRAISE OF THE IMAGINATION

In our world of technical revolution, the power of the imagination is shrinking: not only the power of imaginative insight into the real, but that of imaginative anticipation of the possible.

'THE HEART IS ILLITERATE'

Science and technology appear to outbid the dream and the myth. What is the use of imagination when the television screen has pictures enough – and to spare – to offer to the consumer? And whose sympathetic imagination is powerful enough to withstand the increasing quantity of men, goods, weapons, catastrophes?

The heart in our times has become illiterate [said the Swiss author Hugo Lötscher at a writers' symposium in Vienna in 1965]. How is it to behave when confronted with mass graves? Sympathy is not enough. The heart can be present at the death of one man, when it can directly feel that death; but today it is not the personal dead who are our problem but the unknown dead. How is the heart to react? Does it feel more strongly if there are two hundred thousand dead rather than a hundred thousand? It is powerless, and by its powerlessness it betrays thousands. But with my intellect I can teach my heart and force it to understand that two hundred thousand are more even than a hundred thousand. Spontaneous feeling has got to go back to school, and since I don't know any other teacher, I must employ my own intellect.

But the intellect too is powerless unless the imagination comes to its aid – the capacity, not yet extinguished, to imagine sympathetically the death of the *one man* who is one of the hundreds of thousands. Without this capacity, without the power of the imagination, a hundred thousand and two hundred thousand would really represent only a quantitative difference. The imagination has always been the great mediator between the possible and the real, between sensuality and reason, the past and the future. It reaches out beyond the here-and-now, it complements our fragmentary existence, it can make life be felt as a single whole, it can temporarily replace the *principium individuationis* by a sense of unity with nature and mankind.

Satiated with deceptive facts, blunted by an excess of events, misled by the illusion of 'being present' (press a button and the world comes into your home), the modern consumer is forcing the imagination into retirement.

WHAT FURTHER USE FOR THE IMAGINATION?

The notion that the human species might have developed purely through common sense, without excesses of the imagination – by perfecting tools, working methods and social institutions, without ever having wandered in the labyrinth of dreams and folly, myth and magic, gods and phantoms – is disquieting. Yet having once accepted this labyrinth as an unavoidable part of our history, why should we not, in this scientific age, sweep away all the illusions, the sphinxes and chimeras, the masks and metaphors, the parables and mysteries? What we still need, so we are told, is the combinatory imagination of science and technology (in order to eliminate the disturbance factor of the unaccountable). But does the power of imagination serve any purpose? Vast ranges of reality can no longer be grasped except mathematically, that is to say they are *unimaginable*.

Yet the imagination is a way of *cognition of the world*. Cognition of what world? Of what is not, but *could be*. The unlimited potential. It is not a question of abandoning the *logos* – reason and science – but, on the contrary, of supplementing them by the imagination, by concrete vision and mythical image. Without the imagination there is a world of facts, conditions and events, but no *reality*.

Man, a being who, working within the world, modified it to suit his needs, was forced to acquire a knowledge of the world and a consciousness of himself which outpaced his conservative instincts and his early experiences and methods. By working, man anticipated not only the end-product of the work but also *himself*. For the first time the future affected the present of a biological organism. Work was not only the condition but also the postponement of a desired satisfaction. The desired, being something that had to be worked for, demanded the renunciation of immediate for the sake of future satisfaction. The anticipation of the end-product, the imagined object preceding the finished object, the postponement of satisfaction granting anticipatory pleasure to the instincts and desires, formed a new property in man: the property of imagination. The image, unknown to animals, of what is not present, the possible as an inexhaustible force for producing extended reality, was the beginning of a development which cannot now be stopped. Without the productive force of the imagination, without the breath of the as yet unexperienced, the anticipated – without all this the mere accumulation of past experience retained as unassailable tradition would have led to a standstill.

PRODUCTIVE MEMORY

The imagination is dialectical in so far as anticipating the future is a form of *productive remembering*.

In the work process there is at first an imitation of useful objects found in nature, say a wedge to become an axe. But gradually the object placed before the eye as a model becomes a remembered, an inwardly imagined one; the worker improves, refines the crude model, adapts it more and more closely to his purpose, discovers more advantageous combinations, unrealized possibilities. What was once a material model now appears to the worker as an ideal original image, an *idea* of the thing to be made. The possible as still unformed reality, the stuff that dreams and gods and tools, phantoms and inventions, myths and mechanisms are made of, is the never-ending material of the imagination. The trinity of the creative imagination is there from the beginning. To imagine what has not yet been objectified, what is not yet present; to combine things which are not yet mutually related, to join them together and to establish an interaction between them; to draw what is to be from that which is remembered, to overstep the inadequate here-and-now, to make what has never yet been seen, conceived of or noticed *creatively* visible, conceivable and conscious – that is the imagination's three-fold manner of working. Originating in the working process, it is itself an inward-working process, the simplest and the richest way of working. The imagined, the not-yet present, the *new* is waylaid and captured; not merely the past but the future becomes a cause – an *Ur-Sache* – an original object. But this future is born out of the past, and all that is still to be accomplished is mirrored in memory.

By his work, man destroys his unity with nature. He does violence to nature and fears its revenge. With the increasing division of labour, with the beginning of authority, the division into ruled and rulers, into those who serve and those who enjoy, into haves and have-nots, the memory of a lost paradise, of a golden age, of a time when work was not a curse but a humanizing personal activity, becomes an inexhaustible source for the imagination. Original sin was the fact of becoming man; the imagination works to anticipate a *renewed* condition of the past. Drawing from ancient wells, it transforms a fluid element into something malleable and moulds from it images of the future. The force of the instincts, the power of dreams, the material of memory is enriched by new experience and modified by reason – yet anticipation is always the result of looking back upon a past which appears golden.

Later we will consider how the imagination produces myths and examine the myth as a model of reality, Now, however, we must try to see how the imagination tends to shrink in the highly developed industrial society.

'THE REALM OF FREEDOM'

The imagination, which refuses to recognize as reality the world which rulers of all kinds tell us it is reasonable to accept as such, the imagination which anticipates a 'realm of freedom' outside and beyond socially necessary production and the consumer goods manufactured by it, is said to be antiquated, anarchic, suspect and destructive. The rulers' suspicion of the imagination is by no means unfounded, for it rarely coincides with their wishes; it blossoms in contradiction, withers away in apologetics, and is transformed into a call-girl by publicity. Without supervision, the imagination calls up images which suggest freedom and a full life, instead of the wish-dreams and models which serve the interests of society, that is to say of its rulers. The imagination's critique is more abhorrent to social systems than the critique of reason, because it does not affirm that which is but that which could be, and tries to present what is still unaccomplished and unfulfilled through the power of images.

Those forces which treat man as an instrument of production and use him as a means towards their own ends never let him go. During his so-called leisure hours he is no less subjugated to alienation from himself than during the hours of alienated work. The commercial idea that men outside the sphere of production can be trained to become perfect consumers just as they were once trained to be disciplined workers seems to be linked with the thought, or at least with the notion, that the ruler should never leave those whom he rules entirely to themselves, that their imagination must be guided, directed, manipulated lest it bring men to a consciousness of its liberating power. The needs which the entertainment industry creates and vulgarly satisfies do not merely serve the intensification and expansion of production; they also break up a utopia into a million fragments and hand them out in doses large enough to make an addict of the apparently free consumer and small enough to integrate his consequent addiction into the prevailing order. The hope that the reduction in working hours and the extension of leisure, which have been made possible by improved technology and rational organization of work, would expand the scope of the imagination – the 'realm of freedom' – has proved deceptive.

SEMBLANCE AND SHOCK

The effortless reception, the industrious passivity, the killing of time into which leisure has been turned – how can the imagination how can art prevail against it? How can art pierce this smoke-screen of recognized 'facts', this surrogate of reality – when it is itself defined as illusion, as unreality or as the 'reflection' of a reality, vague and ill-defined in comparison with science? In order to operate effectively against a commercial, pre-packaged, de-realized reality, the imagination has to use shock methods. It must shock in order to make people look up and listen. It needs a public which has been shaken, startled, activated.

Thus an exchange of roles is apparently taking place between art and reality. Art, which exists beyond the reality determined by necessity, compulsion and labour – 'for the simplest way of living is in art', said Bertolt Brecht[1] – can no longer avoid intervening to oppose a distorted and disjointed reality. Art, whose nature it once was to liberate man from the pressure around him, to take him out of harness and to anticipate the 'realm of freedom', is now obliged to reveal the *real* world behind the *apparent* one, to drive men who are escaping into irresponsibility back into reality, and to make them conscious of their share in a universal responsibility.

The intention of art, writes Georg Lukács, 'is to rise above the confines of mere everyday life'. 'A further feature of this intention is directed against every schematizing routine, every fetishization.'[2] The fetishes of our time are objects of external life: mechanisms, institutions, clichés, 'facts', phrases. To get rid of the fetishes means to break through this *substitute reality of connivance* and to reveal the latent reality. But the fetish formations in a highly developed industrial society are so dense and strong that without the help of shock the imagination can scarcely hope to break through them to reality. The entertainment industries continually and successfully feed the market with rubbish which releases and satisfies the lower instincts suppressed by civilization. Whilst pretending to 'liberate' men, it in fact dehumanizes them. How can art, using old methods, challenge if not defeat the barbarism which is establishing itself in the midst of civilization? Is it within the nature of art to enter such a struggle at all? Why should art throw itself into the turmoil which threatens it? Why not withdraw into quietude, into 'pure being'?

Many writers and artists have chosen such withdrawal without much ado. They put forward the well-founded argument that 'pure being' comprises 'being otherwise', that beauty existing for its own sake is a kind of protest against utilitarianism and dehumanization. They ask: does not art, when it undertakes a direct, immediate attack upon the fetishes, run the risk of desecration? It does – and not only today. It has done so ever since the technical and industrial revolution, ever since the end of a culture which was the privilege of a tiny minority, when the masses entered as a force into a world of increasing alienation. The risk of desecration casts doubt on what art, in Europe at least, has been supposed to be for more than five centuries; it casts doubt upon the great illusion of a 'reflected' reality come to rest in its mirror image, in which it enjoys permanent being, removed from the process of becoming. If art is determined to fight against the fetishes, it must adapt itself to the conditions of that struggle and risk breaking with the old categories of aesthetics.

SHOCK THERAPY?

We read in Lukács that ancient aesthetics recognized the connection of aesthetic activity with social life, yet

did not see this social function as being related to this or that concrete, actual purpose, but rather believed that its significance lay in the fact that the practice of particular arts was a formative force in the development of human, and therefore of social, life; that art was a way of influencing men in a direction which would promote or impede the development of certain types of human beings.[3]

Little has changed in this *general* social function of art (although we should not forget that there existed works such as the *Miletus*, a tragedy of which Themistocles was one of the co-authors, the purpose of which was topical and concrete). But in order to influence the direction in which men can develop, is it not necessary first of all to undermine the indifference, the irresponsibility, the genuine or simulated ignorance which are characteristic of our time, by presenting the public with what it cannot imagine?

On 3 November 1965 the play *Saved* was given its first performance at the Royal Court Theatre in London. The play contains a scene in which a gang of young toughs torture a baby and finally kill it. The critics, worried less about the baby than about art, rejected the play almost unanimously. Art, they said, must, for aesthetic reasons, respect certain limits which harsh reality ignores. The unbearable is a prerogative of reality; art, if it cannot avoid such subjects, must ennoble them until they become bearable. The theatre critic of *The Financial Times* wrote: 'If such things are really going on in South London they are properly the concern of the police and the magistrates rather than the audiences of theatres.'[4] The author, Edward Bond, replied in a letter to his critics: 'I wanted to show that all violence, wherever it occurs, in Europe, in Asia, in prison, in the back garden, in the living room, in joke or in anger, in war or in peace, has the effect of making people corrupt, and if the act of violence is a serious one then this corruption is a permanent state.'

Kenneth Tynan and Sir Laurence Olivier came out in favour of the play and its author. Erich Fried, the German poet, wrote to the critic of *The Financial Times*:

This aesthetic approach . . . would mean that we must be spared all knowledge of the dreadful things with which the police, the magistrates' courts and other specialized institutions have to concern themselves. Basically this means a refusal to face such things. And such a refusal can in the long run encourage precisely those forms of alienation and dehumanization which are described in the play.[5]

Erich Fried points out that the disgusting James Bond films and the equally disgusting books by Mickey Spillane and others, with their mixture of sex, sadism, and political reaction, provoke far fewer protests than plays like *Saved* or *The Investigation*. In the latter, Peter Weiss uses authentic material, arranged to attain an extraordinary poetic intensity, in order to conjure up the Auschwitz which so many millions are still suppressing from their consciousness or trying to dismiss as 'Jewish exaggeration'.

It is not my purpose, in this connection, to analyse *Saved* or *The Investigation*, but rather to touch upon the problem of artistic commitment in an age when the imagination is shrinking. The entertainment industry appeals to the 'lower' instincts in order to gain higher profits. The material production of modern industrial society encourages the destructive instinct in order to increase the turnover of consumer goods. Durability and permanence are the commodity's enemy; the more quickly it is consumed, destroyed, thrown on the scrap-heap, the nearer it comes to its ideal form. The rulers fear that imagination and, with the possibility of total war in mind, demand a rough, aggressive, unimaginative public. Their accomplices therein are *kitsch* and trash.

KITSCH AND TRASH

In my boyhood, when we were short of money, we used to 'flog' (or 'kitsch') various objects at the second-hand dealers' or antique dealers' shops. The practice exists in the arts as well. The word 'kitsch', which came into circulation in the 1890s, undoubtedly originated in the jargon of the art trade. Kitsch is the cut-price sale of devalued ideals. The beautiful is reduced to the agreeable, the noble to the pretentious, the sublime to the pompous, feeling to sentimentality. The sublimating function of art is watered down; through its complicity with the 'lower' instincts, kitsch demands incomparably less effort than the beautiful, the noble or the sublime. And yet kitsch presupposes a desire for higher things, a longing for a harmonious world, idyllic happiness, tenderness, gratification, the solution of all conflicts through the happy end, the triumph of good over evil. Kitsch pretends that we are really living in the best of all possible worlds and encourages a vague optimism, rather than any wish for social change. Through the passivity of those who enjoy it, through their cheaply bought reconciliation with a world which is anything but lovely, kitsch serves the requirements of the rulers.

If kitsch, then, is a bromide, trash is a violent stimulant. Kitsch still promises a world which, not yet shaken to its very foundations, continues in a twilight state, a state in which humane ideals, however shop-soiled they may be, have not yet completely forfeited their credibility and are accepted as a dud cheque might be. But the masses of the younger generation neither believe in a possible harmony nor seek gratification in idyllic dreams. Harnessed to the double yoke of alienating monotonous work and a 'leisure' filled with gaudy promises, they want stimulants of a stronger kind. Noise and speed have numbed, if not destroyed, any longing for peace or quiet, for the serenity achieved through beauty, however cheap the beauty is. Trash appeals to all the aggressive instincts, to cruelty as a proof of vitality, to brutality as a test of strength, to ruthlessness as force of character, to sex as cold power. Trash is an education for future killers, rapers, 'supermen', members of a master race for whom the killed and the raped are mere objects, cannibalistically consumed with sadistic pleasure.

Kitsch is no less common in the socialist world than in the capitalist; trash, however, belongs to the latter alone. In a society oriented towards profit, possessions, success, art has little hope of becoming an effective power. In such a society it is not kitsch but trash which is the most vicious enemy of art. I do not know whether it is possible to drive out the devil with Beelzebub; but when coldness,

hardness, cruelty have become fetishes, the attempt must be under-
taken to defetishize them by divesting them of every trace of
pleasure, temptation or satisfaction, exposing them to revulsion and
ridicule as the cowardly, shabby, contemptible *conformism* that they
are. It is necessary to show, not the demonic quality of the horrific,
but its utter poverty, its mean wretchedness. Trash can teach us
the lesson of how to destroy trash. Important writers such as
Dashiell Hammett, Ernest Hemingway and Graham Greene have
all done something of this kind.

ART AND SOCIALISM

Socialist society creates the *objective* conditions which art requires
in order to be a power capable of gripping, moving and changing
men. The production of *kitsch* and trash offers no commercial
benefit. Leisure is not raped by an unrestrained entertainment industry. Socialism is not oriented towards *having* but towards *being*.
Criticism is nourished by an idea, the idea of socialism; the imagination is able to grasp the dynamics of a society in process of
creation.

In a paper (*Marxism and Literature*) delivered at the Congrès
pour la défense de la culture in Paris in 1935, Ernst Bloch spoke of
these possibilities:

Genuinely realistic literature is concerned with a process from
which facts have been artificially isolated and immobilized; the process demands a precise imagination in order to reproduce it, and is
itself concretely bound up with that imagination. When once one
has tasted marxist criticism, one is repelled by empty ideological talk
and rejects it; but the true poetic aura, the only one still possible and
alive today, the imagination without lies, emerges all the more clearly
and needs envy no previous period its subjects.[6]

Behind every great work of literature 'lies the sea of the process in
whose depths reality is least inaccessible: and with which marxism
is sufficiently familiar to provide access precisely to the *thing
attaching to the process* – minus the ideological lie, plus the concrete
utopia'.[7]

Socialism, then, carries within it the force of a forward-reaching,
active, powerful imagination which can become the co-determina-
tor of man's future. It is all the more painful to find that results
have lagged far behind the possibilities, that the apparatus which

rules in the name of socialism is afraid of the creative imagination whose nature is freedom, that it condemns art to impotence precisely because it recognizes or even over estimates its power. No 'guideline', directive or legislation is capable of pressing the imagination into the service of a state, a party or a ruling apparatus so that it agrees with that which exists *as it is* or so that it pretends that what has not yet been accomplished is already part of daily life.

During the Russian revolution, the imagination merged with reality. Revolutionary action, by which all alienation is destroyed, corresponds in this respect with the arts, which lead alienated man back to himself. Art was on the side of the revolutionary masses, even if its forms were unfamiliar to them. A sense of community was present even in words which were not understood. But when the revolution entered the period of construction with all its difficulties, the relation of the literary and artistic *avant-garde* with the masses became a problem. Art as the voice of the revolution lost its unified purpose and became differentiated in response to the multiplicity of tasks to be achieved; it was as if a fist had been opened and the hand reached out for heterogeneous things, both near and far. The *èlan* of the revolution remained effective in the arts until the end of the 1920s, producing an abundance of films, poems and novels which used new means of expression to deal with the new subjects and gave a foretaste of the inexhaustible possibilities of socialist art. But there was a growing tendency to control the arts, to administer and manipulate them, to drive out the spirit of criticism and free imagination and to transform artists into officials, into illustrators of resolutions. The demand for 'party-mindedness' became linked with the formal one for 'universal comprehensibility'.

THE PROBLEMS OF MARXIST CRITICISM

Lunacharsky wrote in his *Thesis on the Problems of Marxist Criticism* in 1928:

The criterion of universality must be treated with great care. In our press, in our propagandist literature we range from very complicated journals and papers, which demand considerable intelligence from the reader, to the most elementary popular level; similarly, we cannot bring all our literature down to the level of the as yet uncultured peasant masses or even of the workers. This would be a very serious mistake.

In the same work Lunacharsky affirms the writer's need to go beyond 'the ideas of our programme which have already been fully developed'.

The artist is valuable when he turns up virgin soil, when he intuitively breaks into a sphere which logic and statistics would find hard to penetrate. To judge whether an artist is right, whether he has correctly combined the truth and the basic aspirations of communism, is by no means easy; here, too, perhaps, the correct judgement can be worked out only in the conflict of opinions between critics and readers.[8]

So long as this is the spirit which determines the attitude of a ruling communist party – although encroachments by the apparatus are always a danger – the conditions are nevertheless present for the artistic imagination to penetrate areas which logic, statistics and the practical experience of politicians and administrators cannot penetrate. Socialism, more than any other system, needs criticism to correct its mistakes and false steps, and imagination to anticipate the future and not merely to 'reflect' but to participate actively in the development of man; for socialism aims at the *whole man*, at the humanization of all relationships. If the artist is denied the right to discover new realities beyond 'ideas which have already been fully developed', if he is forbidden to contradict the ruling powers, if the judgement of a work is not the result of a conflict of opinions between critics and readers but is decreed by a body deemed infallible, then socialist society is *in practice* destroying possibilities which are *in principle* one of its advantages over capitalist society. The fact that there are 'arrogant' artists, as the officials who invoke the common man are always telling us, is undeniable; but the real threat to the development of socialist art are the arrogant amateurs who believe that their office entitles them to teach painters how to paint and writers how to write: those officials for whom the truth is always 'already fully developed'.

'PARTY-MINDEDNESS'

For a socialist artist, art will always be a weapon in the class struggle.

He will use the manifold means of art to make his contribution towards the strengthening of the G.D.R., towards increasing the G.D.R.'s prestige, towards the successful accomplishment of the construction of socialism in all fields, and towards impeding the aggressive forces of imperialism and militarism from realising their plans.

That is what we understand by party-mindedness in art.[9]

Even a frying-pan can on occasion serve as a weapon in the class war: how much more so the arts, whose possibilities and means are indeed more manifold than those of a frying-pan. They can do so on the condition that they are not ordered to so so; and even then the question must be asked: a weapon – in what way? Is a drum a weapon? Or a battle song? Or a military march? The 'weapon in the class struggle' which it is prescribed that art should 'always' be is, then, a weapon only in a metaphorical sense. It neither hits nor terrifies the enemy, but encourages the combatants on its own side. Yet if it does only this and nothing else, it will end up by terrifying the undecided, boring rather than encouraging the combatants, and possibly even tempting Central Committee members to read American thrillers or console themselves with a West German cigar rather than take part in aesthetic arms drill.

And how is art to 'contribute to the strengthening of the G.D.R. and increasing the G.D.R.'s prestige'? Bertolt Brecht was not able to contribute to the strengthening of the G.D.R., although he certainly increased its prestige – because, as an artist, he went his own way, refusing to toe any line. In many of his works a poet of the class struggle, he achieved world fame as a writer, not as a bearer of ideological weapons. Others, who constantly rattle their class-war sabres, have contributed nothing to the G.D.R.'s reputation. A socialist state gains esteem not by drilling its artists to proclaim the party right when it is wrong, but by granting them the freedom which art requires. Artists, therefore, will contribute towards the prestige of their society to the extent that the party apparatus refrains from preventing them from doing so, either by 'guidelines' or by direct persecution.

As for the 'construction of socialism in all fields', this must surely mean not only industrial combines, schools, hospitals and research institutes (all of which are necessary and praiseworthy), but also greater *freedom*, not the 'abstract' freedom of which the rulers speak with so much scorn, but a highly concrete freedom of information, of thought on the basis of acquaintance with mutually contradictory ideas, of choice between alternatives, of a possibility to contradict the authorities by the spoken and the written word.

Regrettably, art is only rarely and only partially in a position to 'impede the aggressive forces of imperialism and militarism from realizing their plans'. Art committed to this cause usually only affects people who are already against imperialism and militarism. It influences those who are as yet undecided only when the work of art speaks for humanity and not for an 'ideological front', when it takes sides with that which is humane and reasonable, that which rises above the interests of class and state: that is to say, when it is not 'party-minded' in the prescribed sense. The principle of 'party-mindedness' in the narrow and strict sense deprives an art which is already wilting of the strength even to serve as a 'weapon in the class struggle'.

There is no art that does not take sides – even if it is only against taking sides. Such 'taking sides against taking sides' is often directed against utilitarianism, doctrinaire thinking and over-simplification; it can also, however, be a carefully disguised con-formism, a taking of sides on behalf of the existing order in the form of a 'sensitive' refusal to be concerned with mundane things. Yet what is called 'party-mindedness' in countries ruled by com-munists is not the artist's free decision to take sides for or against an event, a cause or an idea, but only the decision to behave at all times in such a way as the party may consider appropriate.

THE ABUSE OF QUOTATIONS

During the period when every thought was considered a possible conspiracy against Stalin, there used to be a joke in Moscow: 'What is a thought?' – 'A thought is the shortest distance between two quotations.' This shortest distance, too, was usually a disguised and shamefaced quotation. The Lenin quotation concerning 'the party-mindedness of art' has thus come to claim authoritative power. Let us be clear first about the following points:

1. A quotation, even from a great man, is never a proof of truth; it can, however, reinforce a well-thought-out idea.

2. It is necessary to know the context of the quoted sentence – the situation which gave rise to it.

3. It is also necessary to know whether the quoted sentence has been taken from a fundamental work or from an article, a pamphlet or a letter.

4. Lastly, it is necessary to know whether the quoted sentence is being applied in an appropriate sense.

The Lenin quotation, which has been inflated to a postulate of 'marxist–leninist' aesthetics, is applied in an inappropriate manner and contrary to Lenin's meaning. Lenin's demand for party-mindedness was not meant to apply to literature in general but to political writings. Nadezhda Krupskaya, the companion of Lenin's life and struggle, wrote (not later than 3 May 1937) a comment-ary on a project by E. Buzkova to issue a 'Collection of Lenin's articles and statements on literature', objecting to an article en-titled 'The influence of Lenin's articles and statements on literature upon our pedagogical practice' on the grounds that it merely strung together quotations taken out of context and not illustrated by examples. She wrote:

It is necessary to say for what motive an article was written, and in the context of what events. Lenin's articles *On Proletarian Culture, Party Organization and Party Literature* and *The Tasks of the Youth Leagues* do not concern literature as a fine art.

Nadezhda Krupskaya was personally close to Lenin, unlike Stalin and Zhdanov who only arranged quotations from his works. The Soviet journal *Druzhba Narodov* published her significant commentary in its No. IV issue for the year 1960. Not even this commentary, however, should replace an analysis of the situation which gave rise to the relevant article, *Party Organization and Party Literature*.

REVOLUTION AND PARTY

In the autumn of 1905 great masses of people were set into motion in Russia. The revolution was elemental and spontaneous. Who was to lead it to ensure the fall of tsarism and the triumph of a democratic republic?

The Bolsheviks emerged from illegality. Their small militant groups had to unite with the non-party masses and with progressive, for the most part socialist, intellectuals who had been publishing articles in 'Aesopian' language in various journals and newspapers and who represented a hotch-potch of radical and reformist views. Organizations whose experience was small and whose leadership was accidental were formed all over the country.

In an article entitled *The Socialist Party and Non-Party Revolu-tionism* Lenin described the situation as follows:

The revolutionary movement in Russia, which is rapidly spreading to

M

ever new sections of the population, is giving rise to a number of non-party organizations. . . . All sorts of organizations, frequently loose in form, and most original in character, are constantly springing up. They have no hard and fast boundaries, as have parties in Europe. . . . Strict adherence to the party principle is the corollary and the result of a highly developed class struggle. And, vice versa, the interests of the open and widespread class struggle demand the development of the strict party principle.[10]

In a democratic revolution which demanded an end to barbarism, savagery, corruption and other 'Russian' survivals of serfdom, it was unavoidable that the idea of non-party revolutionism should become extremely widespread. 'The urge for a "human", civilized life, the urge to organize in defence of human dignity, for one's rights as man and citizen, takes hold of everyone, unites all classes, vastly outgrows all party bounds. . . .' The non-party principle was

the product – or, if you will, the expression – of the bourgeois character of our revolution. The bourgeoisie cannot help inclining towards the non-party principle, for the absence of parties among those who are fighting for the liberation of a bourgeois society implies that no fresh struggle will arise against the bourgeois society itself . . .

The non-party idea is a bourgeois idea. The party idea is a socialist idea. This thesis, in general and as a whole, is applicable to all bourgeois society. One must, of course, be able to adapt this general truth to particular questions and particular cases; but to forget this truth at a time when the whole of bourgeois society is rising in revolt against feudalism and autocracy means in practice completely to renounce socialist criticism of bourgeois society.[11]

PARTY ORGANIZATION AND PARTY LITERATURE

The Bolshevik party, emerged from illegality, faced the tremendous task of leading the masses engaged in a revolutionary rising towards two goals: a democratic revolution and, at the same time, the preparing of the socialist proletariat for a proletarian revolution.

In order to succeed in this double task, it was necessary to lay great emphasis on the question of the party press and party literature. In an article entitled *Party Organization and Party Literature*, Lenin wrote:

So long as there was a distinction between the illegal and the legal press, the question of the party and non-party press was decided extremely simply and in an extremely false and abnormal way. The entire illegal press was a party press, being published by organizations and run by groups which in one way or another were linked with groups of practical party workers. The entire legal press was non-party – since parties were banned – but it 'gravitated' towards one party or another. Unnatural alliances, strange 'bed-fellows' and false cover-devices were inevitable. . . . An accursed period of Aesopian language, literary bondage, slavish speech, and ideological serfdom![12]

The unfinished, the half-finished semi-revolution, in which there still existed 'the unnatural combination of open, forthright, direct and consistent party spirit with an underground, covert, "diplomatic" and dodgy "legality" ' forced the party to demand that those writers and journalists who were party members should openly declare their allegiance. 'Literature must become part of the common cause of the proletariat, "a cog and a screw" of one single great Social-Democratic mechanism set in motion by the entire politically conscious vanguard of the entire working class.'[13]

It was Lenin's way to use extreme formulations in extreme situations. But he immediately supplied a well-considered commentary to the extreme formulation.

'All comparisons are lame', says a German proverb. So is my comparison of literature with a cog, of a living movement with a mechanism. . . . There is no question that literature is least of all subject to mechanical adjustment or levelling, to the rule of the majority over the minority. There is no question, either, that in this field greater scope must undoubtedly be allowed for personal initiative, individual inclination, thought and fantasy, form and content. All this is undeniable; but all this simply shows that the literary side of the proletarian party cause cannot be mechanically identified with its other sides.

Thus it was no longer a matter of literature in general but of the 'literary part of party activity', of party literature, of political writing. What Lenin demanded was this:

Newspapers must become the organs of the various party organizations, and their writers must by all means become members of these organizations. Publishing and distributing centres, bookshops and reading-rooms, libraries and similar establishments – must all be under party control.

The decisive thing for Lenin was the press, the activity of the publicists belonging to the party. His fundamental demand was: 'We want to establish, and we shall establish, a free press, free not simply from the police, but also from capital, from careerism, and what is more, free from bourgeois-anarchist individualism.' To the anticipated objection: 'You want workmen to decide questions of science, philosophy, or aesthetics by a majority of votes!' he retorted:

Calm yourselves, gentlemen! First of all, we are discussing party literature and its subordination to party control. Everyone is free to write and say whatever he likes, without any restrictions. But every voluntary association (including a party) is also free to expel members who use the name of the party to advocate anti-party views. Freedom of speech and the press must be complete. But then freedom of association must be complete too. I am bound to accord you, in the name of free speech, the full right to shout, lie and write to your heart's content. But you are bound to grant me, in the name of freedom of association, the right to enter into, or withdraw from, association with people advocating this or that view. The party is a voluntary association, which would inevitably break up, first ideologically and then physically, if it did not cleanse itself of people advocating anti-party views. . . . Freedom of thought and freedom of criticism within the party will never make us forget about the freedom of organizing people into those voluntary associations known as parties.[14]

FREEDOM AND VOLUNTARY CHOICE

If I quote Lenin so extensively, I do not mean to elevate the quotation to the status of dogma or to make absolute something that was originally conditioned by a situation, but to oppose the abuse of this question. It is evident from the context that Lenin was not concerned with an aesthetic principle of 'party-mindedness' but with the press and party political literature. The freedom of speech and of the press must be complete. *Only one* freedom is not permitted to the party member: that of exploiting the party press in order to express views directed against the party. The party is founded on voluntary choice. Anyone who has freely chosen to join it cannot take sides against it by the spoken or written word. He is, however, entitled to complete freedom of thought and criticism within the party. To belong to a revolutionary party carries no advantage with it; if it expels a member, that member loses no professional opportunity, no academic career, no possibility of saying and writing what he likes. The principle of freedom and free choice works both ways. At a time when centralization was a revolutionary necessity, it was unavoidable that party literature should be subordinated to the party organization. Yet how much open discussion there was at that time, even in the party press and in party literature! And even then, Lenin defended that literature against 'mechanical adjustment or levelling . . . the rule of the majority over the minority'. Still less would he have dreamed of submitting the whole of literature to such a rule.

After a brilliant polemic against the hypocrisy of the 'absolute freedom' of the writer and artist in the capitalist world, Lenin contrasts the 'hypocritically free' literature of capitalism with the 'really free one that will be *openly* linked to the proletariat'. He is not expressing a demand but a dream when he says:

It will be a free literature, because the idea of socialism and sympathy with the working people, and not greed or careerism, will bring ever new forces to its ranks. It will be a free literature, because it will serve, not some satiated heroine, not the bored 'upper ten thousand' suffering from fatty degeneration, but the millions and tens of millions of working people – the flower of the country, its strength and its future. It will be a free literature, enriching the last word in the revolutionary thought of mankind with the experience and living work of the socialist proletariat, bringing about permanent interaction between the experience of the past (scientific socialism, the completion of the development of socialism from its primitive, utopian forms) and the experience of the present (the present struggle of the worker comrades).

This paragraph, in contrast to all the preceding ones, speaks of literature in general. If we compare the formulation of this passage with works in which Lenin, on the basis of a vast mass of material and of profound reflection, developed his theories, the agitational tone, the pathos of a publicist at the end of a well-considered article betrays that what we have here is not a principle but a wish dream. Yet even from the disputable sentence: 'All Social-Democratic literature must become Party literature!' it is far-fetched to deduce that the whole of literature must become social-democratic or, worse still, that art must put itself under the tutelage of some party authority. Lenin never presumed to prescribe subjects or means of expression to art or literature. He did not admire Mayakovsky with his background of futurism; but the last word, he said, should be left to the revolutionary young. Since so many of them admired this poet, there was doubtless something in him.

AGAINST READY-MADE FORMULAE

Since the thunderers of 'party-mindedness' in art sometimes also invoke the speech which Lenin delivered on 20 October 1920 at the Third Congress of the Communist Youth League, I should like to quote from that speech, too.

If a communist took it into his head to boast about his communism because of the cut-and-dried conclusions he had acquired, without putting in a great deal of serious and hard work and without understanding facts he should examine critically, he would be a deplorable communist indeed . . .

You are faced with the task of construction, and you can accomplish that task only by assimilating all modern knowledge, only if you are able to transform communism from cut-and-dried and memorized formulas, counsels, recipes, prescriptions and programmes into a living reality . . .

It is necessary to abjure both caution and lenience in criticizing the 'arts policy' of certain socialist countries, with their regimented aesthetics, misinterpreted 'party-mindedness' and the bureaucratic dictatorship of amateurishness over the creative imagination, because socialism is incomparably better placed than capitalism to inaugurate a new period in the arts. During the brief 'interglacial periods', literature and art in the Soviet Union, Poland, Hungary and Czechoslovakia have unfrozen with astonishing speed, almost equalling the West in their means of expression and, sometimes, surpassing it in their subject-matter. This is why a socialist can only speak with sorrow and anger of the boots and hooves which, again and again, trample upon the green wheat.

THE AUTHENTIC

Doubting Thomas, who doubted the identity of the man risen from the dead and who laid his finger in the wound, is our contemporary. The news has gone around that not only does propaganda lie, but that art and literature also falsify and deceive. Naïve sceptics who believe appearances to be more credible than what they hide and what the artist tries to reveal, insist on the 'real', the authentic, the documentary: letters, diaries, memoirs, minutes, photographs, live broadcasts. Such material, honestly chosen and arranged, can give many people a notion of the world they live in, can influence, move and activate them, can even become a work of art.

Yet it seems to me that literary or even poetic reportage can give form to the reality of our time only within narrow limits and then only occasionally. Literature and art are searching for a deeper authenticity, for maximum intensity and concentration. (Even accuracy can sometimes be lost in what is too precise, too detailed, too quantitatively diffuse.) What they are searching for is related by its nature and suggestive force to the *myth*.

In order to prevent this concept of the *modern myth* from being misunderstood, it is necessary to rid it of all mystification and other-worldliness – but not of the *mysterious*, for a work of art without mystery, a work which begins and ends with its message, is not permanent or lasting. A work of art is an equation whose unknown factors are incapable of unequivocal solution, and its result is never *Q.E.D.*

Antonio Gramsci saw an early form of the modern myth in Machiavelli's *The Prince*. The fundamental characteristic of that book, he wrote, is 'that it is not a systematic treatment, but a "living" book, in which political ideology and political science are fused in the dramatic form of a "myth"'.[15] The 'mythic' quality consists in the fact that this prince does not exist as a whole person but only in a few traits here and there, scattered, fragmentary; that Machiavelli by no means idealized his 'model' but portrayed him with extraordinary realism, yet in an aura of greatness, of an un-indulgent dream, of the precise imagination. Myth does not moralize. It is a suspended state between 'It is so!' and 'It could be so!' It is the historical possibility projected from the past and the present into the future.

That which is recognizable even in early myths – the desire to overcome chaos, to bring order into the world, to arrange objects and phenomena into classes, groups, mutually related systems – has been intensified to the utmost by the complexity and density of our time and its contradictory nature which threatens to lead to disaster. The urge for new myth formation is, in part, a desire for simplifica-tion.

The most extreme form of simplification is agitational propa-ganda. In it, reality is reduced to a tendentious, party-minded, neatly black-and-white pattern – to a *false myth* (similar to the false consciousness of ideology). The agitational myth recognizes only good and bad men, heroes and monsters, and encourages the masses to believe in an old-fashioned myth, the leader myth of the celebrity becoming a god. It is precisely against this that the *modern* myth in art and literature is protesting. The modern myth reveals the horror of apparently everyday things and people's self-protection and self-assertion against them, the resistance of the weak and the nameless, the maid Grusche and the surveyor K., the servant Clov and the convict Ivan Denisovich. By poetic, not agitational, simplification the modern myth is capable of revealing the invisible reality between an obscured and objectified world of established powers, authorities, and institutions. In contrast to the visible documents and records, these myths are effective through the *authenticity of the invisible*. It is possible that the most careful and accurate description of that reality, overlooking not the smallest detail, could reach through appearances to the truth of the myth; but it would require thousands of pages in order to gather what the myth can concentrate into a single situation; and something diffused over thousands of pages is difficult to appreciate as a whole.

THE MYTH

D.-H. Kahnweiler said of Picasso that the attitude implicit in his art was 'not the subjection of man to destiny, whose course he has not the power to alter, but the affirmation of human greatness which opposes itself to destiny'. This is the attitude characteristic of myth, and we observe that when a mythical hero accepts his destiny (e.g. Oedipus) he is not subjecting himself to it but growing beyond it. In modern myth destiny is not an unchangeable, super-human power but *politics* in the broadest sense of the word, i.e. the struggle for the conservation or the changing of the man-made world of economic, social, or political conditions which, in its total alienation, wears a mask borrowed from the ancient destiny of the past.

I agree substantially with Roger Garaudy when he says:

This creating of myths, this essentially human act of transcending nature and the provisional technical means of mastering it, which is the essential function of art from Homer to Cervantes, from Goethe's *Faust* to Gorky's *Mother*, which questions the world and at the same time challenges the order of the world in the name of that heroic image which man at all times has made of his destiny and his future: this Picasso had the audacity to see in the profound vocation of painting.[16]

A little more cautiously, I would add that although I see the creating of myths as an essential function of art, I do not regard it as the only or essential one. For example, art can carry out one of its functions – that of criticizing the *status quo* – by the use of myth, but equally well by the use of anti-myth. (*The Marriage of Figaro*, *Madame Bovary*, and *Anna Karenina* are all, it seems to me, entirely devoid of any mythic character.) Morever, since the concept of the myth is currently much bandied about, it is important to distinguish the *secularized* myths of our time from the earliest myths, which originated somewhere between magic and religion. The distinction can enable us to recognize the essential thing which the two kinds of myth have in common, and to avoid confusing the true myths of our time with the pseudo-myths of metaphysical mystifiers.

The origin of the myth lies in some shattering experience – an earthquake, a flood, a volcanic eruption, an epidemic, a fire, an outbreak of hysteria, an intoxicated vision, a dream or an historical event.

'A phenomenon such as that which we have experienced,' wrote Emmanuel Kant about the French revolution in 1798, '*is never forgotten. It revealed a capacity in human nature that no politician, arguing from the earlier course of events, could have guessed.*'[17] Not only in the early history of mankind but also in periods of advanced social development there have been and still are phenomena which *are never forgotten* and which continue to exercise a shattering effect beyond the clever guesswork of politicians. These phenomena lend themselves to the forming of myths. It was not only William Blake who attempted to transform the American War of Liberation and the French revolution into mythical works of the imagination.

This hypothesis of the origin of myth does not contradict the view that the myth is a comment on ritual actions. Some believe that the spoken word came into being simultaneously with the magic rite; others believe that it was added at a later stage when the rite, which represented some natural or working process, was no longer self-explanatory because memory, having become creative, now began to make the demands of imagination. Yet others believe man came to feel less directly about natural events (as a result of division of labour, class separation, increasing individuation) and the ancient rites acquired a new content from historical events. Every explanation which claims to be the only one has an element of arbitrariness about it. Systematization requires reflection and a readiness to accept correction; yet the refusal to recognize any common factor ends in trivial statistics, a well-ordered but uninterpreted mass of 'facts'. Without the courage of imagination there is neither art nor science.

Three elements are combined in the myth: it speaks of *nature* in grand images; it tells the *story of mankind* through unforgettable situations and figures; nature and history serve as a *parable* of the life of man, of birth and growth, conflict and death. In myth, everything becomes a symbol. Unlike allegory, nothing dead or rigid enters the circle of living symbols each enhancing the significance of the other. In this interweaving of nature, history and human existence, in its profoundly *symbolic* character, lies the power of the myth; it is this which makes the myth indispensable.

Nature becomes man's experience of the world: his identity with it and his divorce from it, the felt unity and the division into contrasts: light and dark, day and night, man and woman, spring and harvest, the living and the dead, the upper and the lower. Has he not torn to pieces what was once a whole (as the Titans did to Dionysus)? Has not his labour led to his ambivalent relationship with nature: the hope that nature will prove merciful and the fear that it will avenge itself upon him for the damage he has done it with his weapons and tools – for the offence of Prometheus?

In the symbol of the original unity, Erebus, the 'tail-eater', the snake biting its own tail – rounded and safe, the embryo in the mother's womb, man in community with all living things – there is an ambivalence not to be overlooked. The original snake, the original mother, the unity in the flesh, is simultaneously the all-generating and the all-consuming. The womb, which swallows up the penis, gives birth to the new being and swallows it up again into darkness. The phallus of the 'spring youths' is offered to the 'Great Mother': she is the life principle, but at the same time she is castration; she is conception and at the same time emasculation. She is fertility and death. In her, eating and being eaten merge into one. The natural law according to which life requires killing takes on a new and disturbing meaning.

In the *Upanishads* it is said that the world was made to feed the Godhead.

Everything, whatever he created, he decided to devour; because he devours all (*ad*), therefore he is called infinity (*aditi*). He who thus understands the nature of the Aditi shall become a devourer of the universe; to him the universe shall serve as food.

At the side of Osiris holding judgement sits the monster Amam ('Devourer', 'eater of man'), made up of a crocodile, a hippopotamus and a lion; a variation of the Great Mother, he devours the heart of a dead man if the scales prove it to be too light.

Hundreds of myths speak of this 'natural condition' of man, this being-embedded in a totality, mother's womb or protective cave. Nature is feminine.

Woman is the given fact, man is only the product of that fact. He belongs to visible but ever-changing creation; he exists only in mortal form. Woman alone is present from the beginning, given, unchangeable; man is the result of *becoming*, and therefore is doomed to death. . . .[18]

A. P. Elkin, the investigator of Australian totemism, 'opposes', as Claude Lévi-Strauss says,

the totemism of matrilineal clans to that of patrilineal clans, and with good reason. In the former case, the totem is 'flesh', in the latter it is 'dream'; organic and material in one case, therefore, spiritual and incorporeal in the other. Morever, matrilineal totemism attests the diachronic and biological continuity of the clan, it is the flesh and blood perpetuated from generation to generation by the women of the lineage; while patrilineal totemism expresses 'the local solidarity of the horde', i.e. an external link, no longer an internal one, territorial and no longer biological, which synchronically – no longer diachronically – unites the members of the clan.[19]

THE NATURE MYTH

The development of man's imagination from identifying a person with other beings (especially with animals) to a partial, temporary sense of unity with a dead man or with a divinity – a unity regulated by rites; from the discovery that similar and contrasting things are directly related to himself to substituting a symbolic action for a real one; from the observation of real or fictitious connections to the creation of a store of productive memory from which myth, poetry and art eventually emerge – this development cannot be traced with scientific precision, and much must inevitably remain hypothetical. What is undeniable, however, is the fact that social development has modified, enriched and deepened the myth – that the historical element has more and more taken over the natural element.

The original nature myth, whose form is bare and artless, relates what is in reality already a conflict between men, clans and tribes as a conflict between totem animals. Thus Radcliffe-Brown in his study *The Comparative Method in Social Anthropology*[20] tells of a dispute between an eaglehawk and a crow, which were the totems of the two moieties of a dualistic Australian clan organization. In similar myths, the eagle and the raven, the coyote and the wild-cat are opposed to one another as totem animals of dualistic clan organizations. Whether the totem animal was at first a particularly desired or particularly dangerous one, whether the social group sees their ancestor – their unity – in the flesh or in a complex re-lationship, whether the totem is identical with the tribe or only its emblem – the struggle for food remains the decisive element in most of these rather meagre myths.

The imagination humanizes nature; it incorporates it in society. But by making the work process magical, it also encourages the hope of mastering and appeasing nature, of reconciling nature with the injuries done to it with weapons and tools, or of outwitting nature with deceptive words or acts.

The Ainus, before they slaughtered a bear, expressed love and veneration for it and promised it resurrection and bliss. The Djagga Negroes, before they fell a tree, try to convince it that its wedding is being prepared, and as soon as the axe is laid upon it the work leader says: 'O departing child of man, we are not felling you but marrying you! And we are not marrying you with violence and tyranny but with loving kindness!' As soon as the tree has been felled, its owner approaches it as though by chance and breaks out in lamentations: 'You have robbed me of my sister!' According to certain Malayan tribes, the crocodile drags its prey into the water and drowns it, but instead of devouring it there and then pretends to have come across it by chance and calls upon sun, moon and stars as witnesses: 'It was not I who killed you, it was the water which killed you.'[21] In all these cases the imagination is working not only as a preserver of an all-embracing unity, but also as a wily conjuror convinced of the power of illusion.

This power of illusion has become an aid to human development. By way of analogies, the imagination acquires the power of inventing substitutes. Just as the tree is addressed as a sister, so it can represent a sister. In a suspended state between belief and deception, between the identity sensed in the analogy and the distancing *principium individuationis*, the imagination discovers the *symbol*. Imagination teaches man to be extravagant in the as yet unaccomplished and moderate in his actions. The symbols transcend the past, which is no longer appropriate to man's new social condition.

Lévy-Bruhl tells of a case of blood vengeance reduced to a purely symbolic act. The attack of the avengers takes place, but what really happens is not known. No one is killed and no one asks any questions. 'The affair is over, the act has sufficed. . . . The equilibrium of the social group has been re-established . . . by mystical compensation for the wrong it has sufficed.'[22] A death is considered unnatural, suggesting the intervention of some outside force, an act of violence, brought on, not by nature, but by man, through direct or magic action. The balance can only be restored by expiation; expiation is achieved by blood vengeance, by agreement between the tribes or by a rite, a spectacle, the play of appearances.

By the play of appearances, the imagination attempts to deceive not only death but, above all, the dead person. The dead are unpredictable, unaccountable and aggressive. They are afraid of being cheated of their rights, and they do not love the living. Whether they continue to belong to the tribe as invisible beings, vanishing only very gradually, or whether they return to the animal kingdom from which their ancestors once came, they retain the power of rising up again from the deepest abysses and untrodden forests, in the shape of murderous beasts. So long as they remain on earth, they are highly dangerous. The custom of making up the faces of the dead so that they may appear as glamorous, as alive as possible while they lie on their bier, reaches back into the earliest times. The imagination of the true 'primitives' was, however, incomparably more inventive than that of civilized man.

THE FALL OF THE GREAT MOTHER

George Thomson points out that myths developed with the

development of production. Before the discovery of the potter's wheel, it took many days to make a jar, and so this was housework, woman's work. After the invention of the wheel, pottery was practised by men, at first for their own village, later for the market. With this displacement of the woman from the old sphere of labour, the myth of the jar-mother also changed. 'Pandora, the woman in the form of a jar, became a woman *with* a jar, the oppressed woman of patriarchal society, seductive, deceitful, the root of evil, and her jar was filled with curses.'[23]

In the beginning was the night, repose within the mother, the rounded circle of the snake that bites its own tail. The myth of creation, the separation between light and dark, is at the same time the myth of the *birth of man*, biologically and historically. At first the night is goodness, comfort, motherliness: then comes the *victory of day*, the domination of the masculine over the feminine. The Great Mother is overthrown, the division of labour between man and woman ceases to be a natural one and becomes an enforced one. The hero representing the new social order has to vanquish the snake, the dragon, the Great Mother and her brother, the old king. (Malinowski has shown that many primitive peoples do not desire to kill the father but only the mother's brother, who represents discipline, authority and executive power within the family.) The victorious hero revalues his values. The Great Mother becomes the principle of evil, a witch, a magician; the snake becomes an object of horror which must be destroyed. In many heretical movements which protested against what they saw to be the evil world of their time and dreamed of putting a world of their own making in its place, the snake was rehabilitated as the principle of goodness fighting against the eagle of power. In Romanticism, rebelling against the puritanical father-god whose power is based on money and the machine, the snake also regains its old meaning (Blake, Shelley, E. T. A. Hoffmann).

The conqueror of the mother-snake, the dragon-killer, takes the hidden treasure of the matriarchy and often also the virgin who has been the dragon's prisoner. (The vagueness of the distinction between the Great Mother and the virgin has been frequently remarked.) The virgin thus liberated from the matriarchy becomes the liberator's property. In certain myths she betrays the ancient powers, the Erebus, to her liberator who is a state founder (Jason and Medea). But her liberation from bonds, flames or a hedge of thorns is also her humiliation; she is reduced to the status of a man's chattel. Together with her, the liberator liberates himself from endogamous, maternal rule; but the bonds he destroys once also protected him. Without such dualism there would be no development. The myth prefigures the dialectic of history.

Apollo is the essential god of light who conquers the night. He subdues the avenging goddesses of matriarchy and liberates Orestes whom they pursue. He kills the dragon Python and seizes the Great Mother's oracle shrine at Delphi. He flays the satyr Marsyas who worships the Great Mother Cybele. He subdues the wild muses and settles them on Mount Helicon near Delphi to instruct them in moderation and chastity. As a result the dream, instead of ecstasy, becomes the source of prophecy and art. The unity of flesh guaranteed by the Great Mother is destroyed by the *principium individuationis*. Unlike ecstasy, the dream is an *individual* experience and an appeal to the individual.

Very early in their history, people dimly realized that dreams are memories, a '*déjà vu*': that the imagination is the recognition of an invisible reality that was once seen. W. Colenso reports of the Maoris in New Zealand: 'They believe in the reality of dreams. . . . They are convinced that dreams are memories of what they have seen in the Reinga (the invisible country of the dead). . . .' In the *Relations des Jésuites de la Nouvelle-France* it is stated that the dream is the 'absolute ruler' of the Indians. 'If a chief commands one thing and a dream another, then the chief can shout until his head bursts, the dream will be obeyed first.' The Hurons and Iroquois follow the command of dreams with extreme punctiliousness. 'All their huts are filled with their dreams.' Fr. de Charlevoix reported of the Iroquois in 1744 that every dream must be fulfilled whatever the price

because every dream is a wish of the soul and if that wish is not fulfilled one dies. . . . They believe that our soul manifests these natural wishes through dreams as well as through words; it is therefore satisfied if these wishes are fulfilled. If, on the other hand, one does not give the soul what it demands, it becomes angry; not only does it not grant the body the well-being and happiness that it would like to have, but often it actually turns against the body and becomes the cause of diseases and even of death.

Thus the dream is regarded as a language whose origins lie deeper than those of the word – in instincts and desires suppressed by daylight and taboo, morality and law: desires which recall a 'natural' state older than patriarchal society. Thus dreams mediate ambiguously between the 'rule of the Mother' destroyed by the division of labour and private ownership, and the reality principle of a new society. In Apollo, too, there is the same ambiguity: with his hermaphrodite's features he is a little reminiscent of the chorus leaders and priests who continued to wear women's clothes for the sake of tradition. His victory over Python, the mother-snake – who lives on as Pythia, the ecstatically prophetic virgin – is also ambiguous.

We read in Robert Graves of the historically conditioned transformations of myth:

Python is said to have been sent against Leto by Hera, who had borne him parthenogenetically, to spite Zeus (Homeric Hymn to Apollo, 305); and Apollo, after killing Python (and presumably also his mate Delphyne), seized the oracular shrine of Mother Earth at Delphi – for Hera was Mother Earth, or Delphyne, in her prophetic aspect. It seems that certain Northern Hellenes, allied with Thraco-Libyans, invaded Central Greece and the Peloponnese, where they were opposed by the pre-Hellenic worshippers of the Earth-goddess, but captured her chief oracular shrines. At Delphi, they destroyed the sacred oracular serpent . . . and took over the oracle in the name of their god Apollo Smintheus. Smintheus, originally an oracular ghost who took the form of a mouse, had been made a god of healing and destruction; but they now agreed to identify him with Apollo, the Hyperborean Horus, worshipped by their allies. To placate local opinion at Delphi, regular funeral games were instituted in honour of the dead hero Python, and his priestess was retained in office.[24]

Thus Apollo, like his antagonist Dionysus, preserved some traits of the pre-patriarchal age. Pythia, intoxicated by the exhalations of the earth, utters confused prophecies. An aristocratic priesthood interprets her stammered utterances, imposes form and measure upon her prophecies – ambiguously, yet generally in such a way that the interpretation corresponds to the interests of the conservative landed nobility. As social development proceeds, Apollo becomes more and more the representative of the new order.

Friedrich Schlegel and Friedrich Nietzsche contrasted the Apollonian and the Dionysian – the individual dream and the intoxicated state of *being beside oneself* – without recognizing that in the

Dionysian myth it is the Great Mother, the ancient night, the vanquished snake, the mass of the dispossessed and disenfranchized, who revolt against the rulers and their gods.

The rulers modify or change the myths. Dionysus was torn to pieces by the Titans. Like the Babylonians, the Orphics taught that man was descended from the blood of Dionysus. Yet Hesiod, the great authority on myths, is silent about this. To the proud families of the landed nobility, the suggestion that they might be descended from the blood of the rough god of the peasants was altogether too vulgar. They were descended from the gods. It was only the mob that was descended from the blood of the dismembered Dionysus![25]

In the myths of the rulers, the *principium individuationis* towers above the primitive collective. The mythical hero detaches himself as a personality from the community (although he still represents it). In him, the community must recognize itself: the ancient myth is preserved but transformed. The memorable, timeless quality of mythical figures may be due precisely to this precarious balance between the collective and the personality, between nature and history. The individual hero, who represents the community, generally embodies only one exemplary or sinister characteristic (strength, beauty, courage, power-seeking, *hubris*, wisdom, cunning, etc.). Although they originate in an historical period, all these light-bringers, dragon-killers, fratricides, seafarers and conquerors, men pursued by destiny and men returning home after long voyages, seem timeless; fundamental human situations and characters recur again and again in a multitude of concrete forms; and this effect of timelessness is due to the simplicity, transparency and directness of the conditions in which they are portrayed. Again and again Cain murders Abel, Prometheus is chained to the rock, cunning Odysseus is shipwrecked and Antigone resists. The conflicts are not obscured by objectification, by object relationships removed from sensory perception, but are acted out directly between gods, heroes or monsters as persons and personified natural forces. And, at the same time, they signify (as a legacy of the unity of all existing things which is the hypothesis of magic) the struggle between light and darkness, fertilization and destruction, death and rebirth.

Thus myths tell the story of man in a sequence of images and 'symbolic' situations. Myths are not 'eternal images' which man

N

projects into his past. The music of the myths is the *true history of man*, heightened and intensified. The myth is not 'being as verbal content', nor the 'processing of being'[26]; it is the experience of reality. Manifold images, capable of many interpretations, images whose origin lies in memory and experience, encircle reality, become concentrated into symbols and, finally, into clearly defined signs of cognition.

MYTH, LOGOS, EPOS

In his work *Form and Being*,[27] Walter F. Otto points out that there are three words for 'the word' in the Greek language. *Epos* is the narrator's word; the present is reported, conjured up in images, without being present. Between the Homerid and his epic narration there is *distance*. Sometimes it may happen that the singer begins to improvise, and it is precisely this which indicates that he is entitled to introduce changes, i.e. is not bound by the sacredness of his matter. *Logos* is the word as the fruit of reflection, 'excellently suited to express that which is thought-out, consequent, rational'. *Mythos* signifies the 'word' in an entirely different sense, namely an objective one. Here it is not something considered, calculated or rational that is meant, but the real and actual. '*Mythos* is the thing itself, "history", for that is how we describe the authenticity of past events and the account given thereof.' Myth is 'the word as direct testimony of that which has been, is and will be, as self-revelation of being in the time-honoured sense which makes no distinction between word and being'.

Mythos, then, is the *magic* word, unified with that which it stands for, the truly poetic word: it is neither recitation like *epos* nor reflection like *logos*. *Mythos* is, by its very nature, poetry: the giving of poetic form to what really happened and is happening now. It represents historical matter, not as something irrevocably past but as the present anticipating the future. Mythos, created by certain historical conditions and having undergone changes together with these, transcends the 'then' and 'now', the 'here' and 'there', and preserves the core of ever-recurring conflicts, situations, and decisions. *Mythos* is the 'word' of reality emerging in pure form, not disguised or disfigured by the accidental: reality as the *essential*.

In *mythos* man is not yet alienated from himself. He is present, both actively and passively; he engages powerful beings, gods and demons, in battle, and his nature is akin to theirs; if he is defeated, he is capable of greatness and dignity in his fall. The divine is not really situated in the beyond: it assumes many forms in order to visit man on earth, and man in turn is not prohibited from dining, sleeping, and fighting with the Olympians, nor from raising himself to their stature by his actions and his suffering. It is only when *mythos* solidifies into dogma, when the archaic rites no longer tolerate many commentaries but only one, that the rule of religion establishes man's alienation from himself. Yet even in religion *mythos* is the mediator, the secularizer of the divine. The divinity descends to earth in order to share man's joys and sorrows. The myth of the Son of Man, the suffering, dying, resurrected God, is moving because man feels that it is about himself: he is the prisoner of his alienation: and he is being appealed to to unite with his fellowmen, to form a community in which *mythos* and *logos* fuse into one.

The 'true' myth, says Walter F. Otto, is indissolubly linked with cult and rite. Indeed this has been the case in the past: but need it always be so? In Greece, the poet rose above the priest, and myth separated itself from the religious rite. Yet when myth takes the form of literature, must it not be *believed* in order to retain its evocative powers? More than that: must the myth, its situations and characters, already exist or can the poet invent them? He cannot invent them out of nothing – but is anything in literature invented out of nothing? Does not the stuff of literature derive from memory as well as from the events of its time, endowing these with the dignity of myth? There have been and still are many 'false' myths, from Racine to Wagner and Jean Anouilh; but Don Juan and Faust have become *true* myths, and Blake, Hölderlin, Melville, Kafka, Brecht, Faulkner, Beckett, Genet are myth-making writers who yet have nothing to do with religious cult and rite. If, as we have assumed, the origin of myth lies in great shattering events in the history of mankind, how should it be alien to our own time, this time of violent convulsions and extreme alternatives: the end or the renewal of mankind? annihilation or liberation? powerlessness or responsibility? man or machine? All conditions are present for secularized myth not bound up with religion or rite.

SECULARIZATION OF INFINITY

Poetry cannot exist without myth.

Necessary as it was for the *logos* of the Enlightenment to defeat a decaying mythology, the Romantics were right – although their right instinct was obscured by a confused attempt to inject an artificial new life into myth – when they felt that with the loss of the myth the dimension of infinity also was in danger of being lost. This was the beginning of the arduous effort to secularize myth and infinity.

What was no longer believed, or believed only under duress, was retained as a cypher, a sign pointing beyond the here-and-now. Great Romantic works took up the myths of Lucifer, Prometheus, Faust, Don Juan – those myths which gave expression to a dissatisfaction with the momentary and a hunger for infinity, as the revolt of the individual. Balzac in his later novels, Stendhal and other novelists critical of their society renounced mythological figures; yet the mythical was invisibly present in the apotheosis of 'pure', unquenchable passion. The Duchess of Sanseverina and Vautrin are mythical characters. But novels such as *Madame Bovary* and *Bouvard and Pécuchet* expressed a direct refusal to incorporate the faintest echo of the mythical. The decision to be only critical has enriched literature by an experience it could not have done without; yet Flaubert himself groaned under the burden he had shouldered.

The exponents of naturalism were at first convinced that precise and critical representation of the here-and-now, without the dimension of infinity, would prove the myth to be useless. Yet it was naturalism which, threatened with premature old age, retreated into symbolism and into legends and fairy stories of all kinds. Meanwhile, myth would allow itself neither to be domesticated as family drama, nor reduced to psychological research, nor revived through neurosis. The shudder, the nervous excitement, the aesthetic pleasure obtained as a result of such experiments was the breath of decay, not of infinity. What Goethe achieved in *Faust* – the raising of man to infinity – could succeed only because the ancient divine myths had been transformed into the *new myth of humanity*.

Über allen Gipfeln
Ist Ruh',
In allen Wipfeln
Spürest du
Kaum einen Hauch;
Die Vögelein schlafen im Walde.
Warte nur, balde
Ruhest du auch.

(Over all summits there is silence, in all the treetops you feel scarcely a breath; the little birds are asleep in the wood. Only wait, soon you shall rest too.)

In the poem *Wanderer's Night Song* Goethe expressed the new relationship of man to infinity more intensely than any of his contemporaries. Within the apparent directness of the new feeling for nature, within the restless 'I' weary of wandering and the silence above the summits, the new social situation lies concealed. Lonely individuality escapes from society, elevates its loneliness to a cosmic experience and by so doing elevates itself above the futility of 'wandering' to a state of composed melancholy. That which the German Romantics later called 'romantic irony' – fragments transcended by the whole, infinity transcending the passing moment which yet is so convinced of its own importance – Goethe anticipated sublimely. Theodor W. Adorno says in a remarkable essay:

In face of nature in repose, with every trace of man wiped out, the subject becomes aware of its own nothingness. Imperceptibly, soundlessly, irony touches the comfort of the poem: the seconds which precede the delight of sleep are the same that separate our short life from death. This sublime irony degenerated, after Goethe, into a vulgar one.[28]

Or into a fearful one which 'becomes aware of its own nothingness' with horror and feels the finite to be a ghastly farce. Goethe drove out such fears with beauty.

A century later Rimbaud wrote a poem which is more violent and more desperate, yet has something in common with Goethe's:

Elle est retrouvée.
Quoi? – L'Eternité.
C'est la mer allée
Avec le soleil.

Ame sentinelle,
Murmurons l'aveu
De la nuit si nulle
Et du jour en feu.

Des humains suffrages,
Des communs élans
Là tu te dégages
Et voles selon.

Puisque de vous seules,
Braises de satin,
Le Devoir s'exhale
Sans qu'on dise: enfin.

Là pas d'espérance,
Nul orietur.
Science avec patience,
Le supplice est sûr.

Elle est retrouvée.
Quoi? – L'Eternité.
C'est la mer allée
Avec le soleil.

(It has been found again. What? – Eternity. It is the sea fled away with the sun.

Sentinel soul, let us whisper the confession of the night full of nothingness and the day on fire.

From human approbation, from common urges, you free yourself here and fly off as you may.

Since from you alone, satiny embers, Duty breathes without anyone saying: at last.

Here is no hope, no *orietur*. Knowledge with fortitude, torture is certain.

It has been found again. What? – Eternity. It is the sea fled away with the sun.)[29]

The alienation from the self, which Goethe already sensed, is expressed without Goethe's power of reconciliation but in its most intense form. There is no longer any hope; only torment is certain. The comfort of Goethe's 'Only wait: soon . . .' has become the breaking of all bonds with the 'common urges', flying off anywhere, nowhere. The weightlessness, the serenity of the first verses, spoken in the reedy voice of an angel or a child, the astonishment at the unbelievable return of eternity, reveals a contrast incomparably more painful than the Wanderer's. What is only hinted at in the Night Song is here expressed: the night is full of nothingness, the day full of fire, and Duty comes from you alone. The dissonance is too great to allow of conciliation. Eternity is, simply, the 'other' which suddenly overpowers despairing man and takes him back into the sea and the sun.

MYTH AND MODEL

The secularization of infinity, the 'oceanic sense' without religious dogmatism, makes secularized myth possible.

Science produces models of a possible reality. 'A picture contains the possibility of the situation that it represents.'[30] Every phenomenon is reduced to its structure. The model of a crystal or an atom does not represent the phenomenon but the structure which is common to groups of objects. Models of crystals or atoms serve to demonstrate the possible structures of crystals and atoms.

By adopting this scientific method, art – which shakes our whole being to its foundations when it is the experience of a latent reality – has acquired the ability to create myths in our time. What it shows as a model is neither an individual case nor idealized reality, but the possible structure of a situation. The model has the exemplary quality of myth, free from mystification and moralizing intent. In the model, the literature of our time can combine *logos* and *mythos*, Enlightenment and Romanticism, the exemplary and the poetic.

Yet this – it may be objected – means the impoverishment of the arts; art needs the superfluous in order to give plenitude to the essential. The objection is a weighty one, for art is indeed a state of plenitude. Yet in our time the accumulation of external objects is so enormous, existence so obscured, so walled in by object relationships, that literature and art face new difficulties. A car dump is not a symbol of plenitude. It is necessary to shake off the accumulated objects, to aim for spareness, austerity, concentration, in order to achieve artistic mastery in our time.

The work of art as model refers to objects and at the same time endeavours to *express* them, so that the word may become the object itself. It wants to make what has happened so resonant that it happens once more: then we will not only experience it but actually recognize it as present. The work of art as model reveals the structure of a situation, a way of behaving, without claiming that it must be thus but merely as a possibility which allows other possibilities to be conceived of. What has just taken shape is immediately put in doubt. An appeal is made to the reader's intelligence.

What makes the modern myth – which is essential for literature – possible is its synthesis with the *logos*. The chorus of mythic tragedy, that voice of collective memory, becomes the reader's emotional and intellectual awareness of his own self.

The imagination gained nothing by the 'destruction of reason' (Georg Lukács): on the contrary, it too fell victim to destruction. The imagination does not lisp, it speaks; its word is *mythos*; it is not concerned with a return into the abyss of the past, but with memory which speaks of the future. The imagination needs its alliance with reason.

The dimension of infinity which is necessary for literature as an art is no longer a divine one, with its alienation and dogmatism; it belongs, as Hölderlin saw it, to the *whole*, 'and one thing connects with another, compensates for the lack of the other – the other, which it needs in order to be wholly that which it can be as a separate thing. . . . For man is a god as soon as he is man.'

Man, as he becomes aware of his alienation, does not desire merely to be a spectator of himself and a witness of his own works: as he searches, he longs to make his contribution to the myth of mankind.

TO START AGAIN FROM ZERO?

Jean-Paul Sartre said of Alberto Giacometti that 'a glance at [his] antediluvian face reveals his arrogance and his desire to place himself at the beginning of time'.[31] A contemporary of the cave painters of Lascaux and Altamira? What matters is that Giacometti was not their contemporary but tried to be one, in the midst of the twentieth century, reflecting upon the traditions of the sculpture of three millennia, almost despairing of them, questioning, with a high degree of consciousness, what art had been and what it had become: what matters is that he was not unconsciously groping in the past.

We have come to an end in art, and not in art only; we face an abyss over which we must leap if we do not want to turn back, to retrace the same road step by step, falling into mere imitation or repeating the same experiments in ever-contracting circles. But if we leap, where shall we land? In the depths – apparently – where art began.

It is therefore necessary to start again from zero. After three thousand years the task of Giacometti and of contemporary sculptors is not to glut galleries with new works but to prove that sculpture is possible. . . . If the undertaking should end in failure, it would be impossible to decide under even the most favourable circumstances whether this meant the failure of the sculptor or of sculpture; others would come along, and they would have to begin anew. But involved here is more than an infinite progression; there is a fixed boundary to be reached, a unique problem to be resolved: how to make a man out of stone without petrifying him.[32]

This specific problem of sculpture contains within it a general one: to make a man out of stone without petrifying him, to transform the living into a work of art without its slipping away into the beyond, escaping from the process of *becoming* into pure *being*, a complete, perfect, final thing.

'To start again from zero.' To leap from the height of three millennia into the depth of prehistory, into a state when art was not yet fully art, when it was still magic, practised in order to humanize nature, put a spell of fertility or death on plants, animals and men. It is not the naïve or incompetent artists who try to break away from civilization, to immerse themselves in the archaic, to start again at zero, but those most familiar with the problems of art, the most thoughtful and most conscious. This leap into the abyss in order to cross the abyss is a little reminiscent of the blinded Gloucester's leap in *King Lear*, when Gloucester thinks he is jumping to his death over the edge of the cliff, yet only falls where he has stood. His imagination makes him experience the fall in such a way that his survival seems to him an omen and a miracle. Edgar comments upon the event:

> *And yet I know not how conceit may rob*
> *The treasury of life when life itself*
> *Yields to the theft; had he been where he thought*
> *By this had thought been past . . .*

The leap is made. The artist belongs to our epoch with all its works, experiences and the traditions of three millennia. Yet he is opposed to these, and this opposition is not a beginning *ex nihilo* but a continuation which refuses to imitate the past, a revolution which refuses to deny the past as though it had never existed: for had he been where he thought, by this had thought been past.

THE PROBLEM OF DISTANCE

In the development of art, as in social development generally, there are periods of gradual change and others of sudden change, of violent breaks with the past. Everything suggests that we are living in one of these latter periods, where there are problems peculiar to the visual arts, music, literature, the theatre, etc., but also a wider problem common to them all. Although art is a social phenomenon, it would be a simplification incommensurate with the scale of that common problem to describe traditional art, which in its motives, methods and means of expression is no longer adequate to our time, as 'bourgeois' art, and the new art, which is developing in so many different ways as the result of so many contradictions and experiments, as 'socialist', 'collective' or 'activist' art. It is not only the bourgeois period which is ending but a whole development in the arts in which the distance between the work and the public (the latter being no longer a community but a conglomerate) has become too great. Art without distance is inconceivable. There is the external distance necessary, for example, for looking at a visual work: but there is also a kind of inner distance necessary for all types of art without exception. Without distance there can be no art: art would become one with life, and even then a new distance would have to be created to enable life to be 'beside' itself, to become aware of itself, to reflect, recognize and enjoy its own nature.

A child 'shows off' in order to gain importance, to get his capacities noticed, to *make himself* by producing an effect on others, to create his own pleasure by heightening his existence. The dances of prehistoric man had a similar, though deeper, meaning; they not only 'imitated' battle, courtship or work in order to acquire magic power through mimesis, but helped the dancers to 'produce themselves' by rhythmic unrestraint, by the experience of their own bodies and the common rhythm of the collective. It was a work process freed from the objective product; the usefulness of the process lay not in the product but in the joy of being man.

Christopher Caudwell wrote in his pioneering work *Illusion and Reality*:

The body has certain natural periodicities (pulse-beat, breath, etc.) which form a dividing line between the causal character of outside events and the ego. . . . Any rhythmical movement or action therefore exalts the physiological component of our conscious field at the expense of the environmental.

Rhythm produces an emotional introversion as opposed to a rational one (e.g. that achieved by concentration upon a mathematical problem). In dance, song and music man puts himself into a condition in which he plays with the outside world, forming and transforming it. Yet he does so

according to the laws of the social ego, and he does this because in the dance and the chant, while withdrawing from the world of external reality, he maintains touch with the subjective world of his fellows by moving his body in rhythm, by repeating the same words in unison, by weaving between them an emotional network of common feelings . . .[33]

Thus the collective self strengthens and intensifies itself. The inner rhythm of the body is fused with the rhythm of the work process. Within the collective rhythmically uniting itself with the external world, work, too, becomes a work of art, whose producer is simultaneously its product, creator and enjoyer.

The unity of the tribe was destroyed by increasing division of labour, the division into rulers and ruled, into those who served and those who enjoyed. In art, too, the more it separated itself from magic, the division of labour became predominant, not only as between different forms of art but above all between those who produced art and those who passively received it and 'aesthetically' enjoyed it. We read in Georg Lukács: 'Only when human beings are confronted with an – evocatively mimetic – work which is pure reflection and not at all reality, is there a clean division between creative and receptive subjectivity.'[34] The mimetic work confronts the receptive spectator

not only as a closed system, but as something unchangeably given, something existing independently from his consciousness, which he can reject as a whole or in part, but in the process of which he cannot

intervene. . . . Thus the receptive spectator concentrates entirely . . .
upon the contemplation of the work as an entity . . .[35]

The revolt of modern art (more precisely, of one of the principal
movements in modern art) is directed precisely against this
'clean division between creative and receptive subjectivity', against
the work of art as a 'closed system' allowing only contemplation
and never the spectator's active participation. This revolt contains
many infantile, exaggerated, hysterical elements, such as 'Happenings' and similar attempts to induce an audience to direct
participation, to provoke into spontaneous being a work of art un-
separated from life. Yet in the early phases of the break with
tradition such exaggeration is unavoidable, and even indispensable.

The separation has not fully affected the dance. Only in the *art
dance* – dance performed for others, for kings and their courts,
culminating in that quintessence of the courtly which is the ballet –
were the 'receptive' and 'creative' roles separated from each other;
in folk dancing and social dancing those who execute the dance
are at the same time those who enjoy it; there is still 'aesthetic'
enjoyment, but permeated with the elemental consciousness of one's
own corporeal nature. This special characteristic of the dance is
denied to other forms of art; yet in all the arts we see a return to
the idea of participation, with a less clean division between creative
and receptive. An activation of the spectator's imagination and
reason, so that, by way of art, he takes part in the transformation
of the object and of the world at large – this is an aim in all the
arts now. Bertolt Brecht wanted his spectators to be 'productively
disposed even after the spectacle is over'.[36] Sculptors like Giacometti, Zadkine and Neizvestny likewise want their spectators to be
'productively disposed'. This is achieved above all by the art work
no longer being presented as a 'closed system', as something 'unchangeably given', but as something still in the process of becoming, unfinished and incomplete. 'The characteristic of the work of
art is an incompleteness which is the crown of all perfection.'[37] I
am convinced that the best artists of our time would agree with
this proposition.

Giacometti, in a conversation with his publisher Peter Schifferli,
said that the difficulty of describing the artistic work process con-
sisted in the fact that 'what one is searching for is itself engaged in
a search while one is searching it; that one attempts in vain to
catch up with reality and capture it, because reality itself is always

developing and changing. . . .' Those who sat for Giacometti's portraits used to say that 'it was tiring because you had to work too . . .'.

We find this incompleteness, not merely intended but skilfully attained, in Giacometti's delicate works ('figures made of the dust of space', as Sartre has described them). They have the transparency and fragility of human beings as yet barely in existence, still fragmentarily sketching themselves, imaginary in their transience. We find the same poetic incompleteness in Zadkine's powerful Rotterdam Memorial, rising from debris and destruction, a synthesis of mutually opposing movements, the coincidence of collapse and advance; and the same in many sculptures by Neizvestny as the unresolved metamorphosis, the creation of a double being resulting from the interaction of man and machine, of hard, metallic, structural elements and soft, living, human ones. With a sculptor's means of expression, Neizvestny poses the question: will the machine conquer man or man humanize the machine? Will the work become its creator's prison or the creator become the master of his work?

'YOU MUST CHANGE YOUR LIFE!'

It is precisely through this incompleteness, in which the work of art is not yet petrified into Being but is still engaged in Becoming, that the spectator is drawn into the creative process. Within this process, the artist is changing not only his subject but also himself, and his aim (conscious or unconscious) is to change the spectator also. The artist's attitude to his subject is not merely that of one who contemplates and reflects it; through the creative process, he makes the subject his own.

In the first of his eleven *Theses on Feuerbach* Karl Marx noted that 'the chief defect of all materialism up to now . . . is that the object, reality, what we apprehend through our senses, is understood only in the form of the *object* or *contemplation*; but not as *sensuous human activity*, as *practice*; not subjectively'.[58] It was not only a major failing of materialism until that time that it overlooked reality as 'sensuous human activity', as 'practice'; in the aesthetic sphere, too, in the determination of what was art, what was a work of art, what was aesthetic enjoyment, the subjective activity was underestimated. For vulgar materialism or crude individualism, art is, quite simply, the incomprehensible. The world as such, existing independently from us, becomes *reality* only as a world *for us*. Yet the one who experiences, investigates and creates the world cannot simply be considered in terms of empty individuality. The 'I' which experiences, recognizes, appropriates the world goes far back into the pre-human, the animal, the vegetative, and reaches far forward into the not yet accomplished; it is the whole of everything that has come about historically and all that is still engaged in becoming; in the last analysis, however fragmentarily, inadequately, and accidentally, it represents *humanity*. The work of art, by conceiving of its subject as a process and transforming this subject, by the process of artistic creation, into something that is constantly changing, developing and staying imperfect, becomes an evocation and so acquires the power to activate the spectator.

> *Sonst stünde dieser Stein entstellt und kurz*
> *unter der Schultern durchsichtigem Sturz*
> *und flimmerte nicht so wie Raubtierfelle;*
> *und bräche nicht aus allen seinen Rändern*
> *aus wie ein Stern: denn da ist keine Stelle,*
> *die dich nicht sieht. Du musst dein Leben ändern!*

(Or else this stone would stand deformed and squat under the shoulders' transparent drop, and would not shimmer thus like pelts of beasts of prey; and would not burst out at all its edges like a star: for there is no place here that does not see you. You must change your life!)[39]

In Rilke's poem it is the Greek archaic torso which issues this command. The torso forms itself into a whole in the spectator's imagination and forces him to complete the fragment and turn it into a god: and thus to anticipate his own self, to anticipate the man he could be if he changed his life.

PROMETHEUS AND ORPHEUS

In our world of alienated labour, in which production overwhelms man and does not allow him, even in his leisure time, to be himself, but only to let the entertainment industry kill time for him; in our protest against the fetishization of 'productivity', whether it serves preparation for war, production of superfluities or of essentials, there is good reason to recall a work process which allowed man to develop instead of crippling him, a way of producing which was not forced upon him but liberated him because it was creative. Work has always meant the struggle for existence, defence against hunger, homelessness, catastrophe. Yet many discoveries of ethnology and anthropology justify the assumption that at first it was also a pleasure, a self-affirmation through the rhythm of the community and through the ability to transform what was already given, for the sake of an anticipated future.

We may presume that the 'paradise lost' of idleness, the *dolce far niente*, became a nostalgic alternative only when the relationship between master and servant was established and work assumed a repressive character, becoming a social compulsion. I believe that Prometheus and Orpheus – Prometheus as the 'cultural hero of effort, productivity and progress by oppression', Orpheus as the herald of a world of peace, the standstill of time, 'silence, sleep, night, paradise – the Nirvana principle not as death but as life' – are not so harshly opposed to one another as Herbert Marcuse suggests in his important work *Eros and Civilization*.[40] Prometheus and Orpheus were not only antagonists; they were also profoundly akin to one another as the representatives of a pre-Apollonian, pre-patriarchal world, as defenders of the old laws of unity and equality against the new aristocratic gods.

In social orders founded on domination, the 'Apollonian' remoteness of a work of art from real life is seen as perfection; their aesthetics encourage movements culminating in repose, the ideal of a totality resting within itself. But in times of revolt against the rulers, the 'Dionysian' element usually breaks through, with its tendency towards the disquieting, the restless, the moving, the incomplete and the activating – until finally it may deny art altogether as something misleading and deceitful, the snare of tyranny and hell. (It was in this mood that the heretics and, later, Rimbaud, Duchamp and Breton condemned the Aesthetic as the 'Olympus of illusion'.)

PRODUCTIVE LOVE

In his first work *The Birth of Tragedy* Friedrich Nietzsche speaks of the 'Dionysian magic' through which each man feels 'not only united, reconciled, fused with his neighbour, but actually one with him' and man expresses himself 'as a member of a higher community', adding: 'Man is no longer an artist, he has become a work of art.' In Dionysian states of intoxication, in the spontaneous union with a collective which cancels out the *principium individuationis* and in which each man becomes one with nature and with his neighbour, man only temporarily becomes a work of art unto himself. He can only become a work of art of permanence and substance, a solid work of his own making, through a work process freed from compulsion, alienation and dehumanization, through a form of productivity whose prototype is the work of the artist. Bertolt Brecht speaks of such productivity in his fragment *Meti, Book of Turnings*:

Kin-Jeh on Love. I do not speak of the joys of the flesh, although much could be said about them, nor of being in love, of which there is less to say. The world could get along with these two phenomena, but love has to be considered separately, because it is a kind of production. It alters the lover and the beloved, whether for good or ill. Even from the outside, lovers appear as producers of something, and, indeed, as producers of a high order. . . . It is the nature of love, as of other great forms of production, that lovers take many things seriously which others treat lightly, the smallest touch, the most imperceptible nuance. The best succeed in putting their love into complete harmony with other forms of production; then their well-disposedness becomes a general one, their inventiveness becomes one that is useful to many, and they support everything that is productive.[41]

Art is by no means the only form of productivity whose purpose is man himself, whose purpose is not to have more but to be more; but it is in art that the greatest experiences and inventions of such productivity are accumulated. The work process in which man becomes his own purpose combines the Promethean with the Orphic, the pleasure of active change with the enjoyment of fulfilled being. Many modern artists who suffer because the work of art is so distant from life, because the command: 'You must change your life!' seems so futile, hope to find unity in the primeval depths. Their return to the archaic is an attempt to regain the sources of that unique productive force, the imagination.

The shrinking process of the imagination is among the most alarming phenomena of our time. Having developed together with work (the postponement of satisfaction and the anticipation of that which is to be accomplished), it has withdrawn from alienated labour into a no-man's-land beyond the sphere of material production which can one day become the 'State of Freedom'. Reality, reduced to a merely factual one, will then be transformed into a total one, made complete by the possible, the unaccomplished. The power of the instincts, the stuff that dreams are made of, the material of memory is enriched by experience and modified by reason, yet it is always a looking back that leads to a looking forward, and the backwards-turned utopia is always transformed into a forward-turned one.

Overfed with deceptive 'facts', blunted by the quantity of events, led astray by the illusion of 'You Are There', the modern consumer has sent the imagination into retirement. To activate it and, through it, to activate man (since the imagination tempts man to take part inwardly in the creation of the work of art and so to think and work further) is the desire of many modern artists. 'To start again from zero', therefore, means also the opposite of what it seems to mean. It is to anticipate a world in which the socially necessary material production demands only short working hours, and the 'State of Freedom' is extended.

The work process, if no longer founded on scarcity but on plenty, if removed beyond material production, could become pleasureable, artistic and creative. But on such a foundation the aesthetic, too, would change its nature, and the work of art would, if it did not remove the division between production and reception, life and art, being and illusion, at least resolutely transcend it. In such a way man could – perhaps – become a work of art for his own enjoyment. In the twenty-seventh of his letters *On the Aesthetic Education of Man* Friedrich Schiller had the courage to give expression to this vision:

The State of Beauty . . . where mankind passes through the most complex situations with eager simplicity and tranquil innocence, and has no need either to encroach upon another's freedom in order to assert his own, or to display gracefulness at the cost of dignity.[42]

In the midst of modern industrial society, Brecht, who was not a particular admirer of Schiller, continued the same thought. It is the task of actors, he wrote,

to entertain the children of the scientific age, and to do so with sensuousness and humour. This is something that we Germans can-

o

not tell ourselves too often, for with us everything easily slips into the insubstantial and unapproachable, and we begin to talk of *Weltanschauung* when the world in question has already dissolved. Even materialism is little more than an idea with us. Sexual pleasure with us turns into marital obligations, the pleasures of art subserve general culture, and by learning we mean not an enjoyable process of finding out, but the forcible shoving of our nose into something. Our activity has none of the pleasure of exploration, and if we want to make an impression we do not say how much fun we have got out of something but how much effort it has cost us.[43]

Let the theatre and all the other arts, then, affect consciousness through entertainment, activate reason through the senses and arouse a desire to change the life of human beings in society. 'Like the transformation of nature, that of society is a liberating act; and it is the joys of liberation which the theatre of a scientific age has got to convey.' Neither the content nor the form of what is thus conveyed can be laid down by authorities (and not even science, let alone the party or the state, may be recognized as an authority in this context); they belong to the sphere of artistic freedom and the imagination. That which is portrayed – the life of human beings together as it really is, behind the illusion of clichés, imitations and counterfeits, and the vision of life as it could be if it meant living *with* one another, not *against* one another – achieves truth and completeness within the work of art only through the workings of the freely ranging imagination. 'And the pleasure . . . must be converted into the higher pleasure felt when the rules emerging from this life in society are treated as imperfect and provisional.'

In the desire to demolish the footlights between art and life, the desire for spontaneity and pleasure, for participation 'even when the spectacle is over', for activity and being in the midst of what is happening, we recognize the same double aspect as in the technical and scientific revolutions of our time. The technical inventions *can* lead to a world where the machine becomes truly the servant of man and the 'State of Freedom' is developed on every side; but they can also lead to the annihilation of the human race. The new discoveries of natural science can liberate man from poverty, hunger, disease, physical and psychological inadequacy: but they can also, if abused by power, make man wholly manipulated, depersonalized and dehumanized. The tendencies of modern art which aim in a multitude of ways at creating a new unity of art and life can prepare a new epoch in the arts in which aesthetic experience, as a form of sensual, psychological and intellectual productivity, captures the masses: but they can also lead towards a vacuum, towards art despairing of itself.

With this double aspect always before our eyes, we must clearly understand that it is impossible to turn back. Behind the experiments of technology and science in all countries stands death, and yet they are promoted at fantastic expense. Who, then, has the right to reproach artists with their experiments – not carried out under any military auspices but simply in order to try to find means of expression which will make it possible to give artistic form to what has become unimaginable?

To land on the moon requires imagination: most of all, however, imagination is needed to discover the earth, not by firing rockets into the Milky Way but by finding man and anticipating his future.

SPECIES AND HUMANITY

The species man is distinguished from all other forms of life by work and language, imagination and consciousness. Yet the special nature of man's fundamental situation and contradictions has not yet – fragmented as it is into tribes and peoples, races and classes, nations and systems, the hungry and the satisfied, the oppressors and the oppressed – constituted itself as humanity.

The great religions, Christianity and Buddhism, recognized the principle of humanity; they were followed by the Enlightenment and socialism. The principle of the equality of all men in the eyes of God, the gospel of loving one's neighbour and the 'tat vam asi', were a revolutionary transcending of barriers, an anticipated integration. The Enlightenment and socialism secularized the great religious messages: humanity is present in every man and grants him the right to an equal opportunity of realizing himself as a human being.

Neither the great religions on the one hand nor the Enlightenment and socialism on the other have so far been able to make the possible humanity which is implicit in the species man into a real one. Technology, it is true, can supply all nations and continents with the same machines, weapons, hotels, means of transport, plastics and other products; but it cannot bring about human

o*

unification through the unification of objects. There is no *humanitas ex machina* any more than there is a *deus ex machina*. Technology and economics are no more than the pre-conditions of new alternatives. It is always people who decide. In order to influence the decision towards *humanization* rather than *objectification*, the great religions, the tradition of the Enlightenment and socialism must work together.

Science and the arts must be part of this collaboration. In science it is the common content, the questions addressed to nature and the methods employed in answering them, which overcome the separation between men and lead humanity as a working community established through international teamwork towards an awareness of itself. In art it is the realization of what is existentially common to mankind in all its diversity, the common dangers, hopes, fears, dreams and utopias, through which man alienated from the 'other' suddenly becomes aware in that other of himself, a man alienated from himself, and experiences humanity as unity in multiplicity.

HUMANITY IN MAN

Georg Lukács describes art, which is opposed to fetishization, as

a significant liberation from the utilitarianism of everyday life. . . . True art liberates from habits, unavoidable in everyday life, which yet can, and often do, damage the humanness of human beings. But art not only discovers this new immediacy, it also nourishes it. Thus art becomes not only the seeing, hearing, feeling organ of humanity – of the humanity which is in every human being – but also, at the same time, its memory.[44]

Elsewhere Lukács says:

As the work of art, which is the central construct of the aesthetic sphere, moulds and establishes an organic unity between the inwardness of man and the outside world, between the human personality and its destiny in the world, the opposition between the terms is cancelled out to make a world of man, of humanity.

Such a synthesis can only be 'striven for and approximately achieved in a rationally objective way by the whole of humanity'.[45] The difficulty in

grasping the relationship between individual consciousness and that common to the entire species is due to the fact that the latter is not given as a subjective, immediate fact, or at most is only given in prophetic, utopian terms. People experience at first hand social bonds such as family, clan, caste, tribe, class, nation and so forth; they do not, or very rarely, experience with any immediacy *humanity as the unity of the species.* . . . Of course it has existed *objectively* ever since man became man, and is developing more and more strongly, but intensively and extensively.[46]

By its 'appropriateness' to the deepest needs of man,

art can strip off those masks which appear to be part of the organic life of man, but which in fact only distort his nature, and so can reveal man's true nature which establishes reason and the unity of his existence. . . . Freeing from fetishization is the same thing as the artistic salvaging of what is lasting and worthy of being preserved in the species Man.[47]

Is it not misleading to speak of the 'reality of humanity' which is 'sure evidence' of 'the coordination of all the best things which occur in life'? Is 'humanity as the unity of the species' objectively present from the outset? Or must it necessarily become conscious of itself through the development of productive forces, through the extension of units from the clan and the tribe to the nation, through the progressive overcoming of false consciousness? Is not the process of technical and economic unification so contradictory that its completion may mean the explosion, the mass grave of a humanity dying before it has ever come into being? Lukács, too, speaks of the fact that 'humanity', after it had 'consciously appeared upon the horizon of man', for a long time and frequently assumed 'the form of a mere ideal, a postulate'. But was it really only false consciousness when early man thought of and experienced himself not as a member of 'humanity' but of a family, a clan or a tribe? Did not the species have to spread across the world in order to survive, and was it not consciousness of reality when small groups saw themselves as a unit and the stranger as an enemy?

And the 'nature of man in man', the 'true' nature of man – what is it? Since the primeval condition of the species man there have existed mutually contradictory conceptions: the sombre one – Hobbes, Freud (man is a wolf unto man, man murders the original father); the bright one – Rousseau, many of the Romantics, the young Marx (the 'noble savage', the native fraternity, the primitive communist community). Ancient and other myths confirm both views: Kronos emasculates his father with a stone sickle and devours his own children: the golden age; Tantalus offers his son to be eaten by the gods: Iphigeneia liberates the house of the Tantlides from its curse; Oedipus solves the riddle of the sphinx, kills his father, takes his mother to wife: Antigone resists Creon's orders and serves not hate but love. Always the same conflict, the 'humanness' of man as darkness and light, as the murderous and as the fraternal.

Is this conflict to be the condition of man for all time, or can it be hoped that, with appalling setbacks, the word 'inhuman' is coming more and more to mean the murderous, the cruel, the selfish, while the word 'human' means the helpful, the fraternal and the selfless? Is it possible that light, goodness, solidarity – or at least the possibility of these – may predominate? I should like to agree with Teilhard de Chardin when he speaks of the evidence:

The fact that, under the combined effect of two irresistible forces of planetary scale (the geographical curvature of the earth which presses us together, on the one hand, and the psychological curvature of thought, which envelops us, on the other), the reflexive capacity of the human mass (i.e. its degree of humanization), far from being stopped in its growth, is, quite on the contrary, entering upon a critical period of intensification and a new upward surge. In the world around us there are not only *men,* who multiply numerically, but also *that which is human,* which is still being formed. In other words, man is zoologically not yet grown up. Psychologically he has not yet spoken his last word. Rather, something 'ultra-human' is on the way, and it cannot fail through the effects (indirect or direct) of socialization to appear tomorrow: there is not only a future which comes and passes, but a future which is building itself in what lies ahead of us. – That is a vision which man, since he once began to glimpse it in our time, will never again – of that one can be sure – forget. . . .[48]

Man on the way to himself, zoologically, psychologically, socially? I dare to hope, though not to assert it.

It seems that we humanists, marxists and Christians alike, have this in common in the present critical period, that we see man as *that which he is capable of becoming.* We see him as the inexhaustible possibility of a living creature who, through work, commenced the attack upon nature and thus upon himself; who does not passively adapt himself to the surrounding world, but undertakes actively to adapt it to his needs and who, by satisfying these needs, multiplies and refines them until they are more than needs; who is not only the creature of the world which preceded him, but the creator of a new world, in his doing and his language, his imagination and his consciousness; who is not only 'an abyss of past things' but also a fullness of future ones; who is not closed within that which befits his species but is open to the new, the far-away, the unknown, always confronted with alternatives, always called upon to make free decisions; who endlessly anticipates his works in his project, and himself in his works; a living creature between totality and individuation, aggression and solidarity, death and potential immortality; a living creature driven forward and striding ahead, restless, incomplete, unrealized.

Thus the 'humanness' of man is the great possibility that the species Man may grow beyond itself, that it will not merely remain an 'in-itself' but will become a 'for-itself': that it will break down its barriers by common experience and the consciousness of itself within each individual. Highly developed technical and economic community is a pre-condition, but it does not make such an experience and such a consciousness a necessity. Unless there is utopian anticipation, unless we fly ahead of ourselves as in a dream, there can be no humanity. And such utopian anticipation draws its strength from the source of productive memory, from the myths of the human race, from the imagination.

The tendency towards humanity implicit in a working, dreaming, thinking, anticipating human being, a tendency towards the development of all material, intellectual and psychological forces, could lead towards a state of termites, a monstrous organism steered with uttermost precision by science and technology. To be fulfilled, the tendency towards humanity requires the vision of a higher unity in which the contradiction between the personal and the collective is not wholly cancelled out but reproduces itself with increasing creative tension and richness on an ever-rising level. Without the prophetic vision of visionaries, poets and artists, the species man will never attain humanity. And this vision of the future transforms the species man (which as a species is 'beyond good and evil') into something qualitatively new, not merely a 'coexistence' of states, nations and cultures or a centralized world social system, but something like a condition of liberty, equality, and fraternity. Men have dreamed this dream again and again, beyond castes and estates, classes and nations, in the memory that such a condition, a golden age, a lost paradise, once existed. Earning his bread in the sweat of his brow, humiliated and oppressed, disenfranchized and exploited, man projects into this 'once upon a time' his longing for liberty, equality, and fraternity, draws from it the hope that all the evil things, *ruling* and *having*, weapons and power, are only a mask covering the true face, nature and humanness of man. This hope has an ally in the arts; and although the alliance has often suffered betrayal, it has always been renewed.

The arts have often praised those who rule, selling 'immortality' to powerful patrons at a cheap price. 'Whose bread I eat, his song I sing.' But more generally and more deeply, more elementally, art has sympathized with the suffering and the persecuted, the beaten and the rebellious – with Hector and Hamlet, with Antigone and Prometheus, with Heloïse and Don Quixote, with Barnabas and the maid Grusche. The artist's 'immediacy', which does not mistake the mask for the face or the fetish for the true nature of anything, is perhaps nothing other than this long productive memory; it reaches further than the memory of other people into childhood, into the sphere of first experience without 'experience' and inhibition, into all the freshness of the unknown and all the terrors of discovery, and thus not only into the artist's own childhood but into the childhood of the human race; and the great refusal to become an adult in the conventional sense, to recognize whatever 'reality principle' may be in force at one's particular time, is perhaps a guarantee of immediacy, of the productive imagination, of the revolt of art against that which goes without saying because it is sanctioned by society.

Thus art is like the child that sees and says what no one dares to see or say: 'The Emperor is naked!' In the story, the remark enjoys a dazzling success; in real life the child is usually slapped, and, as before, only a few people dare to believe what they see and what the child said when it saw the emperor for the first time. But the rumour refuses to die, and it is possible that someone at court will get the idea that it might be advisable to put a few clothes on the emperor, and sometimes it happens that the people get rid of the emperor altogether. Perhaps by this time the child has long since grown up, perhaps he has even entered the emperor's service, perhaps the incident of long ago is almost forgotten, yet the word has continued its secret work and, in a way statistics can never account for, has contributed towards the change.

THE IMPOTENCE AND POWER OF ART

But are we not overestimating the power of art if we believe that in this critical period when irresponsible rulers are prepared to destroy humanity (that humanity which has not yet been born), art can contribute to its birth, rescue and salvation?

The impotence of art is evident, its power is smaller than ever. But was it ever a power? Was it a power *as art* or only in alliance with magic and religion – forces outside the aesthetic sphere? Art has rarely been capable of participating *directly* in social change – and then only when an old order has begun to crumble and the new, not yet clearly emerged, still has need of language, with its images, parables and symbols, in order to castigate that which is worthy of death and to announce and anticipate the future. It was in this way that Greek tragedy contributed to the rise of the urban democracy, the art of the Renaissance to the undermining of feudal rule by commercial capital, the literature of the Enlightenment in England and France and, a century later, in Russia, to the preparation of the great revolutions. Yet the essential power of art does not consist in such direct influence upon events: such social effects can be produced by plays as good as *The Marriage of Figaro* or novels as poor as *Uncle Tom's Cabin*; in other words, they are less the result of artistic than of extra-artistic factors. An appeal, a pamphlet, a leading article can be incomparably more effective than the greatest poem or symphony.

In this critical period of history, art and literature can hardly avoid becoming aware of their educative, ethical and political possibilities, becoming 'committed' to the struggle for the being or non-being of humanity; and the more they are free from any guided 'party-mindedness', the more effective will be the stand they take. But let us not arouse the illusion that a work of art or literature, however important, can swing the opinion of the majority of a country, overthrow a government or prevent a war! Art can do little – far less than the rulers who fear it and try to bribe or crush it. Yet also it can do more than the rulers ever dream of. It can be the tear in which a dream is mirrored, the footstep and flicker of the invisible, the eye of the Medusa which, as she dies, turns the murderers to stone. And all this, tear and dream, footstep and flicker and the breaking eye whose lid will never close mercifully upon the killer, all this that trickles away into the business of the day, that gathers in the unconscious and prepares itself deep below ground, all this can suddenly be more powerful than the Caesars, the living and the dead ones, for it is in stillness that men begin to change and turn. The visionary spirit, the creative imagination recognize that which is to be accomplished by its first sign. He who adds up facts, calculates reality, exercises power, will become aware of it only on the last day, when it is too late.

Hölderlin dedicated this hymn to Rousseau:

> Und wunderbar, als hätte von Anbeginn
> Des Menschen Geist das Werden und Wirken all
> Die alte Weise des Lebens schon erfahren,
> Kennt er im ersten Zeichen Vollendetes schon,
> Und flieget, der kühne Geist, wie Adler den
> Gewittern, weissagend seinen
> Kommenden Göttern voran.

(And wonderfully, as though from the very beginning the mind of man had already experienced all its becoming, all its working and the ancient ways of life, he recognizes that which is to be accomplished by its first sign; and, as eagles fly ahead of storms, so he flies, prophesying, ahead of his coming gods.)

But a book which raises questions in a time as difficult as ours should not end on an exclamation mark.

Have art and literature, beneath the metal hoops that grip the earth to unite or to suffocate it – have they contributed intensively enough to the birth of humanity for humanity to be able to withstand its own inventions? Has the imagination, which is incapable of feeding the hungry, of restraining the lunatics, or of liberating the earth, anticipated humanity in enough persons for humanity to arise, before it is too late, from its ordeal?

Has the imagination, allied with reason, acquired the quiet power to turn people, now left far behind by their own works, into beings who will fly ahead, not of disaster, but of liberation, and accept the difficult demands of 'the simplest way of living', of achieving dignity with the smile of grace, of becoming men?

Utopian hopes? Perhaps.

But what would life be without the breath of inexhaustible possibilities?

Notes

1. Bertolt Brecht, 'A Short Organum for the Theatre' in *Brecht on Theatre*, edited and translated by John Willett (New York: Hill & Wang, 1964)
2. Georg Lukács, *Von der Eigenart des Ästhetischen*, collected works vols. 11–12, (Neuwied: Luchterhand, 1963)
3. ibid
4. Erich Fried, MS.
5. ibid
6. Ernst Bloch, *Literarische Aufsätze*, collected works vol. 9 (Frankfurt: Suhrkamp, 1965)
7. A. V. Lunacharsky, *On Literature and Art* (Moscow: Progress Publishers, 1965)
8. ibid
9. An official at the 11th Plenum of the Central Committee of the S.E.D.
10. V. I. Lenin, *The Socialist Party and Non-Party Revolutionism*, collected works vol. 10 (London: Lawrence & Wishart, 1962)
11. ibid
12. V. I. Lenin, *Party Organization and Party Literature*, collected works vol. 10 (London: Lawrence & Wishart, 1962)
13. ibid
14. ibid
15. Antonio Gramsci, *The Modern Prince and Other Writings*, translated by Louis Marks (London: Lawrence & Wishart, 1957)
16. Roger Garaudy, *D'un réalisme sans rivages* (Paris: Plon, 1963)
17. Emmanuel Kant, *The Dispute of the Faculties*, translated by Gabriele Rabel, (Oxford: O.U.P., 1963)
18. Johann Jakob Bachofen, *Urreligion und antike Symbole*, vol. II
19. Claude Lévi-Strauss, *Totemism* (London: Merlin Press, 1964)
20. Alfred Reginald Radcliffe-Brown, 'The Comparative Method of Social Anthropology', in Lévi-Strauss, *Totemism*
21. Lucien Lévy-Bruhl, *The Soul of the Primitive*, London, 1928
22. ibid
23. George Thomson, *The First Philosophers* (London: Lawrence & Wishart, 1961)
24. Robert Graves, *The Greek Myths* (London: Cassell, 1958)
25. George Thomson, *The First Philosophers*
26. Karl Kerényi, 'Das Wesen des Mythos und die Technik' in *Die Wirklichkeit des Mythos* (Munich: Knaur, 1965)
27. Walter F. Otto, *Die Gestalt und das Sein*, Darmstadt, 1955
28. Theodor W. Adorno, *Noten zur Literatur* (Frankfurt: Suhrkamp, 1961)
29. Arthur Rimbaud, 'L'Eternité', prose translation by Oliver Bernard (Harmondsworth: Penguin, 1962)
30. Ludwig Wittgenstein, *Tractatus Logico-philosophicus*, translated by Pears and McGuinness (London: Routledge & Kegan Paul, 1961)

31. Jean-Paul Sartre, 'The Quest for the Absolute', *Essays in Aesthetics* (London: Peter Owen, 1964)
32. ibid
33. Christopher Caudwell, *Illusion and Reality* (London: Lawrence & Wishart, 1946)
34. Georg Lukács, *Von der Eigenart des Ästhetischen*, collected works vol. 11
35. ibid
36. Bertolt Brecht, 'A Short Organum for the Theatre'
37. Richard Ott, *Urbild der Seele*, quoted in Alfred Andersch, *Die Blindheit des Kunstwerks* (Frankfurt: Suhrkamp, 1965)
38. Karl Marx, 'Theses on Feuerbach' in Marx and Engels, *The German Ideology* (New York: International Publishers, 1947)
39. Rainer Maria Rilke, 'Archaischer Torso Apollos' in *Der ausgewählten Gedichte erster Teil* (Wiebaden: Insel, 1954)
40. Herbert Marcuse, *Eros and Civilization* (Boston: Beacon Press, 1955)
41. Bertolt Brecht, *Meti, Buch der Wendugen* (Frankfurt: Suhrkamp, 1965)
42. Friedrich Schiller, *On the Aesthetic Education of Man, in a series of Letters*, translated by R. Snell (London: Routledge & Kegan Paul, 1954) letter 6
43. Bertolt Brecht, 'A Short Organum for the Theatre'
44. Georg Lukács, *Von der Eigenart des Ästhetischen*, collected works vol. 11
45. ibid
46. ibid
47. ibid
48. Pierre Teilhard de Chardin, *Auswahl aus dem Werk* (Olten: Walter, 1964)

Index